Lionel Decle

Trooper 3809

A private Soldier of the third Republic

Lionel Decle

Trooper 3809
A private Soldier of the third Republic

ISBN/EAN: 9783337137014

Printed in Europe, USA, Canada, Australia, Japan

Cover: Foto ©ninafisch / pixelio.de

More available books at **www.hansebooks.com**

Trooper 3809

A Private Soldier of the
Third Republic

By
Lionel Decle

New York
Charles Scribner's Sons
1899

NOTE

It is right to state that the following pages have not had the advantage of final revision by the Author, as Mr. Decle started on a mission of African exploration without having completed the preparation of his MS. for the press

PREFACE

THE bitter and protracted discussions which have arisen out of the Dreyfus case, and which have divided France into two hostile camps, have concentrated the attention of the civilized world on the French army, but nobody has done more to disgrace it, and to lower it in the eyes of friends and foes alike, than Frenchmen themselves.

Those who, persuaded of Dreyfus' innocence, made superhuman efforts to further the noble cause of justice and to obtain the redress of one of the greatest wrongs ever committed against a human being, spoiled their noble task by indiscriminate and wholesale abuse of the army in general, holding the thousands of French officers responsible for the conduct of a few of their number. Those, on the other hand, who believed in the guilt of Dreyfus, based their conviction upon their blind belief in the infallibility of half a dozen officers who had passed judgment upon the condemned man. Trusting to unworthy subordinates, the highest officers of the General Staff made of Dreyfus' guilt a matter on which they staked their own honour and reputation, and when they discovered that they had been deceived, they found themselves in the position of having either to acknowledge that they had been

PREFACE

befooled, or else of having to stand by those who had led them into their awkward predicament. They chose the latter alternative, and their friends and supporters played into the hands of those who so fiercely attacked the army, by refusing to admit that there could be a single black sheep in it, and by thus linking together the whole body of French officers and making their collective honour dependent on the honour of every individual member.

A time came, however, when even the most determined partizans of this system had to turn against those they had extolled but the day before. First came Esterhazy, the liar, the swindler, and the traitor; then Henry the forger, and de Paty du Clam, his accomplice.

It is a remarkable fact that amidst all these scenes of violent abuse there should be but one man who maintained implicit trust in the good faith of his worst enemies—Dreyfus himself—the victim of this most abominable conspiracy.

His case is, unfortunately, but a greatly magnified example of what daily happens throughout the French army, and the recollections I am now offering to the reader, of the time I served in its ranks, will show that Dreyfus has been a victim not so much of the malice of individuals as of a faulty system. It will be seen how, in a regiment, the Colonel forms his opinion of a private from the character given to him by his Corporal or Sergeant, and how the mere fact of appealing against a punishment is considered

PREFACE

as an act of insubordination. It is always the same principle—*le respect de la chose jugée* (the upholding of a judgment, without considering upon what grounds or evidence it has been delivered).

I wish it to be clearly understood that this little book has not been written for the purpose of attacking the French army as represented by its officers. It is intended merely as a faithful account of the hardships I endured when I served my time in the ranks—hardships which every Frenchman has still to bear. I cannot follow M. Urbain Gobier in his virulent and indiscriminate attacks upon all French officers—among whom individuals differ as in other classes of men; but each one of my readers will be able to draw his own conclusions with regard to the system which, in practice, is universally in force.

INTRODUCTION

I

EVERY Frenchman is liable to military service during twenty-five years of his life—viz., from the age of twenty until he is forty-five.*

In time of peace this period of service is thus divided:

(i) Three years of active service.

(ii) Ten years in the reserve of the standing army, during which two periods of a month each with the colours must be undergone.

(iii) Six years in the territorial army, with two periods of thirteen days each with the colours, and

(iv) Six years in the reserve of the territorial army.

The conscription lists are thus made out:

Every year the Mayor of each " Commune " draws up a list of all the young men who have arrived at the age of twenty during the past twelve months.

These lists must be posted up by January 14 at the latest. The names of the sons of foreigners, if born in France, are included, and unless they claim foreign nationality they are liable to serve, and on failing to do so when called upon are regarded as deserters and punished accordingly.

* For full particulars see "Loi du 15 Juillet 1889, sur la Recrutement de l'Armée." Librairie Militaire L. Baudoin, 30 rue Dauphine, Paris.

INTRODUCTION

Domicile is established by the parents' residence.

Every year the War Minister fixes the number of conscripts required to serve three years with the colours; those in excess of that number are called upon to serve for one year only; but during the following two years they are liable to be called upon to complete their time of active service.

In order to determine those who are to benefit by this arrangement *tirage au sort* (drawing lots) is resorted to.

In time of peace, conscripts falling under any of the following categories among others are also called upon to serve for one year only:

(*a*) The eldest of orphans, or the eldest son of a widow, or of a family whose father is blind, or has reached his seventieth year.

(*b*) The only son in a family of seven children or more —or the eldest son of a family of at least seven.

(*c*) The elder of twins.

(*d*) Brothers of men engaged in active service.

(*e*) Brothers of a man who has been killed, or who has died in active service, or who has been invalided on account of disease contracted, or wounds received, while serving.

(*f*) Young men who have signed an engagement to serve during ten years as teachers in the National schools.

(*g*) Students in law, science, or medicine who have already obtained their admission to the Government Universities or other institutions mentioned in the Act.

(*h*) Students of the religious institutions who are studying to become ministers of one of the religions recognised by the State.

Provided that, in classes (*f*), (*g*), (*h*), such young men have obtained their final degree before their twenty-sixth year, or that religious students have been ordained

INTRODUCTION

before the end of their twenty-sixth year, failing which, they are called upon to complete three years' active service.

Whoever has been convicted of theft, obtaining money by false pretences, rape, and other crimes against morals, and has been sentenced to more than three months' imprisonment for such crimes, or has been sentenced twice for similar offences, is sent to special battalions in Algeria. If, at the time a conscript is called upon to serve, he is undergoing imprisonment, he begins his service at the expiration of his sentence.

Instead of joining their regiment like other conscripts, these men have to report themselves on a certain date at the headquarters of the military district to which they belong, and they are thence taken by gendarmes to the depôt of their battalion. They are subjected to an iron discipline, being commanded by officers and non-commissioned officers picked out from other regiments where they have distinguished themselves for their harshness. Many are the tales of dreadful revenge taken by these conscripts on their officers. It is no uncommon thing for a few of them to play away the life of an officer at cards, the loser being obliged to kill him within a certain time. To quote but a single instance: A few years ago one of these battalions was being marched from Biskra to Tuggurt in Southern Algeria. Before leaving, four of the men had played away the life of their Major at cards. The loser, who was to carry out the deed, pretended to be ill, and kept to the rear of the column. On the second day he kept still farther back, and sat down pretending to be exhausted. The Major, who had fallen far behind, seeing the man, spoke to him kindly, telling him to make an effort. "Oh, sir," said the soldier, "I can't; I am done for." The Major kindly handed the man his flask to take a pull from, and

INTRODUCTION

as he was replacing it in his holster, the man fired his rifle point blank at his officer. Fortunately the horse swerved, and the bullet missed. Thereupon the Major drew his revolver, and blew the ruffian's brains out. A few months later a stone was found on the spot bearing this inscription:

HERE
ON THE 10TH OF DECEMBER 18—
PRIVATE ———
WAS MURDERED BY MAJOR X.

The man who placed the stone there was never discovered, and, although it was removed by order of the military authorities, another one bearing a similar inscription soon afterwards stood in its place. Six times these stones were removed, and six times they were replaced, yet the guilty parties were never detected. It is hardly to be wondered at if the officers of these battalions usually carry loaded revolvers.

To return to our description of the mode of recruiting.

The lists having been duly posted up, a day is appointed for drawing the lots. This public ceremony is presided over by the "Sous-préfet" of the "Arrondissement." Having counted the number of names on the list, the Sous-préfet places a corresponding number of tickets, each bearing a number, in an urn: he then calls out the names of the young men, and each in turn draws a ticket; in case of absence of one of them his lot is drawn by the Mayor. As already explained only a certain number of men being required to serve three years, those who draw the highest numbers stand a chance of serving for but twelve months, besides those who have a right to claim the privilege, although the latter are also bound to draw lots.

INTRODUCTION

All the young men whose names appear in the lists have next to appear before a *Conseil de Revision* (Revising Commission).

This Commission consists of:
  The Prefect of the Department, who is ex-officio President.
  A Conseiller de Préfecture.
  A Member of the Conseil General.
  A Member of the Conseil d'arrondissement.
  A General or Field Officer appointed by the military authority.
  An Intendant militaire (Commissariat officer).
  The chief Recruiting Officer of the district.

A military Surgeon, or a Doctor, is appointed by the military authorities to make a medical examination of all the conscripts, and upon his report the Commission decides by vote whether each individual conscript shall serve or not. It should be added that the minimum height is 5 feet ½ inch.

The Commission also decides upon claims of exemption made by sons of foreigners, and upon the claims of those entitled to a service of one year only.*

Each conscript subsequently receives his *feuille de route,* stating the regiment he must join, and the date on which he must join it, and making an allowance for his journey to the town where he is to be quartered.† From the moment conscripts receive their *feuilles de route* they are under military law, and can only be tried by court-martial for any crimes or offences they may commit.

Men while serving for a month in the reserve, or for a fortnight in the territorial army, are also exclusively under

---

* All who for any cause are considered unfit for service have to pay a yearly tax of 6 francs and an additional tax proportionate to their means.

† Soldiers pay one-third of ordinary fares on French railways.

INTRODUCTION

martial law for the time being. Even in the case of a soldier who has finished his service the fact of his assaulting one of his former superiors (from a Corporal upwards) renders him liable to be tried by court-martial " should such assault be considered the result of revenge for a punishment received during his service."—(Art. 223 and 224 of the Code of Military Justice.) So that a man who has been abominably treated during his time of service and who gives a good hiding to one of his former officers ten or twenty years later, is liable to be tried by the military authorities.

I may add here that the act of striking a *supérieur,* meaning any man superior in rank to one's self, from a Corporal upwards, is punished with DEATH, *even in time of peace.* Two instances occurred while I served. In the first instance a private had struck a Corporal who had bullied him in a most shameful way; in the second instance a Corporal had struck an officer who had called his mother by a vile name. Both men were found guilty and publicly shot in the presence of their regiment on special parade. It very seldom occurs that a man who has struck even a Corporal is reprieved.

In each subdivision of every military district is kept a register in which are inscribed the names of all the men in that subdivision who are serving, or have served.

In this register is stated the date at which each man has been incorporated, as well as the date of his leaving the service, the date of his passing into the reserve, then into the territorial army and into the reserve of the territorial army, until he has satisfied all his military obligations. Every change of address is also noted.

Every soldier receives on joining his regiment a *livret matricule,* a book in which are stated his age, his name, the address of his parents, his full description, the list of

INTRODUCTION

all the punishments he has received, and many other particulars.

It is of the utmost importance for every Frenchman to keep this book carefully, as it has to be produced whenever required by the military, civil, or judicial authorities, and its loss entails several days' imprisonment. Whenever a Frenchman—until he has reached the age of forty-five and has thus satisfied all his military obligations—wishes to absent himself from his domicile he is bound to present his *livret* at the nearest *gendarmerie* and to declare where he is going: this is written down in his *livret*, and on arrival at his new residence he must have this book "*visé*" anew. If he goes abroad he must present it to the French Consul, and whenever he changes his residence for more than three months, he must repeat the operation exactly after the fashion of a ticket-of-leave man in England. To omit to do so renders the offender liable to imprisonment. It is therefore easy to realise the tremendous power of the military authorities in France.

II

The military law I have just explained is that which has been in force since 1889 only. It differs from the previous law chiefly in regard to the length of service. In my time (1879) the period of service in the active army was five years instead of three. Young men, however, who had obtained the degrees of B.A. or B.S., provided they paid £60 to Government, and provided also they contracted a voluntary engagement within the year preceding that in which they became liable to conscription, were allowed to serve only one year instead of five. During the next four years they still belonged, however, to the active army, and

INTRODUCTION

were liable to be called at any time by decree of the War Minister. These young men were officially called *Engagés conditionnels*, but commonly termed *Volontaires d'un an*, or by abbreviation *Volontaires*. It is as such that I served.

I have roughed it a good deal since those days, but I have no hesitation in saying that the time of my active service with the colours was the bitterest experience I ever underwent.

In the case of a nation which possesses no public schools like the great institutions of England, I believe that compulsory military service might be made an excellent moral and physical training for young men in every rank of life. But the French system is vicious. A system in which gentlemen of refinement and the vilest dregs of the city slums are subjected to identical treatment, and ruled by identical measures of discipline, is an impossible one. Take punishments, for instance. " Equality of punishment " may sound well in theory, but in practice it becomes the rankest inequality. A gentleman accustomed to comfort, or perhaps luxury, is for the slightest fault sent to the *Salle de Police* to endure the degrading horrors presently to be described—his companions are perhaps roughs who have never slept in a bed since they were children, to whom dirt is a mere necessary condition, and vermin are " familiar beasts."

Where is the equality of punishment in such a case?

It must not be thought either that some compensation lies in the comparative infrequency of the punishments meted out to gentlemen. The contrary is the truth. For an equal fault the rough usually gets a shorter punishment than the man of higher class.

The German system is very different. In Germany they also have the reduced service of one year for young men who have fulfilled certain conditions of superior education.

INTRODUCTION

But these *ein jahr preiwiller*, as they are called, form a class absolutely distinct from the other privates, and are distinguished by a uniform of better cloth. During the first month of their service they live in barracks, where they learn the routine of a common soldier's duties, but afterwards they are allowed lodgings in the town where their regiment is quartered, and they are altogether treated differently from the rest.

Then, again, in the German army non-commissioned officers cannot punish a private, the Captain alone having the right of punishment, while in the French army a Corporal could give us two days' *Salle de Police;* a Sergeant, four; a Sergeant-major, a Sub-lieutenant, or a Lieutenant, eight; and a Captain could send us to prison. Each of those punishments was usually increased by the Major, and also by the Colonel, and it will scarcely be credited that *no man could appeal against a punishment until he had undergone the whole of it.* Things have altered a little since General Boulanger was Minister of War, but very slightly. There is still no higher appeal than to the Colonel, and such a thing as a private or even an officer having the right to ask for a court-martial in case he considers himself unjustly punished does not exist. But more of this in the sequel.

III

In order to enable readers to understand clearly the account of my adventures, I think it will be necessary to describe somewhat fully the routine of a French cavalry regiment, as well as the rights and duties of officers, non-commissioned officers, and privates.

Any one desiring further particulars can obtain them from a little book called " Règlement du Service Intérieur

INTRODUCTION

des troupes de Cavalerie." (Paris: Librairie Militaire de L. Baudoin, 30 rue Dauphine.)

The following are the titles of the officers and non-commissioned officers of a French cavalry regiment, with the duties and responsibilities which theoretically devolve upon them. How far those duties are carried out will appear in the course of my narrative.

COLONEL.

(Five Gold Stripes.)

The authority of the Colonel extends over every part of the service. He is responsible for the discipline, military education, instruction, police, hygiene, and appearance of the regiment he commands. He directs its administration with the help of a " Conseil d'administration." He appoints all non-commissioned officers, and Corporals.

LIEUTENANT-COLONEL.

(Three Gold and Two Silver Stripes.)

" The Lieutenant-colonel is the intermediary of the Colonel in every branch of the service. He acts on behalf of the Colonel in the absence of the latter. . . . When thus acting he states that the orders are the Colonel's, so that the authority of the latter should be sustained. . . ."

" Among the books he has to keep are those containing the individual notes on each officer, in which are entered twice yearly the punishments inflicted on each officer, and information as to their military as well as private conduct, their instruction, and military aptitude. These notes are countersigned by the Colonel, who adds whatever remarks he thinks fit. . . ."

INTRODUCTION

CHEFS D'ESCADRONS (Majors).
(Four Gold Stripes.)

There are two of these in each regiment, each commanding two squadrons.

"The 'Chefs d'Escadrons' see that the Captains commanding their squadrons carry out their duties, as well as the Colonel's orders, with zeal and intelligence. . . .

"One of them presides over the *Commission des ordinaires* (food supply). The other presides over the *Commission d'abatage* (killing of horses). . . ."

Each of them has also to look carefully into the service of the kitchens of their squadrons, and they must frequently visit the canteens.

They take in turns the weekly duty and are in charge of the general police of barracks. Under their orders they have for this service a Captain and an *Adjudant*.

MAJOR.
(Two Gold and Two Silver Stripes.)

The duties of this officer are chiefly connected with the general administration of the regiment—accounts, purchases, pay, equipment, barrack furniture, &c. He is in command of the 5th squadron,* which forms the depôt in case of war.

CAPITAINE INSTRUCTEUR.

The Capitaine Instructeur is chiefly concerned with the instruction of the non-commissioned officers. He also gives the Lieutenants and Sub-lieutenants lectures on shooting, artillery, topography, hippology, &c., and has to teach the *Adjudants* (to be described later) their duties.

* French cavalry regiments have five squadrons.

INTRODUCTION

CAPITAINE TRÉSORIER (Paymaster).

He receives all moneys for the use of the regiment; he makes all payments authorised by the Council of Administration, of which he is a member.

He keeps the "archives" of the regiment. Every five days he hands over the pay to the Captain commanding each squadron or to his Sergeant-major, and issues the demand for forage supplied through the "Intendant" (an official apart from the regiment).

Under him he has a Deputy, a Lieutenant, or Sub-lieutenant.

CAPITAINE D'HABILLEMENT.

This Captain is in charge of the armoury, clothing, and barrack furniture, keeping all accounts relating to the same.

All the regimental workshops are under his orders: the chief armourer, the master saddler, the master tailor, and master bootmaker.

Under this officer is:

THE PORTE ÉTENDARD.

A Lieutenant who helps generally his immediate chief, and carries the colours on parade.

DOCTORS.

Two Doctors are attached to each cavalry regiment—a *médecin major* (captain-surgeon) and *médecin aide major* (lieutenant-surgeon). Their duties are similar to those of regimental doctors in an English regiment.

INTRODUCTION

VETERINARY SURGEONS.

Two Veterinary Surgeons are attached to each regiment, and their duties need not be described here.

CAPITAINES (Captains).
(Three Stripes.)

There are two Captains in each squadron—the Captain Commanding (*capitaine commandant*) and a second Captain (*capitaine en second*).

CAPTAIN COMMANDING.—This officer is in full charge of the squadron (in time of peace a squadron consists of about 120 men and horses); he is the real chief and almost the only one the non-commissioned officers and men of his squadron know, many of them leaving the service without having ever been spoken to by such an exalted and god-like being as a Major, much less by their Lieutenant-colonel or Colonel. The Captain in command is himself a very great man indeed, who has very little intercourse with such riff-raff as common privates. No leave nor promotion can be obtained except through him, and punishments are usually increased when they reach His Mightiness. When I served my time I think I saw my Captain nearly twenty times in as many months, but nevertheless I must show what his duties are—in theory. Let us quote once more from the " Service Intérieur."

" The chief duty of the Captain Commanding is to inspire the soldiers under his command with zeal and love [!] of the service; to develop among them feelings of duty, honour, and devotion to their Fatherland. He must endeavour to make their duties easy by advice, the equitable use of his authority, and a constant solicitude for their welfare. He is the necessary intermediary of all their

INTRODUCTION

requests. . . . He must repress the familiarity and harshness of his subordinates towards the privates, who must never be illtreated or insulted."

He has also to look after the officers under his direct orders. " He visits his squadron daily, visits the men in hospital, and signs a daily report to the Colonel."

" He is responsible for the military education of his squadron, for the discipline of the rank and file, the condition of the horses and stables. . . ."

He is also responsible for the moneys and supplies handed over to him.

The Captain receives from the Treasurer the money for the use of the squadron on the 1st, 6th, 11th, 16th, 21st, and 26th of each month. This money is divided into two parts: the first being the money to be spent on the men's food, and the second being the men's pocket-money, " which," say the regulations, " must not be less than 5 centimes ($\frac{1}{2}d.$) per day." The money invariably handed over to the men is $2\frac{1}{2}d.$ every five days in the infantry, and $4d.$ every five days in the cavalry! Corporals get about twice as much, while Sergeants get about $4d.$ a day, and Sergeant-majors $8d.$ What would Tommy Atkins say to that?

All the accounts and books are kept by the Sergeant-major, the Sergeant *fourrier,* and the Corporal *fourrier,* non-commissioned officers whose duties will be described more fully later on. All clothes, saddlery, arms, &c., are supplied to the men in the presence of the Captain: all repairs are done on his written requisition.

When the men's food is supplied through the *Commission des ordinaires* the Captain finds every day the amount of supplies required. When, however, he receives money for the purchase of provisions he must see that supplies are bought at the cheapest rate.

INTRODUCTION

The daily rations for each private are as follows:
Ten ounces of meat (bone included).
One pound of bread for soup, which is reduced to $3\frac{1}{2}$ ounces if stew is served instead of soup.
In the same way the ration of meat is reduced if fish, lard, or preserves are given to the men.
The Captain in Command assigns a horse to each trooper, and has to see that the horses are kept in good condition. He reports on all matters to his Major.

SECOND CAPTAIN.—The duties of this officer are twofold: first, in the squadron, and secondly, as Captain on regimental duty for the week—" Captain of the Week."

In the squadron he is under the orders of the Captain Commanding, but he is specially in charge of all matters connected with the food supply.

In case of the absence of the Captain Commanding he takes the command of the squadron. The five Second Captains take " the week " by turn. The " Captain of the Week " is under the immediate orders of the " Major of the Week." He has to see to the roll-calls, the assemblies, and the changing of guards. He is in charge of the cells, and is responsible for the cleanliness of the barracks, and their police and security. The evening roll-call takes place in the rooms, and is made by each Sergeant-major, who hands over his report to the *Adjudant,* who makes out a general bulletin and hands it over to the " Captain of the Week." This Captain may order extra roll-calls in the middle of the night should he think fit to do so.

LIEUTENANTS AND SUB-LIEUTENANTS.

There are four of these in each squadron, and they take in turn the " weekly service " (*service de semaine*). As such they must be, or ought to be, present at " stables,"

INTRODUCTION

drill, &c. Let us quote again from the "Service Intérieur": "They must maintain perfect order in their *peloton*" [company] "excite emulation among their men, advise union" [the only union I ever saw was in the hatred all the men felt against them], "develop the love of service, and always show an impartial example of justice." [But wait until I tell my own story.] "The chief of a *peloton* visits it daily. He inquires into everything relating to it. . . .

"He sees to the cleanliness of his men" [mine must have had peculiar ideas on the subject]. . . . "Often and without warning he inspects the clothes of a man whom he suspects of bad conduct.

"He passes constant reviews of the men's effects" [doesn't he], "and when a man returns after an absence of fifteen days or more he inspects his kit. . . ."

He does many other things—in theory—but chiefly acts on the principle that rules are made to be broken.

PETIT ETAT MAJOR AND PELOTON HORS RANG.

Under these titles are known all the skilled assistants (whether non-commissioned officers or troopers) who are employed as clerks in the offices of the Treasurer, and other officers employed in the various administrative services of the regiment. The Capitaine d'habillement acts as their Captain Commandant.

ADJUDANTS.

The *Adjudants*, although non-commissioned officers, wear the uniform of a Sub-lieutenant, the only difference being that their galoons are striped with a small red thread. They receive from the troopers and other non-commissioned officers the same marks of respect as officers.

INTRODUCTION

There are three *Adjudants* in each cavalry regiment. The first two are the *Adjudants* proper, while the third (*Adjudant vaguemestre*) has different duties. The two *Adjudants* have under their immediate authority all the Sergeants and Corporals so far as the discipline and the general police of barracks are concerned. They have to keep watch over the private conduct and appearance of the Sergeants.

They take "the week" in turn under the immediate orders of the "Captain of the Week." All strangers wishing to enter the barracks are referred to him when he takes "the week." The *Adjudant* receives from the one he has relieved:

(1) The list of all Sergeants and Corporals, so as to arrange their rotation of duty;

(2) The list of the various Sergeants and Corporals who take "the week" at the same time as himself;

(3) The register of punishments of non-commissioned officers and troopers, on which he inscribes all punishments of two days or more of *Salle de Police*, or confinement to the room, or of four days or more C.B.;

(4) The list of men under punishment, which he hands over to the Sergeant of the Guard.

He posts up in the orderly room the list of the officers, Sergeants, and Corporals "of the week."

He is responsible for all trumpet calls.

The Colonel's orders and decisions are handed over to him for dictation to the various Sergeant-majors, by whom they are read aloud to the troopers of each squadron, after afternoon "stables."

He conveys the General's orders to the Colonel. Every morning after *réveille* each Sergeant-major hands over to him a report on the morning roll-call, but this call never actually takes place in the cavalry.

INTRODUCTION

At the same time the Sergeant of the Guard hands over to him the register bearing the names of all troopers who have returned to barracks after the last roll-call (9 P.M.),* and he reports on these to the " Captain of the Week."

He sees that the canteens are closed at the proper time, and that lights are extinguished in the rooms at 10 P.M. He has besides the general control of all men undergoing punishment.

It will thus be seen what enormous power the *Adjudant* has. With his connivance a trooper may absent himself for three or four days without any one being the wiser. Let a Sergeant or a Sergeant-major dare to report the matter to the Captain and he will soon discover what it will cost him. How I made use of the *Adjudant* will be seen when I describe my personal adventures. " Stand well with your Sergeant-major and one of the *Adjudants* and you are all right," is a well-known saying in the French cavalry.

The *Adjudant-vaguemestre* is really the regimental postmaster and postman; he collects letters, cashes money-orders for the troopers, and does all sorts of dirty work others don't care to undertake; he acts as Sergeant-major to the *Peloton hors rang,* and is usually chosen from among old Sergeants who are unfit for anything else.

Of the skilled artisans, armourers, saddlers, tailors, &c., little or nothing need be said, as they are soldiers but in name.

Let us now return to the true inner life of a regiment, the squadron and its units.

* It was 8 P.M. in my time.

INTRODUCTION

SERGEANT-MAJOR (MARÉCHAL DE LOGIS CHEF).

The Sergeant-major is the right hand of the Captain commanding a squadron. In theory he is, of course, far below a Lieutenant or Sub-lieutenant; in practice—at least in most squadrons—he is the real head of the squadron in barracks. He is in hourly contact with the Sergeants, Corporals, and troopers, and it is through the Sergeant-major that the Captain judges them. Most Sergeant-majors will send a man to prison in the Captain's name, knowing well that the latter will approve of and endorse their decision.

"The Sergeant-major," says the "Service Intérieur," "must study the conduct, the character, and the capabilities of the Sergeants, Corporals, and troopers of his squadron, in order to give information to the officers, and chiefly to the Captain commanding the squadron. He gives all orders with regard to duty, dress, and discipline. . . . He is the Captain's agent in all matters of administration and accounts, he is responsible for the proper keeping of all books, registers, &c., and for the proper state of all the *matériel* belonging to the squadron.

"The Sergeant *fourrier* and Corporal *fourrier* do the clerical work under his immediate supervision. He is responsible for the proper keeping of the squadron stores and must supervise the reception, distribution or return of every article, whatever may be its nature. . . ." The Sergeant of the Week hands over to him the list of all sick men and reports to him on every roll-call.

"It is through him that all applications of the Sergeants, Corporals, or troopers must be addressed; after informing the Lieutenant he submits these applications to the Captain. Troopers cannot, without his leave, change their rotation of duty."

INTRODUCTION

SERGEANT (MARÉCHAL DES LOGIS).

"The Sergeants give the Corporals and troopers all orders relating to duty, police, discipline, and military instruction." They take in turn the duty "of the week" in their squadron. Sergeants drill the men of their *peloton*, and are responsible to their Lieutenant for the horses of their *peloton*.

They have to take particular care that the rooms are kept in proper order, that the men have their clothes properly cleaned and arranged above their beds, and that no article of their kit is missing; they take care that the arms and saddlery are always kept in perfect order; they are responsible for the cleanliness of their men, seeing that their clothes are duly mended, and that they are frequently shaved and have their hair cropped short.

Whenever the *peloton* is ordered to assemble, the Sergeant passes through the rooms to see that the troopers are getting ready. If the *peloton* has to be mounted, the Sergeant sees that the horses are properly saddled. He always superintends "stables" and sees that the horses are properly groomed. When the *peloton* is ordered to assemble singly, he calls the roll and reports to the Lieutenant in command; in case, however, the whole squadron is ordered out, he reports to the Sergeant-major.

"SERGEANT OF THE WEEK."—The Sergeant of the Week is under the direct orders of the officer "of the week" and seconds him in every way.

He reports on the morning and evening roll-calls to the Sergeant-major, and hands over to him the list of the sick troopers. At the daily parade of the squadron he notes all duties which are ordered and designates the troopers for the fatigues and distributions. After *réveille* he goes to the stables and superintends their cleaning and airing; he

INTRODUCTION

must see that all head-stalls and stable utensils are in proper order; he transmits to the stable guards their orders, and sees that these are punctually executed. In case of the sickness of a horse he sends at once for the Vet.

The Sergeant of the Week also keeps the key of the oat-bin and is responsible for the proper distribution of its contents as well as of forage. Before the time fixed for the assembly of the guard of the day he sees that the troopers who have been ordered for such duty are properly turned out. He then escorts them to the place which has been fixed for the parade. He takes to the cells the troopers who are to be punished, and those who are sick to the Doctor's inspection.

He has to see that all corridors, staircases, and rooms of his squadron are kept clean, and swept twice daily.

SERGENT FOURRIER.

The Sergeant *fourrier* is under the direct orders of the Sergeant-major, keeping all books and accounts under his supervision; he receives besides, on his behalf, all supplies, and is responsible for them. He escorts every man sent to hospital.

CAPORAL FOURRIER.

This N.C.O. helps generally the Sergeant *fourrier*. He enters in a book all the orders issued by the Colonel, and takes it to each officer of the squadron; he reads these orders out to the assembled troopers after afternoon " stables."

INTRODUCTION

CORPORALS.
(In command of an *escouade* of about ten men.)

" A Corporal sleeps in the same room with the troopers of his *escouade;* he sees that his troopers wash their heads, faces, hands and feet." He sees that the beds are properly made, and that the troopers ordered for special duty are in readiness. Once a week, on the day fixed by the Captain, he gets all the kits thoroughly cleaned.

" He takes particular care that the troopers change their linen once a week."

On pay-day he receives the pay from the Sergeant-major and hands it over to the troopers. He superintends the drill of the recruits, teaches them how to do their packing, and how to clean their arms and kit. He also shows them how to groom their horses.

He reports to the Sergeant the punishments he has given, and reports to him on matters generally.

At *réveille* he compels the troopers to rise, and calls the roll; he sees that all beds are uncovered, and that the great-coats which may have been used at night are properly rolled up. He then sends to the stables a certain number of men to feed the horses and to clean the stalls.

" When the other men are dressed he orders the windows to be opened in order to change the air."

He takes the names of the sick men, and reports on the events of the night.

He designates a trooper in turn to clean and tidy up the room. (When several *escouades* sleep in the same room the senior Corporal is in charge.) It is his duty to keep proper order. He stops all games likely to lead to quarrels, he sends men who are drunk to bed; should they disturb the peace he calls the Sergeant of the Week by whom they are sent to the *Salle de Police.* He forbids

INTRODUCTION

smoking in bed, and sees that troopers take their meals properly. In winter he takes care that the stoves are heated in moderation, and in the evening sees that the water jug is full. When the trumpeter has sounded "lights out," he sees that all lights are extinguished.

When an officer enters the room the Corporal commands "*Fixe!*" (attention). The troopers rise, uncover themselves, and stand at attention until the officer has given the word "*Repos!*" (stand at ease). Should the officer be a Field or General officer the Corporal commands "*A vos rangs—Fixe!*" at which command every trooper stands at the foot of his bed at "attention."

The "CORPORAL OF THE WEEK" helps generally the "Sergeant of the Week," who, in practice, relies upon him for the performance of many of the duties he is supposed to carry out himself.

CAPORAL D'ORDINAIRE.

This Corporal takes delivery of, or purchases, the supplies required for the meals of the troopers of his squadron; he has also the supervision of the kitchen, and collects the washing.

IV

PUNISHMENTS

"The following are regarded as offences against discipline, and punished as such according to their gravity:

"On the part of the superior, every act of weakness, abuse of authority, insulting language, or the unjust infliction of any punishment.

"On the part of the inferior, murmuring, unseemly

INTRODUCTION

answers, lack of obedience (whatever may be the circumstances or the provocation); evading a punishment; drunkenness (even without disturbance); general misconduct, debt, quarrels . . . in fact, every dereliction of military duty, whether it is the result of negligence, laziness, or stubbornness."

The fact of publishing, even under a *nom de plume*, a book, pamphlet, article, or letter, whatever may be its subject, without previous leave from the Minister of War, is considered an offence against discipline.

" *Any man belonging to the army or navy can be punished by another man holding a rank superior to his own, whatever may be the place or the circumstances.*" To be rightly understood this requires some explanation. For instance, a Captain in the navy (who ranks as a Colonel), on leave in Paris, meets at a *café* a Major of a cavalry regiment; if the latter does not salute him, or misbehaves himself in any way, the naval officer can punish him on the spot. It constantly happens, for instance, that a trooper of a cavalry regiment passing a Corporal of the line fails to salute him. The Corporal has the right to punish the trooper forthwith.

" The officer in command of a regiment can increase or reduce punishments; he can even cancel them. In that case, he points out to the officer or non-commissioned officer the mistake he has made, and orders him to cancel himself the punishment he has inflicted. . . ." The Captain in command of a squadron can increase a punishment inflicted by one of his direct subordinates. He cannot, however, reduce such punishment without the Colonel's leave.

INTRODUCTION

PUNISHMENT OF OFFICERS.

The following are the punishments which may be inflicted on regimental officers:
(*a*) Arrêts simples (confinement to rooms).
(*b*) Reprimand by Colonel.
(*c*) Arrêts de rigueur (strict confinement to room).
(*d*) Arrêts de forteresse (confinement in a fortress).
(*e*) Reprimand by a General.

A Lieutenant can inflict a punishment of four days *arrêts simples* on a Sub-lieutenant; a Captain a punishment of eight days on any officer of lower rank; a Captain of a squadron fifteen days on officers of his own squadron; a Major fifteen days, and the Colonel thirty days, on any officer of a rank lower than their own.

An officer thus placed under arrest must attend to his military duties as usual, but in the intervals he must keep to his room, and may receive no visits except official ones.

Arrêts de rigueur (viz., confinement to the room, with a sentry posted at the door) and *arrêts de forteresse* can be inflicted by the Colonel alone. He can give any officer under his orders thirty days of the former and fifteen days of the latter.

(In no case can an officer apply for a court-martial, as in England. In some regiments, especially in the line, officers get punished more frequently than privates get mere C.B. in a British regiment.)

"The punishment begins from the moment it has been inflicted."

Let it be also noted that an officer can inflict a punishment on any other officer inferior in rank to himself, to whatever squadron he may belong, and can similarly punish officers of other regiments; and, as stated before, any

INTRODUCTION

officer in the navy can punish an officer in the army of inferior rank, and *vice versâ!*

Recent events in France give special interest to this subject, and I will therefore give some account of various other punishments which can be inflicted upon French officers without enabling them to appeal to a court-martial.

The question is, indeed, one of such high interest at the present juncture that I will quote verbatim from the Army Regulations:

" When an officer commits a fault, which—without being such as to entail the loss of his commission or his being sent before a court-martial—is still serious enough to require a heavier punishment than those above described, he can be suspended (placed in *non-activité*) or his commission can be cancelled (*ils peuvent être mis en réforme*)."

The *non-activité*, which means the temporary exclusion from the service, is determined by decree of the President of the Republic upon the report of the Minister of War.

The " superior authority " decides as to the causes which may necessitate the placing of an officer in *non-activité*, a disciplinary measure taken in cases of less serious a nature than those for which an officer may lose his commission (*peut être mis en réforme—c'est-à-dire, l'exclusion définitive de l'armée* *).

The place of an officer who has been suspended (*non-activité par suspension d'emploi*) is not filled up during a year, and he can be sent back to his regiment before the expiration of that period.

An officer placed in non-activity *par retrait d'emploi* remains in that position for an unlimited period, but at the end of three years a court of inquiry (*un conseil d'enquête*) is called upon to give its opinion as to whether the

---
* The vagueness of this should be noted.

INTRODUCTION

officer ought to be cashiered or not (*si l'officier doit être mis en réforme*).

When the officer commanding a regiment considers that an officer under his orders cannot remain *en activité* either on account of misconduct or on account of neglect of duty, or else through incapacity, he details his complaint against the said officer in a report he sends to the Major-general commanding his brigade. He specifies whether he considers that the officer ought to be suspended for a time or permanently (*si l'officier doit être mis en non-activité par suspension ou par retrait d'emploi*), and sends with his complaint a list of the various punishments inflicted on the officer, a copy of the officer's notes, and, if necessary, documents relating to the facts upon which the demand is based.

The documents are examined by the General commanding the brigade, who forwards them to the General commanding the division, who sends them in his turn to the General commanding the army corps, by whom they are forwarded to the Minister of War. Each one of the above-mentioned Generals writes his opinion on the case.

An officer who has been suspended (*mis en non-activité*) remains subject to military discipline under the *surveillance* of the General commanding the military district where he has been allowed to reside.* The *Mise en réforme* † (cashiering) is determined by the President of the Republic upon the proposal of the Minister of War as a disciplinary measure.

This punishment can be inflicted upon an officer as an immediate measure without it being necessary that he should have been previously suspended: it can be in-

---
* Which means that an officer so punished cannot travel out of his district without leave.
† Colonel Picquart's case.

INTRODUCTION

flicted for habitual misconduct, serious neglect of duty, or breach of discipline, or dishonourable conduct. It can also become the consequence of three years of non-activity either as a disciplinary measure or through ill-health. When an officer is, as above stated, sent before a commission of enquiry (*Conseil d'Enquête*) the minutes of the proceedings are forwarded to the Minister of War.

The opinion of such a commission cannot be modified except in favour of the office * (*sic*). An officer who has been cashiered (*en réforme*) is liberated from all obligations imposed on officers in a position of activity or non-activity.†

I have wandered far away from the regiment, I have quoted dry law, and I feel afraid that readers will begin to ask; "But what about your own adventures?" I am as anxious as my readers to get to them, but I think it better to get rid of all the dreary details first, and this introduction will enable me to go on with my story without having constantly to stop to explain this or that. I shall not abuse the patience of my readers much longer, but there are still a few details I must explain, and I hope that I shall be forgiven for doing so.

The punishments which may be inflicted on non-commissioned officers are as follows:—

(i) Confinement to barracks after the evening roll-call. This is given to Sergeants who show laziness in, or ignorance of, their work, or who return late to barracks. (N.C.O.s, unless thus punished, can remain out till 11 P.M.)

(ii) Confinement to barracks. Inflicted on a Sergeant

---

* L'avis du conseil ne peut être modifié qu'en faveur de l'officier. ("Service Intérieur," p. 220.)

† It therefore stands to reason that a court-martial could not legally try Colonel Picquart.

INTRODUCTION

whose personal appearance is slovenly, or who allows his men to fail in their appearance.

(iii) Confinement to the room. Inflicted for slight breaches of discipline. For more serious offences N.C.O.s are sent to prison. (Except, in the latter case, N.C.O.s under punishment have to do their duty as usual.)

(iv) Reprimand by Captain commanding the squadron.

(v) Reduction in rank (*retrogradation*).

(vi) Absolute loss of rank (*cassation*).

The appended table explains itself:—

Punishments of N.C.O.s.	Right of Punishment by—					
	Sergeant-major.	Sergeant-major in his Squadron.	Adjudant, Lieut. and Sub-lieut.	Captain.	Majors, and Capt.-commt.	Colonel.
	Days.	Days.	Days.	Days.	Days.	Days.
(i)	4	8	8	15	30	30
(ii)	2	4	8	8	15	30
(iii)	—	—	4	8	15	30
Prison . . .	—	—	—	—	8	15

Corporals in the French army do not rank as N.C.O.s. The latter are far better treated now than they were in my time, the change being entirely due to General Boulanger, and being one of the causes of his great popularity among the soldiers. Until he became Minister of War, non-commissioned officers could be sent to the *Salle de Police* (lock-up). An *Adjudant* could give a Sergeant eight days of *Salle de Police*, or fifteen days' C.B., and a Sergeant-major could give the Sergeants four days' *Salle de Police* and eight days' C.B. Sergeants could even be sent to prison by the *Adjudants*. There existed a *Salle de Police* separate from the one allotted to the men, to which

INTRODUCTION

Sergeants and Corporals were sent together, the only difference being that Sergeants were allowed a straw mattress and blanket, while the Corporals were only allowed one blanket and slept on boards.

The punishments inflicted on Corporals are:
   (*a*) Confinement to barracks.
   (*b*) *Salle de Police* (lock-up).
   (*c*) Prison.
   (*d*) Reduction to the ranks.

Nature of Punishment of Corporals.	Right of Punishment by—						
	Sergeants.	Sergeant-majors.	Sergeant-major in his Squadron.	Adjudant, Sub-lieut. and Lieuts.	Captains.	Field Officers and Captains commanding a Squadron.	Colonel.
	Days.	Days.	Days.	Days.	Days.	Days.	Days.
(*a*) . . .	4	4	8	8	15	30	30
(*b*) . . .	—	—	—	4	8	15	30
(*c*) . . .	—	—	—	—	—	8	15

Corporals are confined to barracks for slight breaches of discipline. For failing to answer the evening call, bad language,* disobedience, quarrels, drunkenness, Corporals are sent to the *Salle de Police*. For more serious faults, especially when on duty, Corporals are sent to prison.

TROOPERS.

The punishments inflicted on troopers are:
   (*a*) Extra work.
   (*b*) Inspection with the guard parade.

* *e.g.*, saying that Dreyfus is innocent. Reading a newspaper—whatever it may be—is also a serious offence.

INTRODUCTION

(*c*) Confinement to barracks.
(*d*) *Salle de Police.*
(*e*) Prison.
(*f*) Cells (solitary confinement).

Punishments (*a*), (*b*), (*c*) were in my time very seldom inflicted in a cavalry regiment, being regarded as too mild for a trooper and only fit for men in the line. I am told that this is still the case.

Nature of Punishments given to Troopers.	Right of Punishment by—						
	Corporals	Sergeants and Sergeant-major.	Sergeant-major in his Squadron.	Adjudant, Sub-lieut. and Lieuts.	Captains.	Field Officers and Captains commanding a Squadron.	Colonel.
	Days.	Days.	Days.	Days.	Days.	Days.	Days.
(*c*) . . .	2	4	8	8	15	30	30
(*d*) . . .	—	—	—	4	8	15	30
(*e*) . . .	—	—	—	—	—	8	15
(*f*) . . .	—	—	—	—	—	—	8

(Until General Boulanger became Minister of War Corporals could give a trooper two days' *Salle de Police*; a Sergeant could inflict four days, a Sergeant-major eight days, and an *Adjudant* fifteen days, or four days' prison.)

Troopers confined to barracks are employed in doing the hardest and dirtiest manual work. They take part in every drill and duty besides. Those sent to the *Salle de Police* are kept at night in the lock-up. Troopers sent to prison do no duty, but undergo special punishment drill for three hours in the morning and three hours at night. They are deprived of pay, of sugar, and of coffee.

Troopers in the cells are kept in confinement day and

INTRODUCTION

night. Only a blanket without bedding is allowed to the troopers in prison or in the cells.

Any Corporal or trooper who, during his three years' service, has been sent to prison or to the cells, must at the expiration of his three years' service, remain with the colours for a number of days equal to those he has spent in prison or in the cells.

I have not yet exhausted the list of punishments which may be inflicted upon French privates. There is another one more terrible than all the others I have described. This consists in sending a soldier to the *Compagnies de discipline*. This means transportation to Algeria. There the soldier is drafted into one of the special companies encamped far away in the interior. The men are drilled for several hours daily, and during the remainder of the time they are employed at road-making and subjected to other hard labour. Officers and Sergeants in command are always armed with loaded revolvers, and at the least sign of disobedience they can blow a man's brains out. For the slightest fault these men are sent to the *silos*—deep holes dug in the ground, and funnel-shaped at the bottom, so that neither standing, sitting, nor lying down is possible. They are left there for one or two days with bread and water. An awful case occurred some years ago in connection with these *silos*, which will be described in the course of my narrative.

"The Minister of War," say the regulations, "has full power to send to the *Compagnies de discipline* any private who has committed one or several faults, the gravity of which makes any other mode of repression inadequate."

Usually, however, such men are tried before a *Conseil de discipline*. When the Captain in command of a squadron considers that one of his troopers has deserved to be sent to a *Compagnie de discipline* he sends a written report

INTRODUCTION

to the Major stating the faults or misdemeanours of the trooper and the punishments which have been inflicted upon him, dwelling upon the recurrence of certain acts which show a perseverance in ill-doing, a danger to the good order of the service.

This report is endorsed by the Major, and the Lieutenant-colonel, who hands it over to the Colonel. The latter can either transmit this report to the Minister of War, who decides upon the case, or (as is usually done) he can assemble a disciplinary commission (*Conseil de discipline*) consisting of the following officers of the regiment:

One Major (who presides over the commission).

The two senior Captains and the two senior Lieutenants, provided they do not belong to the squadron of the trooper to be tried.

The Captain who applies for the infliction of the punishment, as well as the Major who commands the squadrons to which the trooper belongs, lay their case before the court. They then retire, and the trooper is brought in and makes his defence. The court then deliberates and sends its decision to the Colonel. It must be remembered that the court merely gives its advice, and this is sent to the General commanding the division of which the regiment is a unit. Should the court recommend the trooper to be sent to the *Compagnies de discipline,* the General can decline to act upon their advice, but should the court decide that the trooper ought not to be sent there, the General is bound to abide by the decision. This seems, at first blush, an equitable procedure, but when we remember the almost unlimited power possessed by a Colonel over the officers of his regiment, it is easy to realise that a *Conseil de discipline* usually sits for the mere purpose of carrying out the well-ascertained wishes of the supreme regimental authority.

CHAPTER I

I HAVE already explained that twenty years ago, when I served my time in the ranks of the French army, French military law differed from what it is now. It is true that —speaking generally—every able-bodied Frenchman was then, as now, compelled to undergo five years' active service, but for young men who had graduated at a University there was the loop-hole of escape described in the Introduction. Having no ambition to serve for five years as a private, I naturally determined to avail myself of the benefit of the law, and accordingly in the month of August, 1879, I went over to the head-quarters of the military division of Paris, and there, after producing all the papers required by French red-tapeism,* I signed a voluntary engagement for a period of one year (*Engagement conditionnel*).

A month later I received orders to appear before the *Conseil de revision*, held in the town-hall of my district. About two hundred fellows, belonging to every class of society, were waiting in the yard—most of them, indeed, being roughs from la Villette (the Whitechapel of Paris). We were called up by batches of twenty-five, and shown by gendarmes into a room, around which stood long benches with pegs above them. A red-hot stove was burn-

* Birth certificate, father's consent, certificate of degree, certificate of respectability and good morals (signed by the local Police Commissary), father's undertaking to pay £60 on my being accepted by the *Conseil de revision*.

ing in a corner of this room, and as there was no ventilation of any kind, and more than one hundred unwashed ruffians had already undressed and dressed there, the smell was abominable. A gendarme then ordered us to strip off all our clothing, barring our socks, and when we had done so—what a sight we were!—he called each one of us in turn and placed us under a measuring gauge. He first took our height with our socks on, and then without them—except in the case of those who possessed no such garment, and who formed the majority. The gendarme who measured us was a Sergeant, and he dictated to a private the result of his measurements. When my turn came he placed me under the apparatus and then asked for my name.

"Deele," I said.

"And your Christian name?"

"Lionel."

"Lionel," he replied; "that's not a Christian name."

I assured him that it was my Christian name, and, what was more, the only one I possessed.

"Well, it's a queer Christian name, and I don't know where your people fished it out," he remarked. After a glance at the scale he dictated "1.78 metre in his socks," to his subordinate. He then ordered me to remove my socks, and, measuring me once more, pronounced the verdict "1.79 metre without socks."

"But, Sergeant," I asked, "how can I be taller without my socks than with them on?"

"You will perhaps teach me my business!" he angrily replied, and seeing that the private was hesitating to write down the figures, "D—— you," he shouted, "are you going to take that down or not?"

The private silently obeyed, doubtless accustomed for years to passive obedience.

TROOPER 3809

I was then told to stand aside, and another fellow was called up. We were then sent, each in turn, into another room, where sat the *Conseil de revision*, presided over by a General in full uniform, assisted by officials also in uniform, and a few respectable-looking old gentlemen. I confess that I felt rather shy at having to appear without clothes before so ornamental a company, whose uniforms strangely contrasted with the state of nature I was in. A clerk, having inquired my name, fished out my papers from a huge bundle, and asked me a long list of questions about my family history. The President then inquired whether I could show any cause why I should not serve, and upon my negative reply, a military surgeon proceeded to examine me. A paper was handed over to him by the clerk.

"What's this?" he said. "You're one metre seventy-eight in your socks, and a centimetre more without them?"

"That's just what I said to the gendarme, sir," I replied, "but he told me to shut up."

The gendarme was called and questioned about the matter.

"All I can say, sir," he replied, "is that a machine can't lie, and I've had enough experience not to make a mistake."

There was a burst of laughter from all the members of the council, which seemed to greatly astonish the old gendarme. The doctor took me back to measure me himself, and finding that my exact height was one metre seventy-nine without socks, he pointed this out to the gendarme. The latter, however, shook his head. "Well, sir," he stoutly declared, "all I can say is that he was one seventy-eight just now." I was brought back to the council-room and the doctor then proceeded to take my chest and other measurements, dictating to the clerk a list of my various "points." He then asked me about my past illnesses, and inquired into the health of my father, mother, and grandparents. He then tested my heart and lungs, felt my legs, and examined my teeth; concluding the whole performance by making me sit down, walk, and cough. I felt like a horse under examination by a "Vet." The result of this inspection was that I was passed as fit for service. Before retiring I was asked whether I preferred to serve in the infantry, artillery, heavy or light cavalry. I expressed a desire to serve in the Dragoons, and my wish was duly noted. Shortly afterwards I received notice to present myself at one of the Paris cavalry barracks, in order to pass an examination in riding, for *Volontaires,* having then to serve only one year, were admitted into the cavalry only if they could already ride. The examination was a most simple one: we had to mount a horse, which was saddled, but without stirrups, and then had to walk, trot, and canter once round the riding-school. About a score of others passed the examination at the same time as myself, and only one candidate, who managed to fall off his horse while trotting, was rejected as unfit to serve in the cavalry, though of the whole batch hardly three could pretend to a knowledge of horsemanship.

At the beginning of October I received a notification that I was to serve in the 9th Dragoons, at Dinan in Brittany. I was most anxious not to go so far from Paris, and as my maternal uncle then held a most prominent position in the *Senat,* being Leader of the Left Centre, I obtained a letter from him to the Minister of War, who allowed me to choose whatever regiment I liked. One year before, a great friend of mine, Baron de Lanoy, had enlisted for five years in the 50th Dragoons stationed at Noilly,* and he had lately been promoted to the rank of

* All names of persons and places in the narrative are fictitious.

Sergeant. He had strongly advised me to join his regiment, the Colonel of which, the Marquis de Vieilleville, was most favourably disposed towards the *Volontaires.* At my request I was accordingly drafted into that regiment. Unfortunately, shortly before I joined, the Marquis died, and was replaced by Colonel Hermann, who hated *Volontaires,* and proved, as will be seen, a martinet of the worst type.

Towards the end of October I received my *feuille de route,* ordering me to present myself at 10 A.M. at the cavalry barracks at Noilly. It was a dull, dreary, miserable, wet day when I took a train at the *gare du Nord* at half-past seven in the morning, to begin my military experiences—experiences which proved, as will be seen, little short of what I might have had to suffer had I been sentenced to hard labour. An hour later the train stopped at Noilly, where, following the advice previously given to me by my friend de Lanoy, I drove to the Crown Hotel, the best in the place, engaged a room, and hastily swallowed the last decent breakfast I was to enjoy for many days to come. Half an hour before the appointed time I drove to the barracks. The sentry stood shivering in his box, and the thought then flashed across my mind that it would soon become my lot to stand there myself. I passed the gate, and seeing one of the troopers standing outside the guard-room, I was about to ask him where I could find my friend, Sergeant de Lanoy, when a Sergeant, dragging his sword on the ground, stepped out of the guard-room and addressed me:

"Hullo! what do you want, you there?"

"Sir," I replied, "I am a *Volontaire,* and I want to go and see a friend of mine, Sergeant de Lanoy."

"Oh, you're a *Volontaire,* are you? Well, you can wait where you are!"

TROOPER 3809

"But, sir," I asked again, "can't I be allowed to go and see Sergeant de Lanoy?"

"What! Answers, eh? You'll have to be put through your paces at once, my fine fellow, or else you will make the acquaintance of the *boite* (cells) sooner than you care for. Wait there and shut up," he concluded.

There was nothing for it, therefore, but to walk up and down in the drizzling rain. I had already visited the barracks once, a few months before, when I came to pay a call on de Lanoy, little thinking then that I should soon belong to his regiment. Now they presented a much keener interest for me, and I looked anxiously at my surroundings. On each side of the gate stood a small lodge. One of these was used as a guard-room, the other was the residence of the barrack caretaker, a post usually bestowed on an old pensioned non-commissioned officer. The barrack yard itself was about 400 yards long and 250 broad; in the middle of it stood the riding-school, flanked on each side by two rows of huge two-storied buildings running at right angles to the entrance gate. On the ground floor of these buildings were the stables, and above them the men's quarters. The right-hand portion of the barracks was occupied by an infantry regiment, while the remainder was used by the Dragoons. It may here be noted that different names are given to the barracks occupied by cavalry and by infantry, the latter being called *casernes*, while the former are termed *quartiers*. The yard was teeming with life: troopers in stable uniforms were running to and fro, some carrying buckets of water, others empty-handed; in front of me was a group of half-a-dozen men pumping water into a long tank running along the riding-school; other troopers were sweeping the yard, while one of their number collected in a wheelbarrow the little heaps of refuse gathered by the others; then an officer came out of the riding-school and called to a trooper to take back his charger to the stables. In a few moments a man came running to the guard-room, and shouted to the Trumpeter to call the Sergeants of the Week quickly, as the Captain of the Week wanted them. The Trumpeter sounded the call, and had hardly finished when five Sergeants came at a run and went to the Captain, who stood near the riding-school, where I could hear him abusing them with frantic gesticulations. My attention was next called to six troopers in stable dress (but with swords and carbines), their faces turned towards a wall; they were being drilled by a Sergeant, and I was struck by the length of time during which they remained in the same position. While I was looking at them the Sergeant gave a word of command, and the troopers stood with their swords extended at arm's length: two, three, minutes elapsed, and I could see the poor fellows getting so tired that they had to bend their bodies to remain with their swords in the right position; the Sergeant, walking up and down, did not seem to mind this, but one of the troopers having slightly bent his arm, the Sergeant, in a monotonous tone of voice, calling the fellow by name, said, " So-and-so, two days more for not holding your sword straight." This seemed to me little short of barbaric cruelty. I afterwards realised that this exercise was punishment drill for men punished with prison. Soon the Trumpeter sounded " Soup," and every trooper employed in the barrack square hurried to put away his tools, while men rushed from every corner, shouting like school-boys let loose. While I was watching the scene I have described I noticed the arrival of a tall, handsome, and well-groomed young man in civilian attire, who asked me if I was a *Volontaire*, adding that he was himself one, and that he wanted to know where he had to report himself. In order to save him from the Sergeant's abuse,

I warned him that he had better wait with me until the Sergeant of the Guard called us. While we were talking the Sergeant appeared on the threshold of the guard-room, and, at the top of his voice, shouted out, " What the deuce are you hatching there, you idiots? I suppose you're another of these (using a double-barrelled adjective) *Volontaires?*" turning to my companion.

" Yes, sir," replied the young fellow.

" Well, why the devil don't you come and report yourself, you blockhead? "

" Oh, sir," replied Walter—for such we will suppose his name to be—" this gentleman," pointing to me, " told me—"

" This gentleman told you!" howled the Sergeant, " this *gentleman,* indeed; you're really too damned polite. You're another colt who requires breaking in. Now, you two young *pekins,** advance to orders, and show me your papers." We produced our *feuilles de route,* and the Sergeant having examined them told us to go to the Paymaster's office in the town. " Oh! you want to speak to Sergeant de Lanoy, do you? " he said to me. " I'll give you a trooper to take you to him."

Having asked my new comrade to wait a few minutes for me outside the barracks, so that we might go together to the Paymaster's office, I was going with the trooper towards de Lanoy's quarters when we met him coming to look out for me. I told him how I had been treated by the Sergeant of the Guard, and he replied that he was not in the least astonished, as the fellow was a brute, adding that he had no right to keep me waiting when I asked to go and see him. " I'll have it out with him," he remarked, adding: " You go straight to the Paymaster's office and ask to be drafted into my squadron, the 3rd, and I'll see

* An offensive term for "civilian" used by soldiers.

that you're placed under my orders, so that I can look after you." We then parted, and outside the barracks, I found Jack Walter waiting for me. Curiously enough, though he was the first acquaintance I made in the regiment, our friendship, which began that day, has lasted ever since. My friend is of English origin (his grandfather having been an Englishman who became naturalised in France), and were I to mention his real name it would be recognised by most of my readers as that of a rising painter of undoubted genius, whose works have graced many a *Salon*. We went to the Paymaster's office, and, although we were rather upset by the reception we had received from the Sergeant of the Guard, we were both very keen on serving.

The Paymaster made no difficulty about placing me in the 3rd squadron, while Walter was drafted into the 2nd, having a letter of introduction to one of the officers of that squadron. We each received a paper from the Paymaster's clerk with instructions to hand them over to our respective Sergeant-majors; the clerk kindly added that we need not return to barracks before 11 A.M., as the Sergeants were eating their breakfast. When I returned to the barracks I went to the Sergeant of the Guard and told him that I was back from the Paymaster's office, asking him to direct me to my Sergeant-major's office.

" Do you take me for a sign-post?" he answered.

" No, sir," I replied, " but I wanted your leave before asking a trooper to show me the way."

" You long-nosed chap, you're a soldier now, remember that; so do me the honour of calling me ' Sergeant,' and not ' sir.' "

" Yes, Sergeant," I replied. He then ordered a trooper who stood in the guard-room to take me to the office of my Sergeant-major. " By the way," he said, as I was going off, " what squadron do you belong to?"

"To the 3rd squadron, Sergeant."

"It's a pity you don't belong to mine," he answered: "I should like to have had you under my orders; it would have been a real pleasure to lick you into shape. But God help you if you ever cross my path. I don't like your face. When I don't like a man's face it's a poor chance he stands with me. Now go, clear out of this."

I'm sorry to say that it was my misfortune to have this man later on as my chief, and he duly proved that his boast was no vain one. When I reached the Sergeant-major's office I met outside the door my friend de Lanoy, and informed him that I had managed to be placed in his squadron.

"I'm glad of it," he said: "I will go with you to see the Sergeant-major, and try to get you put in my *peloton*" (company).

The Sergeant-major's office was a small room about sixteen feet by twelve, and served as a bedroom as well as an office. Three non-commissioned officers slept in it; the Sergeant-major, the Sergeant *fourrier*, and the Corporal *fourrier*, who ranks as a non-commissioned officer.* At a huge table in the centre of the room sat the Sergeant-major, a cold, stern, and distant individual. He granted de Lanoy's request, and put me in his *peloton*, ordering him at the same time to assign me a bed. De Lanoy, now my Sergeant, took me to the room where the 120 men of our squadron lived, ate, and slept. Two lateral partitions, ten or twelve feet high, ran the whole length of the room, with beds on each side of them. There were thus four rows of beds running along the room, each row being occupied by the troopers belonging to the same company. The beds themselves seemed so narrow that one could

* Corporals do not rank as such.

TROOPER 3809

hardly realise how a man could manage to sleep in one of them. At the head of each bed hung the trooper's sword; on a nail near it was suspended the bag containing brushes and other stable implements, while laid on two shelves running along the whole length of the room, above the beds, each trooper had his clothes carefully folded, and covered with a canvas bag on which the number under which he was registered appeared in large figures. On the top of this stood the helmet, with a pair of boots on each side of it. In each corner of the room the carbines stood on racks.

"Although you are not allowed to have any one to help you," said de Lanoy to me, "it is simply impossible for you to make your bed and to clean yourself, your clothes, your boots, saddlery, and weapons, for, the moment you begin the special work allotted to *Volontaires,* you will only have two hours to spare for meals every day; you must therefore arrange with two men to do your work, and I will place you between two good fellows whom I can trust to look after you. Only mind you," he added, " the new Colonel hates *Volontaires,* and as any man found helping them will be severely punished, you will have to allow ten francs a week to each of the troopers who look after your things." He then gave me an empty bed which was placed between those of the two men he had selected and who were only too glad to look after me. One of them was a Parisian ruffian, nicknamed *Titi de la Villette,* and the other a country bumpkin whom every one called " the old un," on account of his prematurely aged appearance. By de Lanoy's advice I gave Titi five francs to buy a two-gallon jar of wine for the troopers belonging to my *peloton.*

I then returned to the Sergeant-major's room, in order to supply him with particulars about myself such as have

TROOPER 3809

to be registered in the *livret* (regimental book) handed over to every French soldier.

" What's your name? " he began.

" Deele."

" What's your Christian name? "

" Lionel."

" Your profession? "

" I have none."

" Ah, yes," he replied, " a good-for-nothing, like all the *Volontaires.*" He then asked me for my father's name, Christian name and profession. I had also to give him my mother's maiden name, and to tell him whether I had any brothers or sisters. After this followed some rather ludicrous questions:

" Can you read and write? "

" Well," I said, " I suppose so, considering that I am a *Volontaire,* and have therefore taken a University degree."

" I want none of your remarks," replied the Sergeant-major, staring at me from head to foot; " answer my questions. Can you swim? " I replied in the affirmative.

" How many times have you been convicted? " I protested against the implication most energetically, but this only brought down on me a few cutting remarks about my cheek and impertinence. I had then to state whether I had had small-pox, whether I had been vaccinated or not, and whether I meant to re-enlist at the end of my year's service. My reply was in the negative as may well be imagined.

The Sergeant-major having taken down all my answers looked at me once more from top to toe, and then delivered the following little speech: " Look here, my boy," he began, " don't you run away with the idea that military service is all beer and skittles, or you'll soon be disappointed. I know what you *Volontaires* are like; you come here and imagine that you are going to have a good time of it; but I warn you that you will have a devilish bad time of it if you don't keep straight. I'm a good sort of fellow enough, but all the troopers will tell you that I am pretty stiff. I won't punish you often, but when I do, you'll remember it. You're too much of a fine gentleman for my taste, so I fancy it won't be long before you get into trouble. Now you can clear out—Sergeant de Lanoy will tell you what you have to do."

I retired, a sadder but a wiser man.

CHAPTER II

When I returned to my room the Corporal told me to follow him, as I had to undergo another medical inspection. Two other *Volontaires* who had been drafted into my squadron accompanied us; one of them evidently belonged to the middle classes, but the other looked a mere farm hand; he was, indeed, the son of a small farmer who had made great sacrifices to give his son a good education, and the boy, brought up in a Government school, had managed to get his B.A. degree, and his people had with difficulty scraped together the £60 necessary for obtaining the privilege of serving for one year only. The fact of the poor boy having been foolish enough to elect to serve in the cavalry can only be ascribed to his ignorance, as he lacked sufficient means for this branch of the service, and a bad time of it he had, poor fellow.

"I say," the Corporal said to me confidentially, "that chap is a nice sort of *Volontaire*: fancy—he said that he'd be blowed if he was going to pay eight bob a week to get a trooper to fag for him, and he's only given two bob for us to drink his health with, and not a brass farthing to me, his Corporal. Ain't I going to set him to work he won't relish!"

I took the hint and promptly handed the Corporal a ten-franc piece.

"Oh, I didn't mean that as a hint, of course," he said, pocketing the money, "but I know you're quite the gentleman, and the right sort too, and besides, you're a friend of

Sergeant de Lanoy, a real live Count, and the best of fellows into the bargain. I say you, what's-your-name," the Corporal went on, addressing the country bumpkin, " that's the canteen, what are you going to stand us ? "

" Oh," replied the poor fellow blushing, " I thought we were going to the medical inspection ? "

" Yes, of course we are," replied the Corporal, " but I can see that the Surgeon-major hasn't turned up yet, so we've got lots of time."

Taking pity on the poor fellow, I invited the Corporal and my two comrades to accompany me to the canteen, where we each had a cup of coffee, or rather chicory, with a glass of brandy, a refreshment which cost six pence for the four of us. The third *Volontaire* insisted upon standing another drink, and then we hastened to the dispensary. There we were told to wait in a large, bare ante-room, and Walter, whom I had not seen since the morning, joined us.

" A queer lot," he said, looking at our companions (there were fourteen of us, all told). One of them especially attracted our attention, for he had a huge moustache and was apparently a man of thirty. Half-a-dozen at most looked gentlemen, while the others were, to say the least, commonplace. Few of us felt inclined to be communicative, and when the Surgeon-major turned up he found us gazing at each other in silence. The Surgeon-major was a short, active, sharp-spoken man, and having entered his office he sent the Corporal in charge of the dispensary to order us to strip. Once more we were measured, felt, and thoroughly examined, all of us with one exception being passed as sound in wind and limb. The only one who failed to pass was rejected for short-sight, and ultimately invalided by the "*réforme*" commission. Our respective Corporals then took us back to our rooms, mine choosing a route through the canteen, where he insisted upon treating us—with the money I had given him—and he was half-seas-over before we left.

On our return to the room we found the Sergeant *fourrier* awaiting us, and he at once took us to the store, where we were to receive our outfit. The store consisted of a long apartment, along the centre of which rows of shelves ran, reaching from floor to ceiling; on these were classified, according to size, every conceivable article of regimental outfit, each department being under the charge of a skilled regimental Sergeant—a Sergeant tailor, a Sergeant bootmaker, a saddler, and a Sergeant storekeeper. We were first sent to the tailor. When my turn came he cast a glance over me, took from a shelf two pairs of trousers, two tunics, and one morning jacket. A Corporal showed us how to put them on according to regulations. The trousers are made of red felt, the seat and inside of the legs being of double thickness, that is to say, fully one inch thick; from the knee downwards they were covered with soft but thick leather, with straps to fix under the boots. When I first held them in front of me they nearly reached to my chin, but the Corporal said that they would be all right. I therefore got into them, but when I pulled my braces as tight as they would go, the trousers reached my armpits, and were so broad and so stiff that I could only walk with legs apart, to say nothing of their weight, which amounted to a good many pounds. I next got into my tunic, but the sleeves were so long that they reached the middle of my hand, while the collar was several inches too large for me. Under the collar of the tunic we had to fasten twice round our necks a blue cotton tie, two inches broad, fastened in a single knot in front. The tunic, a blue one, had a white collar with the regimental number in red figures embroidered on a blue background. A white strap was also affixed to the outside of the cuffs of the sleeves. The Corporal having examined me, ordered me to go to the bootmaker's department, in another part of the stores. "When you have been fitted with boots," he said, as I was walking off, "you must return to the tailor, who will send you to be inspected by the Captain."

When I reached the bootmaker's special corner, I found him cursing furiously because he could not fit one of my comrades. "Ah ces nom de Dieu de —— d'volontaires faudrait leur y faire des bottes expres. Ah malheur de Dieu vrai!" At last he seemed to have succeeded, and called me forward in turn. Having told me to take off one of my boots he looked at it: "Encore un d'ces malheurs de Dieu qu'a des pieds qu'ca fait suer," he exclaimed. "I shall never find boots for you," he went on, "why have you got a long narrow foot like that? Damnation! damnation!" he kept repeating as he went to look through his stock.

I must mention here that only four sizes of boots are kept in stock; they all are square-toed and immensely broad; the heels are nearly two inches high, with spurs nailed on to them. The top of the boot is made of a soft piece of leather on which two leather tags are sewn, the boot itself reaching half way up the calf of the leg. Most French soldiers are, I suppose, flat-footed. At any rate every boot presented to me was so low in the instep that I could not find a single pair in which I could insert my feet, until, at last, the assistant bootmaker triumphantly produced a pair about two inches too long and an inch too broad for me, explaining that if I put sufficient straw inside them they would fit all right. Finally, I had to pull down the leather portion of my trousers over the boots, not forgetting to fasten the under straps which alone prevented the boots from dropping off my feet. I hobbled as well as I could towards the tailor; he turned me round admiringly.

"It's all right," he said, "go and show yourself to the Captain."

My boots, as I have just said, were only held on my feet by the straps under them, and at every step my spurs caught in the heavy leather coverings of my trousers, but at last I managed to reach the Captain.

He ordered me to unbutton my tunic, and looking at my elephantine trousers: "What's that?" he cried; "put your braces lower," and artistically creasing my trousers from top to bottom, he stepped back a few feet, and having had a good look at me: "They're too short," he said, "go and get another pair from the tailor." As I was hobbling away he called me back. "What are those boots you've got on? They are too big for you. Are you such an idiot that you can't feel they are too big?"

"Yes, sir," I replied, "but——"

"But!" he exclaimed, "now look here, my boy, please understand that we don't allow remarks of any kind in the army. Go and get another pair of boots and trousers, and look sharp about it."

I stumbled back towards the bootmaker. "The Captain says," I began, "that these boots are too large for me and that you must find me another pair."

"Ah, these d——d *Volontaires*, what a lot of trouble they give us!" sighed the bootmaker. After looking through all his stock he chucked three more pairs at me. In vain I tried to get into them, and called the bootmaker to show him that none of them would fit me. "Why the deuce don't you take off your socks, socks aren't regulation," he angrily retorted. Notwithstanding my protests, I had to take them off. At last I managed to get one foot inside a boot, but the other, notwithstanding the efforts of two strong men, resisted. "All right," said the bootmaker, "I'll stretch it a bit later on."

So with only one boot on I hobbled to the tailor. "The Captain says my trousers are too short," I told him.

"Oh, I'll soon put them to rights," he answered. Having pulled my braces lower down he thereupon proceeded to crease the leather at the bottom of the trousers. "Now go back to the Captain," he said.

When I once more appeared before that officer he looked at me in utter disgust. "Why have you only got one boot on? Bootmaker," he shouted, without leaving me time to reply, "can't you find a pair of boots for this man?"

"No, sir," replied the bootmaker, who had hurried up at the officer's command, "he's got an instep like I've never seen."

"What business has a cripple like you in my squadron?" angrily remarked the Captain.

"But, sir—" I began.

"Shut up," he howled; "if you answer me again I'll send you straight off to the cells!" and without looking at my trousers, he angrily told me to put on my tunic, which I had removed at his orders. I did so, and was then ordered to fold my arm over my chest. "What's that?" said the Captain; "how dare you come and show me such a tunic? Are you such a fool as not to see for yourself it's too small?"

Warned by previous experience I made no reply, and returned limping with my single boot to the tailor. I explained to him that the Captain found my tunic too small.

"All right," he said, "I'll soon make it larger." He pulled it about a little and sent me back to the Captain, who once more ordered me to fold my right arm over my chest.

"Sleeves too long, go and change," he said brusquely.
I returned to the tailor and explained matters to him.

"Never mind, my boy," he said; "I'll make you one that will fit you, it won't cost you much, and, of course, you have got money—you're a *Volontaire;* now pull up your sleeve a bit and hold it tight under your arm before the Captain looks at you."

I did so.

"Fold your arms," once more said the Captain, when I returned to him for inspection. I followed the tailor's instruction. "It's too small," yelled the Captain, "go and change."

Without taking the trouble of doing this, I merely walked to where the tailor stood, and came back with the same tunic, letting the sleeve drop a little. This time, when the Captain examined me, he found it was a perfect fit!

One aspect of the grotesque muddle I have just described is a very serious one.

In the event of war breaking out between France and Germany, there is absolutely no doubt that success would depend on the rapidity with which troops could be mobilised in each country. While I was in the regiment, I witnessed more than once the arrival of the men belonging to the reserve. Although they are supposed to arrive with one suit of uniform, which they must take home with them after performing their act of service, their equipment has to be handed over to them, and the process entails all the confusion and trouble which were incurred when our own outfit had to be given out to us. In Germany things are very differently managed; every man belonging to the reserve knows at what barracks he will have to report himself, and every year the reserve men are called together for a few hours, and shown where each man can find his complete outfit. These are stored up in the following way: Long rows of shelves are divided into a certain number of partitions, each one of which contains the complete outfit of a private, every article of clothing having been properly fitted to the wearer, so that in case of mobilisation each soldier would know exactly where to go for his outfit, and no time would be wasted in distribution, in trying on uniforms and boots, and running from one department to the other. The object of calling out the reserve men for a few hours yearly is to teach them exactly where their outfit stands, and also to try on all the garments with a view to making any alterations rendered desirable by advancing years. In France, on the contrary, everything would be in confusion, and the various services, instead of helping each other, would lose valuable time in complicated red-tapeism.

But to proceed:

I went through the same ceremony with all the other clothes which were handed over to me. My outfit consisted of two tunics, two pairs of trousers, one short jacket for drill, one *képi*, and a helmet. The latter is certainly the most comfortable headgear in the French army. It rests on the head by means of a broad leather band, the ends of which are cut into strips tapering towards the centre, where they are tied together so as to form a kind of skull-cap, which bears the whole weight of the helmet. The latter affords a splendid protection against the sun and rain. Although its weight is nearly double that of the *shako* used by the light cavalry, it does not cause any pressure on the forehead or on the back of the head, as the latter invariably does. Besides the above garments, we also received two pairs of boots, two pairs of stable suits consisting of canvas trousers and blouse, with a blue and white cap and a dark-blue great-coat with a huge cape.

TROOPER 3809

Our regulation linen consisted of two shirts of the coarsest material, two pairs of drawers of the same stuff, two towels, and, besides these, two pairs of thick white leather gloves. (All soldiers being supposed to have hands of the same size, the regulation gloves are invariably "nines.") Socks form no part of the regulation outfit; the men usually replace them by bits of rag, which are nicknamed " Russian socks." To complete the list of our wearing apparel, I must mention an enormous pair of wooden clogs for use in the stables, and a canvas bag into which our outfit was shoved; having received this we were told to carry it on our shoulders to our rooms. We did not receive our arms until the following day, when each of us was given a carbine and a straight sword about four feet long, besides a small box of tools with which to take the carbine to pieces. At the same time we received our various trappings—a sword-belt with brass buckles, a sword-strap, a carbine-strap, and a cartridge-box (which in my time was slung over the shoulder and across the breast and back of the trooper). The next day our saddlery and stable gear were served out to us. The saddles then in use were still the discarded ones which had been bought from the British Government in 1870. These saddles had a high and straight wooden back, behind which the portmanteau was attached. This portmanteau was round and made of blue cloth with a red grenade at each end. Two holsters with miscellaneous straps, a leather bag containing a spare iron, and an open cord-girth completed our saddle fittings. The bridle was similar to that used in the English army, with bit and snaffle so contrived that, by removing the straps holding the bit, the head-stall remained on the horse, the snaffle being passed through the rings of the head-stall. Our stable outfit consisted of a currycomb, a soft brush, a hard brush, a chamois leather, a sponge, and a comb for mane and tail, the whole being enclosed in a small canvas bag.

To return to my first day in the regiment. Having brought back all my gear to the room, I was informed by the Corporal that all the things would have to be marked with the number which had been assigned to me. The clothes, linen, and all articles of wear I was supposed to mark, myself, with stencils which could be obtained from the Sergeant *fourrier*. I entrusted, however, the two men who had arranged to clean my things with this tedious work, as I was, myself, most anxious to get into the town. Of course I had to be in uniform. Full dress had to be worn after noon. I therefore borrowed clothes, a helmet, a sword, and even a pair of boots, from my two orderlies; and I received instructions how to behave in the streets. I had to carry my sword in my left hand, the hilt turned downwards and a few inches behind my hip, the tip of the scabbard in front of me. In case I should meet any Corporal, non-commissioned officer, or officer, whether they belonged to my regiment or not, I was to salute them with the right hand, the elbow lifted high in the air, two steps before reaching them, bringing my hand down only when I had passed two steps beyond them. It was not without difficulty that I managed to get down the stairs into the barrack yard, and I found it still more difficult to walk about. The enormous weight and width of my trousers, the looseness of the boots which had been lent to me, their high heels and the spurs which caught at every step in the leather coverings of my elephantine trousers, the tightness of the tunic under the arms, and the wobbling of the helmet, which was much too big for me, conspired to produce such a state of discomfort and insecurity that I only managed to walk with legs apart and arms held stiffly away from my body. I could hardly manage to hold my sword with my No. 9 gloves, which were, moreover, as stiff as a board; and I felt as awkward as a man who, for the first time in his life, tries to walk across a tight-rope. I had just reached, with much difficulty, the gate of the barracks, and was going to walk out, when a stentorian voice proceeding from the guard-room suddenly stopped me.

"Hullo, you recruit, where are you going?" I looked over my shoulder and saw the Sergeant of the Guard. I turned round, saluted, and nearly lost my balance in doing so. "Come here, you booby!" shouted the Sergeant. He examined me from head to foot. "Right about turn!" he then said to me. It was easier said than done; but I was already walking off when the Sergeant called me anew. "Where are you going?" he said.

"Well, Sergeant, I am going into the town."

"Oh, really, are you? Turn round first, I want to look at your back." I turned and stood there for a minute or two. "Go back to your room," said the Sergeant at last.

"But, Sergeant," I replied, "I thought that we were allowed to go out."

"Go back to your room," he said, laughing, "and ask your Corporal why I won't let you go out." Disconsolately I trudged back to the room. There I was greeted with a roar of laughter from all the troopers.

"So," they exclaimed, "the Sergeant has sent you back?"

"Yes, but why?" All the men shouted with laughter. I confess that I felt rather foolish.

"Come here, you recruit," good-naturedly said one of them at last, "let me brush you." And so saying he vigorously applied a brush to my back. It appears that before I went out one of the troopers had drawn a huge chalk cross on my tunic. I then learnt that before leaving barracks, every trooper must present himself before the Sergeant of the Guard, who has to examine him, and see that he is properly groomed; if anything is amiss in his uniform the Sergeant sends him back to put himself straight. This, I may add, often leads to considerable abuse of their power by certain Sergeants, for when one of them has a grudge against a man he will send him back five or six times to his room without telling him what he considers wrong in his attire—the regulations in no way compelling the Sergeant to explain to the trooper where he considers that the fault lies. I have seen a trooper sent back in this way to his room no less than eight times running.

It was a pouring wet day, and when for the ninth time the Sergeant ordered him to return the trooper implored him to tell him what was wrong.

"You dirty pig," replied the Sergeant, "look at your boots, they are covered with mud." The trooper, it must be mentioned, had to walk over a hundred yards from his room across the courtyard before reaching the gate, and irritated beyond measure by the injustice of the Sergeant, he asked, in a sarcastic tone, whether he was expected to carry an umbrella.

"If you like," added the man, "I'll go and fetch my brushes and brush my boots here, and then perhaps you will be satisfied?" For that answer the Sergeant gave the man four days' *Salle de Police,* stating in his report as a reason for that punishment that "the trooper, after presenting himself nine times before the Sergeant of the Guard in a disgraceful state of filth, had grossly insulted the Sergeant who had remonstrated with him." The trooper had often been punished before, and held a bad record, so, upon reading the Sergeant's report, the Colonel altered the punishment into thirty days' prison.

But to return to myself. When I appeared once more before the Sergeant of the Guard, that non-commissioned officer, who was not a bad fellow after all, laughed at the trick that had been played on me and allowed me to go out.

I shall always remember that first outing. I never realised how grotesque a figure I was cutting, until I met another *Volontaire* in the same plight as myself. I had, besides, been so terrified by the warning I had received not to fail to salute Corporals, especially of the infantry— as a feud always exists between infantry and cavalry—that whenever I saw a soldier with a red woollen stripe on his sleeve, I saluted at once. For this I was unmercifully chaffed by some troopers of my squadron who happened to pass while I was solemnly saluting an infantryman just adorned. They ultimately explained to me that only men with two stripes held the rank of Corporal, while those who had but a single stripe were merely first-class privates —*i.e.*, men drawing higher pay for good conduct. For my blunder I had to pay a fine to my comrades, taking them to the nearest café to have a drink.

Although we were not allowed to have rooms in the town, most of the *Volontaires* had engaged lodgings before joining the regiment. As I have already said, I had engaged a room at the Crown Hotel, and, as every year the best set among the *Volontaires* had been in the habit of putting up there, special accommodation was reserved for them: even a private dining-room was retained for us, and when I arrived there that evening, I found six of my comrades having an appetiser in our special room. They were all young men of good and well-known families: besides Walter, of whom I have already spoken, there were Cuffet, whose father had been a Cabinet Minister a few years before; Pager de la Tasherie, whose father had been an Ambassador; Meix, now the head of one of the largest engineering firms in France; de Nevers, who succeeded, some years ago, to a dukedom, and a couple of others, also of gentle birth. The greatest comfort we found at the hotel was the possibility of getting a tub, for we soon discovered the absolute lack of sanitary arrangements in our barracks. We had a pleasant dinner that night, and having taken off our tight-fitting tunics, we almost felt like civilised beings. We were, however, soon recalled to the reality of our position by the rolling of drums and the sounding of bugles. It was the tattoo. In every French garrison town, a quarter of an hour before soldiers have to be in barracks, the trumpeters, and, if there is an infantry regiment in the place, the buglers and drummers, assemble in the principal square and thence march back to barracks playing the *retraite*. We hurried over our coffee and returned to barracks. For fear of being late we walked as fast as we could, but one or two of us got entangled in our spurs or fell head over heels over our swords.

I cannot possibly give an adequate idea of the horrible stench which caught me by the throat when I opened the door of "my" room. Imagine the odour of 80 human beings, 79 of which had not had a bath within the last three months, add to that the emanations from 160 pairs of boots which had been in use for an average of three years, sheets that had not been changed for a month, and crown the mixture with a smell of stables rising through the floor (our room stood over a stable containing 100 horses), and you will perhaps be able to gather a faint idea of what the place smelt like. Five minutes after the trumpeters had returned to barracks the evening "call" took place. In the cavalry, troopers are not called by their individual names in the evening; but every trooper has either to stand at the foot of his bed in uniform if he has been out, or in stable dress if he has not left barracks, or else he can be in bed if he chooses. The Sergeant of the Week walks through the room, each Corporal having to report with reference to absent men, whether they are on guard, or stable duty, on leave, or missing. When the Sergeant has been the round of a room, the men can do what they like throughout the barracks until 10 P.M., when they must all be in bed at the bugle call of "Lights out." In my time the night call was at 8 P.M., but since General Boulanger was Minister of War soldiers have been allowed to stop out until 9 P.M. After the evening call we changed our clothes and the *Volontaires* collected in the canteen. This consisted of a large room, 30 feet by 20; a long table stood in the middle of it, with smaller tables on each side, forms running alongside of each. A kitchen opened on to this room, and the place was crowded. If the smell of our living-rooms was bad, the smell of the canteen was equally so: burnt fat, onions, garlic, wine, and bad tobacco furnished its chief components. A large number of men, and almost every Corporal of the various squadrons in which the *Volontaires* were serving, were collected in the canteen in the hope—which was not deceived—of getting drinks from us. They chiefly appreciated red wine, which was sold at fivepence and sixpence a quart, superior wine fetching eightpence a quart. Brandy could be had at a halfpenny a glass, or 1s. 2d. the quart. These prices left a very good margin of profit to the canteen-keeper, as all wines and spirits sold in French barracks are exempt from excise duty. A table had been reserved for us, and there the fourteen *Volontaires* who were serving that year met in the evening.

That night our chief topic of discussion related to the *Bienvenue* (welcome), a canteen banquet offered by the *Volontaires* to the men and Corporals of their respective *pelotons.* It was at length settled that this should take place on the following Friday.

At ten o'clock, when the trumpeters sounded "Lights out," we returned to our respective rooms, and for the first time I was taught how to get into a military bed. To do this properly is a fine art. The bed, as I have already mentioned, was about two feet eight inches broad, and to guard against its occupant tumbling out blankets and sheets are tightly tucked under the straw mattress. In order to get in you have therefore to stand at the head of your bed, and to gently pull yourself inside as if you were getting into a bag. I got halfway down satisfactorily, but then, notwithstanding my efforts, I was unable to make further progress. Suspecting that a practical joke had been played on me, I got out of bed, and soon found that it had been prepared apple-pie fashion. While I was examining my bed, I heard, not far from me, a tremendous noise, and saw the bed of one of my comrades rolling bodily on the floor. This is another favourite trick played on recruits, and easily accomplished. The bed consisting of three boards perched on two iron trestles, by pulling sharply the trestle which stands under the foot of the bed, the whole of it can be precipitated forward; while the sleeper, thus suddenly aroused, is further terrified by seeing the Corporal (who usually is a party to the joke) near him, threatening to send him to the cells for kicking up a row. In the present case the sufferer was the impecunious *Volontaire* whom I have already mentioned. The poor fellow had to make his bed anew in the dark—no easy matter.

So far as I was concerned, I turned my attention to one of the troopers who had undertaken to look after me. He was a Parisian, a former street arab, and I suspected him of having prepared an apple-pie bed in order to have a laugh at me. He pretended to be fast asleep, although I called him two or three times; but I struck a match and caught him grinning. In order therefore to make him heed me, I went to the foot of his bed and, seizing the iron trestle, determined to bring the whole affair to the floor if he did not get up. This soon aroused him.

"Look here, old chap," he exclaimed, "you don't try any of these 'ere jokes on your seniors, or else you'll smart for it."

"Well, Titi," I replied, "you've got to make my bed over again, so, after all, the joke you wanted to play on me has been wasted, for it only gives you extra trouble."

At first he declined to touch my things, but, as I warned him that if he didn't do it he'd never get another tip from me, he reluctantly set to work. It took me a pretty long time to go to sleep that night; my neighbour snored like a pug dog, and a goodly number of the eighty men who slept in the same room as myself, besides snoring, emitted such an atrocious effluvium that I did not feel able to go to sleep. It takes some time too, to get accustomed to the noise of stables, and I could hear quite distinctly the chargers below constantly kicking their stalls; at last, however, I dropped to sleep from sheer exhaustion.

CHAPTER III

At 5 o'clock in the morning I was aroused by a loud shouting; it was the Corporal of the Week who was passing through the room calling out, " Any sick men here?" The names of the men who want medical attention have to be put down on the Sergeant-major's morning report, on which also figures the morning call, which is merely nominal, as it never takes place in the cavalry. Half an hour later the trumpeters sounded the *réveille* and immediately the various Corporals told off a certain number of men to go and clean the stables. I was one of those selected. Hastily I donned my stable suit, of coarse canvas, and when I reached the stables, was told off to clean the straw under four horses—my comrade Titi, who had accompanied me, being ordered to show me how to proceed. Neither pitchforks nor shovels are used, the men having to separate with their hands the dry from the wet straw, and having also to pick out with their fingers whatever dung may be mixed with the litter. I scarcely relished this unsavory work, and as I did not consider it likely to improve in any way my military training, I tipped Titi a franc to do it for me, while I went to the canteen to have a cup of coffee and a crust of bread. It may be noted here that before *réveille* a jug of very thin coffee, with a pretence of sugar added to it, was brought into the rooms, but few of the men cared to touch it. Those who were unable to afford the canteen preferred to break their fast with a glass of water and a slice of bread—not that the charges of the canteen were high, for a cup of coffee (so called) and a roll of bread costs but three half-pence—but there exists an unwritten but inviolable law that no man may take a drink of any kind by himself. *Faire suisse* is the term used to describe the fact of going to the canteen alone, and this is considered a real crime, to be severely punished by the rest, so that a poor fellow who gets a few francs monthly from his people must always share them with a comrade. It is also a curious fact that, although most men complain of the scarcity of the food supplied to them, few will ever spend in victuals the money they may receive from home—they invariably consume it in drink.

At 6 o'clock the trumpets sounded "Stables," so fetching the bags containing our implements we returned to the stables to groom our chargers. Every man has often two horses to groom—his own charger as well as the horse of any trooper who may be on guard, or otherwise employed.* Our chargers had not yet been allotted to us, so I was told to groom a lively little mare, which I afterwards found out enjoyed the reputation of being the most vicious charger of the whole squadron; however, whether it was that I was not afraid of her, or that she instinctively felt that I loved horses, we got on very well together. The grooming lasted for an hour, and towards 7 o'clock the Lieutenant of the Week turned up and gave orders for the horses to be taken to the watering-tanks. As I was leading out the mare I had been grooming I was ordered by the Lieutenant to also lead two other chargers; holding their reins in my right hand, I tried to jump on the bare

---

* Non-commissioned officers do not groom their own chargers; they are allowed an orderly, to whom they pay 2*s*. per month. Corporals are supposed to groom their chargers, but usually order a trooper to do so.

back of the little mare—she was called "Durance" after the name of a torrent in the South of France, and she well deserved her appellation. The moment I caught hold of her mane to jump on her back she plunged, and, jumping back a few steps, nearly brought her reins over her head. Twice she played me the same trick, and at the same time the other horses, whose reins I held, pulled away from her, but the third time I landed on her back, and although she tried buck-jumping, I easily rode her with the other animals to the watering-tank. When I returned she was lively enough, but it was all play and not vice: and when I jumped off her back the Lieutenant called me.

"How do you like the mare?" he asked.

"Very much indeed, sir," I replied.

"Would you like her as your charger?"

"Certainly," I said.

"Very well," said the officer, "you shall have her, as you seem to be able to ride."

I was quite delighted, and very soon made friends with the little beast (she was hardly 15 hands high); she came to know me so well that at the end of a few months she used to follow me about like a dog. She was, it is true, very vicious at times, and would not let certain men come near her; she also had a hatred of officers, as years before she had been one of the Surgeon-major's chargers, and the fellow used to thrash her unmercifully. She was one of the oldest chargers in the regiment—being eighteen years old—and originally came from Hungary, where many horses were bought just after the Franco-Prussian war, but notwithstanding her age, she was full of "go" and of play. We became such good friends that many a time when I was on stable guard I used to lie alongside of her, my head resting on her neck, and she would remain quite still for hours until I moved. I always bought extra food for her, and kept her in tip-top condition.

After " stables " we were taken to get our arms and saddlery, and shown how to take our carbines to pieces and put them together again. We then had the *gras carbine*, which has long since been discarded.

At the call of " Soup " (10 A.M.) the troopers rushed off to the kitchen, and wishing to taste regimental food, I told Titi to bring me my ration, and waited until it arrived. In those days food came from the kitchen in what was called a *gamelle*—a stout tin pot in the shape of a saucepan, without a handle, but with a tin cover. Each man found his ration ready in the kitchen, with an allowance of salt on the lid of the *gamelle;* the fare consisted that morning of thin soup which tasted like sloppy water in which dishes might have been washed, with lumps of bread soaked in it and a little fat floating about in cold lumps. At the bottom of the pan was a bit of bone with very little meat on it, the ration of meat allowed to each man being four ounces including bone. The mere sight of that so-called soup and the filthiness of the pan which contained it, was too much for me. However ill-fed the men were, very few of them could ever finish the whole of their ration. When a man had finished eating he chucked his *gamelle* into a corner, a trooper being told off every day to take the tins back to the kitchen. In my time men had to feed on their beds, but since the days of General Boulanger things have, as I stated before, greatly altered. The men now eat at table, the food is served in dishes, and the man at the head of each table, who is generally a Corporal, helps each man on his own enamelled plate.

To return to my own experiences: I went to the canteen to get something to eat. Most of the other *Volontaires* were already there, and, although the place was horribly dirty, I ate with great relish a couple of cutlets. We tried the various brands of wine; that at fivepence a bottle was more suitable for use as a dye than as a beverage, but the one at sixpence was quite drinkable, and the one at eightpence quite equal to the so-called claret sold at two shillings a bottle in second-rate London restaurants. We discovered that the canteen-keeper had a yet better brand at a shilling a bottle, and this was really very good. It was a genuine bottled wine, and not drawn from the cask like the others. During my stay in the regiment I was much struck with the fact that hardly any beer is drunk by Frenchmen belonging to the lower classes. To see troopers drinking it was quite exceptional; wine was their staple drink, except when they wanted to get drunk, in which case they went in for brandy, which was served in flasks holding about two-thirds of a pint and costing fourpence. It took about a pint and a quarter of this stuff to have the desired effect.

It was nearly 11 A.M. before we had finished our breakfast, and I then returned to my quarters, most anxious to have a wash, which I had so far been obliged to do without. I asked Titi where the lavatory was.

"Lavatory!" he laughed out; "his highness wants a lavatory. You'll get a lavatory in barracks, old chap. What else do you want?—a valet to dress your royal highness?"

"But," I said, "isn't there any place where I can go and have a wash?"

"Oh! yes, there's the pump."

This seemed rather unsatisfactory, and I could hardly believe it to be the case, so I went to the room of my friend Sergeant de Lanoy and asked him about it.

"It's quite true, old man," he replied; "lavatories do exist in the barracks, but they have never been utilised since '70, and are now used for storing straw, so that the only place where you can go and have a wash is at the pump. If I were alone in my room," he added, " I would lend it to you, but the other Sergeant who lives with me is a beast, and he would kick up a row if he found you performing your ablutions here."

I had therefore to go to the pump, and fortunately found a bucket near at hand, so that I managed to wash at least the upper portion of my body.

There is in each squadron a barber, who has to shave, free of cost, every trooper twice a week; but the mere sight of the fellow, to say nothing of his implements, was enough. It is impossible to realise how men can live in the state of filth which seems natural to French soldiers. Hardly one of them ever thinks of washing his hands after cleaning the stables in the way I have previously described; occasionally some of them wash their faces, necks, and hands on Sundays, or when they have to appear on parade, but many of them remain all the year round (except in the summer season, when they are sent in batches to the swimming baths) without taking a single bath or feeling the want of one. It will be seen how, later on, when we were permanently consigned to barracks, I had to get special leave from the doctor to be able to go out and have a bath in the town.

At twelve o'clock we were all taken to the dispensary to be vaccinated, vaccination being compulsory throughout the French army. That operation concluded, we were taught to fold our clothes and shown how to arrange them on the shelves above our bed. At 3 P.M. we returned to stables, after which the Sergeant-major made us stand in a circle round him while the regimental orders of the day were read out by the Corporal *fourrier,* all the punishments inflicted upon officers, non-commissioned officers, and troopers being announced at the end of the orders.

It has always struck me as a great mistake to let privates learn the punishments inflicted upon officers, as this, of course, tends to lower them in the eyes of their men. That day, for instance, I was much astonished to hear that one of the Captains of the regiment had been punished by the Colonel with fifteen days of *arrêts de rigueur* (strict confinement to his room, with a sentry in front of his door) " for," said the orders, " having been seen walking about in a drunken state, with his uniform in disarray, at ten o'clock at night." This Captain was greatly hated by the men, and it is needless to say that they all rejoiced at the punishment which had been inflicted upon him, expressing their feelings in the coarsest language.

" Stables " over, we hurried to the town, and our set met as usual at the Crown Hotel, where we exchanged impressions on military service. We were all unanimous in declaring it a filthy and disgusting ordeal. After the evening call, we entertained our respective Corporals at the canteen, most of them having to be supported back to their beds.

The following day was enlivened by the arrival of the ordinary recruits coming to serve their five years. Most of them came from Paris, and belonged to the worst set of ruffians imaginable. A few were countrymen, among whom were two or three stupid " Bretons " coming from the remotest parts of Brittany. One of the latter was assigned a bed next to the " old 'un," and therefore close to mine. As soon as he had eaten his evening meal, he sat on his bed, weeping bitterly, and as I asked him the cause of his grief he began with deep sobs:

" Our poor Jeanne; it's the day she ought to calve, and

to think that I shall not be near her! If you saw that cow, sir——"

"Oh! it's a cow!"

"Yes, sir, and when she calves she won't take any food except from my hand, and now I am here, and she calving! My poor Jeanne, my poor Jeanne!"

I tried to console him, but it was in vain. Of course, the other troopers made great fun of him, and one of them remarked that if his cow was as ugly as himself, and as ill-fed, she must be a hideous beast indeed. This drove the fellow into an absolute frenzy, and, seizing the sword hanging at the head of my bed, he would have made deadly use of it had I not forcibly prevented him.

The recruits went, that day, through the routine we had undergone on the day of our arrival—the only difference being that they were marched in batches to the *Capitain-trésorier's* office under the command of a Sergeant—and before evening every one of them had been drafted into a squadron, each recruit being put under the care of a trooper of at least a year's standing, who had to teach his *bleu* (recruit) what to do. The recruits, upon receiving their outfit, have to hand over their civilian clothes, which are sold by auction. This rule did not, however, apply to the *Volontaires*, but we had to remove our civilian clothes out of barracks, and were, under no circumstances, allowed to wear anything but uniform.

That year the recruits numbered about 125, or twenty-five to each squadron.

That night the most elaborate practical jokes were played on the new-comers. First of all an "artful dodger," a typical Parisian blackguard, attired himself in a great coat and an old cocked hat; alongside of him marched two troopers with swords, helmets, and carbines, but devoid of all clothing. The "Artful dodger" went to the bed of each one of the recruits. "Get up," said another trooper, "here comes the Surgeon-major." "You are a recruit, my boy?" queried the "Artful dodger." "Yes, sir," usually replied the recruit, rather awed. "Don't call me 'sir,'" went on the tormentor, "call me 'Monsieur le Major.'" (The way in which military surgeons are addressed.) "Get out of bed," he went on, "and be sharp about it." If the recruit declined to obey, he was dragged out of his bed by other troopers and stripped; many foul questions were then put to him, and the joke ended by his body being blackened all over with a blacking-brush if he took the proceedings ill. When the recruits had gone back to bed, the "dodger" and his companions proceeded to play other jokes on them.

In order to enable my readers to understand what took place, it is necessary to recall the description of our rooms. These apartments were about 100 feet long, with two partitions on each side of the centre, and rows of beds standing on each side of these partitions, which were from 10 to 12 feet high. The "dodger" and his companions, taking a forage-rope, with which every trooper is provided, tied a slip-knot around the bed of the recruit, so as to encircle the three boards forming the base of the bed as well as the mattress and the feet of the man inside it; the end of the rope was then thrown over the partition, being grasped on the other side by three or four men, while the "artful one" was peeping round the corner to see that the man had not moved. He then gave a whistle, the rope was smartly pulled, and the recruit's bed instantly stood straight up against the wall, the man inside it being tightly imprisoned with his feet held up in the air by the slip-knot and his head downwards. After leaving him for a few minutes in this uncomfortable position, the rope was suddenly slackened, and bed and man crashed with a great noise to the floor. This was called "sending a man to heaven," and the unfortunate victim could not possibly find out who was responsible for the "joke."

Another trick consisted in sticking a carbine-rod between the shelf and the clothes on it, over the recruit's head, so that the end of the rod projected above the fellow's face; a drinking-cup filled with water was then slung from the gun-rod by two strings fastened round its rim, while a third and independent string attached its handle to the rod. A piece of lighted paper was then placed on the top of the water, and before it had time to go out it burnt the two first strings, tilting the water down as the cup remained suspended by its handle. The half minute or so which elapsed between the lighting of the paper and the burning of the strings, enabled the men who had played the trick to get back to bed, so that the poor fellow whose face had been deluged with water was unable to find out who his persecutors were.

In every case when the recruit made a noise, the Corporal, who was invariably a consenting party to these rough "amusements," came forward and threatened to send him to the cells for disturbing his comrades. Of course, to complain to the officers was considered by the troopers a heinous crime, and whoever did so was never tempted to adopt that course again.

That same night one of the recruits whose bed had been sent "heavenwards" rushed to the Sergeant's room and complained. The Sergeant came to our quarters, and shouted in a loud voice, "Look here, you fellows, here's a recruit who has come to complain to me of having been bullied, as we have all been on joining the regiment; you had better leave him alone, and don't let him disturb me any more." Thereupon, knowing well what the result would be, the Sergeant retired to his room. Immediately a blanket was produced, round which from twelve to fifteen men stood holding it, while four other men collared the recruit and chucked him into it. Before he knew where he was, he had been sent flying up to the ceiling, and as soon as he dropped into the blanket was again sent up, the operation being repeated a dozen times until all the breath had nearly left the poor fellow's body. The same misfortune, I am sorry to say, befell me that very night. A trooper from the second squadron, whose room was close to mine, sneaked in and pulled my bed down. I saw him go back to his room, and as soon as he had got under the blankets without noticing me, I pulled his bed down with a crash; but some other fellows had seen me, and, unfortunately for myself, I was ignorant at the time of the unwritten law that no practical jokes may be played on the men of a squadron different from one's own, so, before I realised where I was, I was chucked into a blanket and tossed more than once into the air. I must, however, add that the thing was purely done as a joke, and with no ill-feeling—the bed, indeed, that I had pulled down was that of my friend, Walter. I found it by no means a disagreeable sensation to be tossed in a blanket, but I can quite understand that a repetition of the performance, a dozen times or more, may shake a man more than he may like.

The following day we began to drill. After morning stables we were hurried to our rooms. We kept on our stable-dress, but had to exchange our clogs for boots, although we were allowed to wear ordinary shoes if we possessed any. We assembled in the barrack-square, *Volontaires* and recruits together, and three or four of us were told off under the orders of a Corporal, who proceeded to explain to us the difference between our left and right leg. However absurd this may seem, it is absolutely necessary in the case of many recruits coming from remote districts in the provinces, and I have known some of them to take a fortnight before they realised the difference between left and right.

We went through the various preliminaries of drill, we were taught to stand in line, to execute " By the left quick march," " Right turn," " Left turn," " Right about turn " and so on—preliminary exercises, which are the same in all the armies of the world. At the end of two hours, at the call of " Soup," we were to our great relief at last dismissed.

At 11 A.M. we were put through the first elements of *voltige* (circus-riding). A specially-trained horse was brought into the riding-school, and while its foreleg was held up by a trooper, the others had to jump on its back from behind, leap-frog fashion. It was most amusing to see the efforts of some of the recruits to accomplish this feat, most of them at first rushing as hard as they could towards the horse, and ending by merely striking their noses against its tail; as, however, every man who failed to ultimately succeed in getting on the horse's back was sent to sleep in the cells, very few of us remained unsuccessful. We were afterwards placed on a bare-backed horse around which was buckled a surcingle with two handles—a non-commissioned officer holding the animal at the end of a long rope so as to make him canter in a circle. We had to jump on and off while the animal was cantering, and those who failed, or did not try their best, were usually rewarded with a smart cut from the huge circus-whip which the non-commissioned officer carried in his hand. We had also to repeat the same performance on a broad circus saddle, and many were those who, taking too powerful a spring, were sent flying outside the circle. These were merely preliminary exercises, however, and I will describe later on others we were called upon to do in the same way.

Among the recruits there was one so clumsy that he could never manage to alight on the horse's back, and no amount of assistance seemed to be of any use to him. The Sergeant threatened to send the man to the lock-up, but he looked so helplessly stupid, and made such simple and amusing excuses, that his instructor could not find it in his heart to punish him. When placed on the bare-backed steed, he clung to the surcingle like a monkey, and upon being told to jump off, he rolled like an untidy bundle to the ground. The Sergeant began to lose his temper, and warned the man that if he failed to get on again he would certainly be punished. Thereupon the recruit caught hold of the handle and ran round the ring alongside of the cantering horse; at last, with a mighty effort, he got his knee upon the animal's back and finally sat there, looking half exhausted.

"Now," said the Sergeant, "you see you can do it; jump off and try again."

Clumsily the recruit got down, and tripping, fell on his knees at the Sergeant's feet.

"Now then, up you get!" cried the Sergeant; "jump on once more."

"Jump on?" replied the recruit dreamily, as though just aroused from a reverie; "well, here goes!"

And so saying, he took a mighty bound, and alighted on his feet on the back of the cantering horse! In another moment, turning a splendid somersault, he reached the ground, and stood composedly before the astonished Sergeant, amidst universal laughter and applause.

"You have been fooling me!" cried the latter, when he could find words.

"Forgive me, Sergeant," said the fellow in reply; "you

see, it isn't easy for a man to forget his business all at once; and the fact is, I have been a clown. Houp-la!" And, taking a short run, he this time turned a somersault right over the still cantering horse. I may add that the ex-clown became a great favourite with all the officers, and was certainly one of the most wonderful trick-riders I have ever seen.

After *voltige* we were allowed some rest, and before " Stables " we had an hour's physical drill. This consisted of bending the body downwards with extended arms, bending the knees with uplifted arms, and other exercises which are taught in every English and foreign gymnasium. A curious part of the performance consisted, however, in the principles of French boxing. The position in which we were placed would have been the joy of any English schoolboy; we were told to put our legs well apart, one foot twenty inches behind the other, the left arm level with our chin, and the right arm a little lower. The first movement consisted in striking forward with the right fist. We then had to bring forward the right leg, which had been extended the whole time behind the left; as we brought the right leg forward we had to strike it against the calf of our left leg, so as to give a powerful kick with the heel, which then described a circle, bringing our right foot twenty inches behind the left. Such is what is called " French boxing."

In the evening, after " Soup," we were taken to the riding-school, having to dress for the purpose in undress uniform—namely, the red trousers with leather covering which I have previously described, a short jacket, a *képi*, and white gloves—pieces of rags being tied round the rowels of our spurs. We were first taught how to dress in line, and how to stand at our horse's head. At the command of " Prepare to mount!" we had to take a long step backwards, slipping the reins through our left hand and catching hold of the mane with it while we seized the pommel of the saddle with the right, and at the command " Mount!" we had to raise ourselves well up (our weight resting on the wrists), and then throw the right leg over the saddle. Many of us were unable to get on our horses in this way without a good deal of shoving up by the Corporals. Once on our horses, the position we had to assume was explained, and we were also taught how to hold our reins and how to direct our animals (we had only a snaffle on our bridles). We were then marched in Indian file after a Corporal all round the riding-school. Most of the recruits knew something about horses, as those drafted into the cavalry are usually picked out from amongst farm hands, carters, or men who have had something to do with stables. Some of them, however, had never been on a horse in their lives, and when the command " Trot!" was given, two or three very soon tumbled off. I had been warned beforehand by my friend, de Lanoy, that the looseness and roughness of our military trousers would cause me serious abrasions unless I adopted a plan which had succeeded admirably with him. I had accordingly brought with me when I joined the regiment a few pairs of thin doeskin riding-breeches, which I put on before dressing to go to the riding-school, and over these I pulled my trousers, an easy matter if one considers the abnormal size of the latter. I congratulated myself many a time afterwards upon having adopted this plan, as I was the only man who never was galled.

At the end of an hour we were dismissed, and having taken back our horses to the stables, we were shown how to rub them down with straw, and we then returned to our room, carrying our saddles on our heads.

It was that night that the *Bienvenue* (welcome supper)

TROOPER 3809

was to take place. The evening "call" over, we therefore repaired to the canteen, where the fourteen *Volontaires* sat down with about one hundred and twenty of the Corporals and troopers belonging to their respective *pelotons*. As one canteen would not have been able to accommodate this number, it was arranged that as there were *two* canteens in our regiment, the *Volontaires* of the first and second squadrons should give their *Bienvenue* in one, while those of the third and fourth squadrons would use the other.

We accordingly sat down with about sixty of our guests, the Corporals and troopers of our companies. Tables had been laid in a large room and we crowded around them. Cold meats, sausages, coffee, with wine and brandy *ad libitum*, formed the bill of fare. As the meal proceeded, and the men helped themselves to a liberal quantity of wine, they became more and more noisy. At last one of the Corporals, although very drunk, stood on a form and demanded "Order," adding that the company would now be favoured with a few songs; and at the same time calling upon anybody who could sing to add to the pleasure of the entertainment. Nobody responded, so, rising once more, the Corporal, after swallowing a large glass of brandy to steady himself, began in a drunken and cracked voice to sing a sentimental ditty, an old and simple country song which, although interrupted by many hiccups, was greeted with much applause. Next came a lanky country bumpkin whose regimental training had been unable to obliterate his countrified appearance; he sang, with the utmost monotony and an innumerable number of false notes, an atrociously indecent song, the coarseness of which had evidently never struck him. Every one of the troopers took up the chorus, which they all sang in different keys, but with marvellous seriousness. Then came

TROOPER 3809

the turn of a Parisian ruffian, who sang in a voice of thunder an old and also very obscene regimental song, of course with a chorus; he could, however, not get further than the second verse, for in the middle of this he collapsed on the floor, and interrupted for a moment the gaiety of the proceedings by so noisy an attack of sickness that the whole distinguished company called for his removal. (We found him later on soundly asleep on a dung-heap in the barrack-yard.) After his removal, another trooper, also a countryman, sang a religious song, with a mournful tune, which ran into more than twenty verses, but was greatly appreciated. At this point the delightful proceedings were once more interrupted—this time by a fight between two Corporals. They went for each other like madmen, kicking, scratching, and biting one another. They were, however, too drunk to hurt each other much, and everything would have concluded peacefully had not the quarrel degenerated into a free fight, which resulted in the smashing of a good many glasses and plates, for which we had, of course, to pay. The whole bill, however, only amounted to about 35*s.* for each one of the *Volontaires*. Before the call of " Lights out " peace had been restored, and the whole company adjourned to their respective rooms, most of the troopers supporting (?) one another and collapsing a good many times on the way. I shall never forget the scene when we got near the dung-heap. We discovered the fellow of whom I spoke just now, fast asleep in the mire, and four or five of his comrades volunteered to get him out, but, being as drunk as himself, they all fell in a heap on top of him, and it was only with great difficulty that they were extracted from the filth and, in a state that I dare not describe, carried to their room. Some of the men who were boisterously drunk were sent to pass the night

TROOPER 3809

in the cells by a Corporal who resented not having been invited, and having thus missed the chance of a good "booze."

On Friday, at 11 o'clock in the morning, the trumpeters sounded "Forage," and we were all paraded in the yard, each one of us carrying his forage-rope. (Sergeant de Lanoy had previously told me that he couldn't excuse me from this work, but he promised that he would manage to let me slip off in the middle of it.) We were then marched to the forage-store, some two hundred yards away from the barracks; and there stood the officers of the week of each squadron, whose duty it was to get delivery of the forage required for the next seven days. Each of the troopers was told to pick out of a heap eight huge bundles of straw, and to fasten them together with his forage-rope, the end of which is fitted with a kind of metal pulley so as to form a slip-knot. The rope being thus tied round the eight bundles of straw, we were supposed to take the load on our shoulders and to carry it to the squadron store. To peasants and men of the lower classes, such as were most of the troopers, men who had been accustomed from their boyhood to carry heavy and cumbrous loads, this entailed merely a little extra exertion, but to one who, like myself, had never been used to manual work, it was almost an impossible task. The other troopers enjoyed, of course, the sight of a gentleman carrying on his back a cumbersome weight of nearly one hundred and sixty pounds. I did my best to go on with it, but I had not covered fifty yards before one of the bundles began to drop out of the heap, and the whole load soon came to the ground. I did my best to tie it together again, but when it came to hoisting it on to my back I found that it was out of the question. In vain did I ask some of the troopers who had already carried one load, and were returning to the stores, to help me; they all laughed, but none of them would give me a hand. To my great relief, however, my friend Titi soon appeared on the scene, and, telling me to wait a few minutes, he promised that when he returned with his own load he would relieve me of a few bundles. While I was waiting for him a Captain chanced to pass; I saluted him, but he did not return my salute, and merely said:

"What the devil are you doing here?"

"I cannot manage to carry my load, sir," I replied.

"Now catch hold of it at once, you blasted lazy beggar!" he cried, standing in front of me, and waiting to see me execute his order.

I renewed my efforts, but was unable to hoist the enormous bundle on to my shoulders. The Captain then called out to two troopers who happened to pass by: "Stick me that load on that lazy dog's shoulders!" he said to them. They lifted the bundle, and dropping it on the top of my head before I was prepared for it, they brought me to the ground under the heap. This put the Captain in a fury; he swore at me and cursed me, and said that it was all obstinacy on my part, and that I would "d——d well have to carry it." At last I managed to get it on my shoulders, and went twenty-five yards farther with it; but it was too much for me, and I had to put it down once more. Fortunately, the Captain had disappeared, and Titi soon came to my relief. Although he was carrying seven bundles, he took three of mine, and I was then able to carry the five remaining ones as far as the squadron stores. These, I found to my astonishment, to have been originally built as a lavatory, with a number of large basins for the use of the men. I stopped there a little while, hoping to escape a repetition of my previous experience, when our Sergeant-major looked into the place.

"What are you doing there, you lazy dog?" (the actual expression which is constantly used in French regimental slang, by officers and non-commissioned officers alike, cannot be translated into English for more than one reason).

In reply to the Sergeant-major's civil question I told him that I was putting the straw in order, but he told me to return at once to the stores. All the straw had already been carried away, so I was told off to carry four bundles of hay, each one of them tied up in the shape of a ball and weighing about fifty pounds. I told the Corporal that I should be unable to bear such a weight, especially considering the enormous size of the load. He abused me, called me a lazy dog, and as he was raising his voice an officer came to see what was the matter.

"The fellow refuses to carry his load," said the Corporal.

"Refuses!" exclaimed the officer.

"No, sir," I interrupted; "I merely said that I was unable to bear the weight of such a load."

The officer, who was one of the exceptionally just and gentlemanly lieutenants in our regiment, told me to try and carry two bundles, and to show him that I appreciated his manner towards me, I did my best to go on with them. I only succeeded, however, in going half way to the barracks, and then I tipped another trooper to carry my load as far as the stores. I escaped having to carry any more, de Lanoy having considerately ordered me to sweep the straw in front of the buildings.

The following days were devoted to drill, stables, and the routine I have already described; on Sundays we had no drill, but, unless we had obtained leave, we had to at-

TROOPER 3809

tend stables. The first Sunday, I obtained midnight leave, so that I was able to have a quiet dinner and to enjoy the luxury of a thoroughly good wash. The second week passed off very much in the same way, but at the end of it I obtained twenty-four hours' leave, so that I was enabled to go to Paris. I can hardly describe the delight I felt at wearing civilian clothes, in which I felt a gentleman once more.

CHAPTER IV

AT the end of about three weeks the Colonel decided to form the *Volontaires* into a separate *peloton*, as, according to the usual custom, they had to follow a special course of instruction besides learning the ordinary regimental duties of a trooper. A Sergeant, assisted by a Corporal, was put in charge of us under a Captain selected to supervise our instruction. Sergeant Legros, who was placed in command of the *Volontaires*, was well known as one of the sulkiest brutes in the whole regiment. Our Captain, whose name was Hermann, was the Colonel's nephew. When this " *décision* " appeared in the regimental orders, read after " Stables," all the troopers had a good laugh at us. " Well, old chaps," they said, " now you're going to have a grand time of it. By Jove, won't you ! "

I went to de Lanoy's room and asked him what sort of a fellow Legros was. De Lanoy told me that he was the son of a small farmer, and was a stubborn, vindictive man, who positively enjoyed punishing his men and doing a bad turn to his fellow Sergeants whenever he got a chance. This picture, indeed, was but too accurately drawn. Our Captain was in command of my own squadron, and I had already had a specimen of his manners when I went before him to try on my clothes. Notwithstanding his rough and abrupt manners, I must concede that he was a gentleman; but, unfortunately, for the future he scarcely ever came to see us, and left to the Sergeant the entire control of the *Volontaires*, merely signing the daily reports drawn up by Legros. The following day the Colonel paid one of his rare visits to the barracks, and had the *Volontaires* mustered in the riding-school. We waited there for him more than an hour. When he appeared he walked past us, surveying each one of us with a disgusted look on his face. He was a harsh, stout, sulky-looking officer. For a few minutes he walked up and down in front of us, talking with our Captain and striking his boot with his riding-stick. Then, suddenly turning towards us with one hand in his pocket and the other on the handle of his riding-whip, which was stuck under his arm, he addressed us.

" So," he said, " you're the *Volontaires* who have been sent to demoralise my regiment. Well, there are a few things I want you to remember; you are serving five times less than other troopers; you will therefore have five times more work, five times more punishments, and five times less leave than the rest." Then turning towards the non-commissioned officer: " Dismiss your men," he said, and at the same time he walked away with our Captain. Before dismissing us our Sergeant also thought fit to address us: " You are now going to be under my orders," he began, " and you may have been told that the *Volontaires* who served last year had a good time of it, but if you think that you are going to be treated as they were, you are jolly well mistaken. I mean to make you work, and to make you work hard too. There are a few hard-mouthed ones among you. I will use the curb with them so as to soon break them in." With these words he dismissed us.

As we were running off to the canteen he recalled us. " At eleven o'clock," he said, " you will have to be at the gymnasium without arms." So saying, he dismissed us once more. It was then a quarter to eleven, so that we hardly had any time for our food. At eleven o'clock sharp we were all standing where he had ordered us, and the Corporal, having dressed us in a single file, stood grumbling at not having had time for his meal. It was raining hard, and as the Sergeant had not appeared at the end of a quarter of an hour, the Corporal took us inside one of the stables. Nearly three-quarters of an hour elapsed before Legros turned up. He marched us to a room specially reserved as a schoolroom for *Volontaires*, and also used as a lecture-room for those troopers who aspired to pass the examination necessary for obtaining the rank of Corporal.

At the end of the room stood a raised platform with a desk for the Sergeant, while we sat at tables, twelve to fourteen of which stood in pairs facing the Sergeant's desk. Having been ordered to take our seats, we placed ourselves as we liked, all those belonging to my set selecting a table far away from the Sergeant's desk. He began by giving us a list of books we were to purchase—viz.:

1. " General Instructions as to the Service in Barracks" (*Service Intérieur des Troupes de Cavalerie*).
2. " Cavalry Drill Regulations " (*Réglement sur les Exercices de la Cavalerie*).
3. " The Duties of Cavalry in the Field " (*Service de la Cavalerie en Campagne*).
4. " Moral Duties of the Soldier."
5. " Dismounted Cavalry Drill Regulations " (*Réglement sur les Exercices de la Cavalerie à pied*).

Besides these there was another book, the title of which I cannot remember, and which is now out of print. This book contained most interesting information as to the composition of the French army, the details of the rations allowed to troopers, as well as the principles of topography, and many other matters of use to soldiers. The Sergeant then explained to us what our daily work would consist in. We should no longer have to groom our horses, except on Saturdays* and Sundays. But this was to be our time-table:

    From 6.30 A.M. to 8 A.M. school.
    From 8 to 10 A.M. drill on foot.
    From 10 to 11 A.M. breakfast.
    From 11 to 12, school.
    From 12 to 1 P.M. gymnastics.
    From 1 to 2 P.M. *voltige* (circus-riding).
    From 2.30 to 5 P.M. school.
    From 5 to 6 P.M. dinner.
    From 6 to 8 P.M. mounted drill.

As will be seen by the above, we had only two hours to ourselves during the whole day, and we had absolutely no chance of being able to leave barracks. We were to begin this programme at once, but as it was necessary that we should purchase the books of which a list had been handed over to us, the Sergeant told us that we should have no *voltige* that day, but that we could, instead of it, go to the town to purchase our books. We hurried to dress, and at 2.30 every one of us was once more in the schoolroom. The Sergeant, however, gave us leave to smoke during our lectures, a concession which we all greatly appreciated. We were first given to study " The Moral Duties of the Soldier." This little book begins with an outline of the origin of the first permanent French army created by Charles VII. in 1439. It tells how this army was recruited at first on the principle that each parish had to supply one man, and how this small force continuously and rapidly grew in numbers under the following reigns: how in the time of Louis XIV. the French army already num-

* Saturday being inspection-day.

TROOPER 3809

bered 279,000 men; how Vauban, the greatest engineer of modern times, fortified the frontiers of France, drew up new rules for carrying on the siege of fortified places, and was alleged to be the inventor of bayonets; how Louvois, when he became Minister of War, compelled the officers to be punctual in their service, improved the armaments, erected the first barracks, established regular pay, and devised new uniforms. The book then went on to tell us that before the great Revolution of last century the active army was recruited by Recruiting Sergeants; while the provincial militia consisted of men called under the flag by conscription, the poorer classes alone being compelled to serve. The highest commands were granted to incapable courtiers, commissions being exclusively granted to noblemen; corporal punishment was in force, and the condition of soldiers was a most miserable one. Thus desertions were of constant occurrence. With the Revolution came great changes; the provincial militia was abolished and corporal punishment was suppressed, bravery and military worth entitled any citizen to reach the highest ranks; and this enabled eminent soldiers to reveal themselves—men such as Hoche, Kléber, Desaix, Jourdan, Masséna, Lecourbe and many others, most of whom became Field-Marshals and Generals under Napoleon.

As will be seen, the drift of all this was to try and impress our minds with the fact that we were entirely indebted for our present happy (?) condition to the Republic. This sketch was read to us by the Sergeant, who, taking no more interest in the matter than we did, soon stopped, and told us to read the remainder carefully, while he himself proceeded to enjoy a novel. The rest of the booklet contained a summary description of the various wars of the Republic, and of the First Empire, special stress being laid on the persistent antagonism of " perfidious Albion." A brief summary of the War of '70 was also given, concluding with these words:

"Do not let us forget this terrible lesson; do not let us slumber in apparent security, lest on our awakening we find the soil of France invaded by the enemy. Let us therefore adopt and put in practice this fine motto, the basis of a strong army,

"'WORK AND DISCIPLINE.'"

Then came a pompous dissertation on the duties of citizens towards *La Patrie,* and on the duties of soldiers towards their superiors, beginning thus:

"What is subordination and discipline?" The answer consisted of three pages of high-sounding phrases, among which I may quote the following: "Orders must be executed to the letter without hesitation or murmuring, the authority from which orders come being alone responsible for them; *the inferior has only the right to complain after he has obeyed and carried out his orders* . . . unquestioning and blind obedience is absolutely necessary to enable every individual effort to work towards a common aim."

Curiously enough, duelling is officially countenanced in these regulations, which are still in force: "If a soldier has been gravely insulted by one of his comrades, and the insult has taken place in public, he must not hesitate to claim reparation for it by a duel. He should address his demand to his Captain, who should transmit it to the Colonel; but it must not be forgotten that duels must be the exception, and that a good soldier ought to avoid quarrels." The passage relating to cleanliness is rather interesting: "Troopers are sent to the swimming-baths in the summer, and are allowed to have tepid baths in winter, in order to scrape off the deposit formed on the surface of the body by perspiration and dirt (*sic*)." I must add that, as in many other cases, theory and practice differ vastly, for in my time there existed but one dilapidated bath in the whole of our barracks, where 1600 men were quartered. No appliance for admitting hot water into the bath existed, so that, when it had to be used for a sick man, hot water had to be carried from the nearest kitchen 300 yards away! I need dwell no longer on this little book, evidently written with the best intentions, but entirely ignored by every French soldier.

At the end of an hour or so the Sergeant closed his novel, and told us to learn by heart two pages of the regulations dealing with drill on foot. In order to show how narrow-minded Sergeant Legros was, I must mention that he expected us to learn *verbatim* every single sentence of those regulations. So far as I am concerned (and I am not the only one who suffers from this defect in memory), I am totally unable to learn anything *verbatim*, so that, when an hour later, the Sergeant called upon me to recite what I had learnt, instead of reciting the following: "At the command of 'Cavalerie en Avant—Marche,' the trooper *places* the whole weight of his body on his right foot, *after which he*. . . ." &c. &c. I recited, "At the command of 'Cavalerie en Avant—Marche,' the trooper *puts* the whole weight of his body on his right foot *and then*. . . ." &c. &c. The Sergeant stopped me: "You blockhead," he exclaimed, "what the deuce is that you are reciting?"

"What you gave us to learn, Sergeant."

"What I gave you to learn! Go and look at your regulations, and you'll see if it's right, and as you can't learn the thing in an hour, you will be confined to barracks next Sunday, and that will give you plenty of time to ponder over it."

TROOPER 3809

In everything we were given to learn it was always thus. Legros cared little or nothing whether we understood what we learnt or not, but he attached the greatest importance to our repeating it *verbatim*, notwithstanding the fact that he was himself unable to do so. Even when we had to learn the principles of surveying, he expected us to know word for word every explanation given in the book. Later on, before we were dismissed, the Sergeant called me up once more, and finding that this time I could answer his question to his satisfaction, he cancelled my punishment, telling me, however, that he would deprive me of the right of applying for leave on the following Sunday.

As the routine of our daily work made it impossible for us to dine out in future, we made an arrangement with the canteen-keeper, who agreed to supply us with board at the rate of £5 a month, and henceforth a table was permanently reserved in the canteen for us.

We had been more than two hours in the schoolroom, and it was with real relief that we heard the trumpeter's call of "Soup" (dinner). Before dismissing us from school, however, the Sergeant read us the regimental orders for the day, which contained a reference to ourselves. "The *Volontaires*," said the Colonel, " are warned that they are, under no circumstances, to ask for another trooper's help, either to clean their outfits, or their arms, or to get their horses saddled. Any *Volontaire* receiving assistance from another trooper will have eight days' '*Salle de Police*' and the trooper who has helped him will receive a similar punishment."

"Now you're warned," commented the Sergeant, "and although I have no right to interfere with those who don't belong to my squadron, I'll see about those among you who are in it, and I'll take jolly good care that the Colonel's orders are strictly carried out."

Here was a nice state of affairs! We had but two hours to ourselves every day, and we were expected, not only to take our meals during that time, but also to do work for which an ordinary well-trained trooper was supposed to require three to four hours of steady application! That we could carry out the Colonel's orders was physically impossible, and the only result was that the two men who looked after our things insisted upon getting two francs more a week, as a compensation for the risk of punishment to which they were exposed.

That evening we had our first mounted drill in the riding-school under our new Sergeant, and we were able to realise what a bully the man was. He frequently kept us trotting without rest for a quarter of an hour at a time, though it may be remembered that we had no stirrups, and riding as we did on hard saddles with coarse trousers was a terrible strain on most fellows who had very little previous training on horseback. It was then that I appreciated the precaution I had taken of donning doeskin riding breeches under my trousers. One of my comrades fainted from sheer exhaustion, while three others dropped off their horses, but every one of them was immediately ordered to remount, and the trotting went on for fully five minutes longer. When our Sergeant commanded a halt and let us dismount for a few minutes' rest, some of my comrades sat on the ground, completely exhausted; they were coarsely rebuked, and ordered to stand up at once, the Sergeant commanding "Attention!"

"There's a fine lot of troopers," he said, "who can't even stick on a horse and trot round a riding-school without coming a cropper! Now I warn you that, if one of you falls off again, I'll keep you on the trot until every blessed one of you drops from exhaustion—you blasted recruits!" and forthwith he gave the command to "Mount," starting us immediately at a trot. On we went round and round the riding-school, and God knows how long we should have been kept on the move had not our Captain appeared on the scene. The Sergeant's manner altered immediately; he made us halt and spoke gently, carefully explaining to each one of us the right position on horseback, and while the Captain was there, never kept us trotting or cantering for more than a couple of minutes at a time. During one of the rests the Captain said that he could not congratulate us, as a body, on our riding, "Out of fourteen of you," he said, "there are not five who understand a horse, and I see but three who can really ride." I am glad to say that I was among the three that he pointed out with his whip. How one of the *Volontaires* could ever have been foolish enough to join a cavalry regiment passes my comprehension; the poor fellow was absolutely ignorant of the first principles of riding; he was, besides, terribly afraid of horses, and never managed to get over his dread; in fact, it was through sheer luck that he stuck on his horse for five consecutive minutes. Hardly a day passed during the first two months of his service without coming a cropper, although he was allotted the quietest horse in the regiment.

    I must mention here that our horses were changed every day, and that, besides, while we drilled in the riding-school, we were told to change horses in the middle of the lesson. The first day, I was mounted on a mare, who was the worst kicker I ever came across in my life; she could kick so high that at times she almost stood perpendicular with her hind legs in the air, but fortunately she had a very tender mouth, so that with judgment and good handling it was easy to check her antics. When we were told to exchange horses I handed over the mare to my neighbour, the son of a farmer, who had never ridden anything but plough-horses; the moment he got on the mare's back she gave a tremendous kick and he was sent flying in the air, and turning a complete somersault he landed on his back. He soon got up and was ordered to mount again, but he had no sooner done so than the mare, guessing his lack of confidence, gave another furious kick, with her hind legs so straight in the air that he slipped over her head to the ground, where he sat in front of his charger. It was fortunate for him that in these two instances the animal was immediately caught by a Corporal, as that mare was such a vicious brute that she never failed, after having thrown her rider, to turn round and try to kick him. I was therefore ordered to take her back, and having asked leave to remove the rags covering my spur rowels, I was allowed to do so. As soon as I got on her back she tried her kicks once more, but I gave her such a dressing with the sharp points of my spurs, holding her head well up at the same time, that she became as quiet as a lamb for the remainder of the evening. I often rode this charger afterwards, having a particular liking for her, as she ambled easily, and one hardly moved on her back while trotting, a great boon when one has to ride without stirrups. When we were dismissed that evening several of my comrades were almost unable to walk, and one of them had his knees so terribly scraped that he was losing a large quantity of blood, and was literally leaving a red trail on the ground behind him! Notwithstanding this, he was compelled to ride the following day, as he did not wake up in time to report himself sick, and was therefore not allowed to attend the Surgeon-major's visit.

CHAPTER V

So far none of the *Volontaires* had been punished, and it fell to my lot to be the first to become acquainted with the *Salle de Police*. I had been ordered to ride that evening the kicking mare I described just now, but the revengeful beast, remembering the lesson I had given her on the previous day, let out with her hind legs the moment she saw me coming near her stall with a saddle. I laid it on the ground and tried to get into the stall in order to tie her head up before saddling her. Try as I would, I could not possibly manage to get alongside of her, the stalls being very narrow, and consisting of wooden partitions hung up by a chain fixed to the ceiling. These partitions, which are two feet broad, stand about four feet from the ground, so, getting into the next stall, I climbed over the partition and got alongside the charger and caught her by the head-stall. A more vicious beast I never came across; not only did she try to bite me, but she also tried to stamp on my foot, then she kicked me with her near hind leg, and while I was tying her head up she gave me a forward kick with her foreleg; and when I brought the saddle to put it on her back, she lashed out so furiously that she broke the rope by which I had tied her head high up and bit me viciously. She was Titi's charger, and he alone was able to manage her, so I sent a trooper to call him to help me. Titi came, and I was holding the mare's head while he was putting the saddle on her back when the Sergeant-major suddenly appeared.

"What are you doing there?" he asked Titi.

"Sergeant-major," I replied, "I could not manage to saddle the beast, and as I have to ride her to-night, I asked Titi to help me."

"Very well," answered the Sergeant-major, "you will both have eight days' *Salle de Police,* and if I catch you another time," he went on, addressing Titi, "it's eight days' prison *you* will get." So saying he walked away pompously, evidently well pleased with himself.

"Well, old chap," said Titi to me, "so you've got it at last."

I felt very crestfallen, but I had no time to think much about the matter, as I was already late and had to rush to riding-school. The drill over, I hastened to de Lanoy's room and asked him to intercede for me with the Sergeant-major. He promised to do so at once, and I anxiously awaited the result of his interview. At the end of a few minutes I was called into the Sergeant-major's room.

"I am very sorry for you, Decle," said the latter; "de Lanoy has spoken to me on your behalf, and if he had done so sooner I might have overlooked the matter this time, on account of the special circumstances, but your punishment has already been put down on the report, so the best thing you can do is to go through it with good grace."

When I returned to my room all the other troopers chaffed me unmercifully, but Titi was practical and sympathetic, "Now look here, old man," said he, "let me give you a few tips. First of all, as you've got warm drawers, I advise you to put on two or three pairs one on the top of the other, and I also advise you to wear two or three thick vests, because you know you'll have to be searched before you go to the cells, and you are not allowed to wear any regimentals under your canvas trousers and blouse.

You'll have to put on your clogs, and all the covering you are allowed is your bread-bag" (a canvas bag I have already described, and called a bread-bag because it is generally used for fetching the loaves of bread from the bakery. It afforded very little covering, being only about four feet by two). At a quarter to eight the trumpeters called "The men under punishment," and I went down with Titi to the guard-room. There were a dozen troopers punished with *Salle de Police* that evening, and we were drawn up in front of the guard-room. The Sergeant came out with a lantern, and having called out our names he began to search us. He felt us all over to see that we had neither matches, tobacco, candles, nor spirits concealed under our clothes. But he was a good fellow, and did not make as thorough a search as I have seen made by some others.

One trooper only, who had his riding trousers under his canvas ones, was ordered to pull them off, getting two days more for wearing them. We were then marched off to the cells. We first reached a huge door which the Sergeant opened with an enormous key. This door led into a passage, on the left of which were five heavily-bolted doors leading into the cells reserved to the men punished with solitary confinement. At the end of the corridor stood a solid door reminding one of the traditional prison portal of the old melodrama; it was locked with two gigantic iron bolts, each one closing with a key; when these had been drawn, a key half a foot long and more than an inch thick was inserted in the centre lock, in which it turned with a grating noise. The door itself was at least six inches thick and covered with heavy iron nails. We had to stoop to pass through the doorway, and were immediately greeted by a dreadful stench. The light of the lantern being turned on our faces we could hardly see where we were going, but when we had all marched in the Sergeant gave a look round with his lantern and thus enabled me to get a glance at the place. The room, a kind of cellar, was about twenty feet square. On each side of it ran a sloping wooden platform about seven feet broad, its base standing a couple of feet above the cement floor; at the top of the platform was a raised board about two inches high and one foot broad, which was meant as a pillow; this platform was our bed. The room was about ten feet high, and at the extremity of it, near the ceiling, was a small window, perhaps three square feet in area, strongly and closely barred. The only furniture consisted of an earthenware jug containing water and an iron cup. In a corner of the room, in a small recess, stood a large barrel about four feet high, with two steps leading to the top of it, and with two iron handles on each side. This, in regimental slang, is called "Jules," and is the only sanitary (?) convenience at the disposal of the prisoners. The whole place, having no means of ventilation, was musty and slimy. We all stretched ourselves on the platform, and the Sergeant, having seen us thus comfortably settled for the night, retired.

As soon as the key had been removed from the outer door I heard the cracking of a match, and a candle was lit by my friend Titi.

Having stuck the candle on the flat edge at the top of the bed he at once jumped to the floor and addressed us. "Look here, boys," he began, "I am the chairman of this 'ere meeting, as I hold the record for attendance in this hall, where I have already presided over many a merry gathering. As chairman, and as your senior, I must warn you that my authority has to be recognised by every one of you, and in my capacity of commander of the place, I may as well remind you of the regulations. Remember that 'refusal to obey is a most heinous crime, the offender being liable to be tried by court-martial.' As I notice that there are a few uninitiated members here to-night, I will let them know what are the rules and regulations of the place. I will first proceed to the inspection."

So saying, he ordered us to stand in a single file in the middle of the room; and all the troopers, scenting fun, readily obeyed. He then commanded four of us, who were making our first appearance in the place, to step forward, allowing the others to sit down. "Troopers," he said, addressing us and mimicking the Colonel capitally, "you have the honour of being admitted for the first time to these ancient precincts, which have sheltered many a great man, and it now becomes necessary that you should pay due homage to our military patron, the great and noble Jules. In order not to interrupt the sanctity of your devotions, we shall leave you in *tête-à-tête* with our noble patron, whom you will have at the same time to guard. Trooper Deele," he concluded, "right turn by the left, quick march!" Having been warned beforehand of this traditional farce, I executed the movement, and when I came within a step of "Jules," was ordered to halt. "Now," said Titi, closing the door upon me, "here are your orders: In case any one knocks at the door you are to challenge the fellow and inquire what he wants, and you must also see that Jules does not run away." The door was then closed upon me, and I was nearly stifled. At the end of a minute or two came a knock. "Who goes there?" I said. "Your commander," replied Titi from outside; "have you followed my instructions, and has Jules inspired you?" he went on. "Yes," I replied, "he told me that the distinguished company would feel thirsty in the morning, and he advised me to allay their thirst." "That's right," answered Titi, opening the door; I then handed over to him a five-franc piece to pay my footing. "Boys," he exclaimed, "'tis a hind wheel" (*une roue de derrière*—the slang word for a silver dollar). "Three cheers for Decle." The cheers were duly given. The three other recruits were still standing in the middle of the room. "Now what may your name be, you pug-nosed, carroty villain?" demanded Titi, addressing one of the fellows standing up—a recruit. "Dieudonné, *présent*," shouted the boy, adding to his name the answer given at a roll-call. Promptly he was marched to Jules as I had been, and locked in, but he was left there for ten minutes at least. When Titi went to release him the lad only offered one franc. "It won't do, my boy," said Titi. The fellow replied that this was all he possessed; but on his promising to give fifty centimes more in the morning, "to make up the price of a quart of brandy," he was released. Then came the turn of the third recruit: he was a tall and magnificently-built fellow, 6 feet 1 inch high. "Now, you *Colonne de la Bastille*,* what name has your father transmitted to his pillar of a son?" "Look 'ere you," cried the recruit, "don't imagine that I am going to let myself be bullied like those two other idiots." "I say, Tommy," remarked an old trooper of four years' standing, "don't be an ass; we're having a bit of fun, and even the *Volontaire* has played the game like a man: we've all been through it; if you don't go willing, you'll be made to go unwilling. Go on, old chap." It was of no use; the man sulked and would not budge. Thereupon Titi began another speech, giving this time an imitation of one of our lieutenants. "Ahem, I warned you, my friend, of the—as I might say —disastrous; yes, disastrous consequences of disobedience; you, er—understand well—disobedience—well, as I said, I shall have you removed where you won't—or,

* A high monument in Paris, somewhat like the Nelson Column.

rather, where you decline to—go. Now, boys," he added, turning towards the other men. Four of them had already jumped up, and among them a certain Piatte, a kind-hearted, clumsy-looking chap, but a most powerful man. The first who approached the recruit were knocked down, but Piatte, catching him by the legs from behind, brought him to the floor. The three others at once seized him by the arms and head, while Piatte held his legs, and so carried he was roughly bundled into Jules' corner, and the door locked upon him.

To make it the more secure the door was then tightly held by four men, while the recruit inside kicked and hammered at it in vain. "You cowards," he howled, with curses; "you took me unawares, four to one, and from behind too; wait until I get out! You don't know who I am. I am *Jeannot the butcher, the Terror of Belleville!*"

"Shut up, Jeannot, and listen one minute," cried Piatte, in his deep bass voice. "If you like I'll stand up to you; fair fight, mind you; square fall, both shoulders touching. Is that a go?"

Jeannot ceased hammering upon the door. "All right," he shouted. "Now, you fellows, open the door!"

"Let go, boys," said Piatte.

Slowly the tall recruit stepped out; his face was flushed, his eyes bloodshot. Folding his arms on his chest he looked round. "Where's the idiot who dares challenge me?" he said, surveying us with contempt.

"I am that 'ere idiot," said Piatte, good-naturedly.

Jeannot looked at him and laughed. "So," he said, "you want me to crush your bones? You fancy yourself pretty strong, but presently you'll be sorry you spoke, putty-face!"

"Very well, my boy, very well," quietly replied Piatte, beginning to strip.

Jeannot followed his example, and as he had but a shirt under his blouse, he was soon naked to the waist. He was a magnificent specimen of humanity. His muscles looked as if made of cast-iron; his chest was broad, his body supple, and his wrists and hands were not coarse like those usually found among the labouring classes.

Piatte took longer to strip, having a couple of flannel shirts and three heavy vests to remove. When he was bare to the waist, he appeared immensely powerful indeed, but lacking the manly beauty of Jeannot. He was thick set, with a short neck, breasts like a woman's, and a tendency to stoop. His hands were enormous (he could not get on No. 9 gloves). He was fully two inches shorter than his opponent. Both men were, however, equally matched in weight, each being about 14 stone, but at first sight I felt sure that Jeannot would easily win the day.

"Who is to be umpire?" said Jeannot.

"Titi, of course," answered Piatte.

"Titi? Who is Titi?"

My chum came forward. "You don't know me, old fellow," he began, "but you've often heard my name. I was one year with old Blanc the wrestler. 'Titi de la Villette,' don't you remember now?"

"What," cried Jeannot, "Titi de la Villette, the champion light-weight? Shake hands," and so saying he extended his palm, which Titi firmly grasped.

"Now, boys," said Titi, addressing the adversaries, "here are the conditions of the match: No grasping below the waist or by the clothes; no foul tripping, and both shoulders to touch the ground."

"Right you are—agreed," answered Piatte and Jeannot simultaneously.

The two adversaries shook hands, and immediately stood in an attitude of attack, with their knees bent, and both arms half extended forward with open hands. Then Titi gave the signal "Go!"

Jeannot thereupon advanced towards Piatte, who did not shift his position. The assailant then laid one hand on Piatte's shoulder, while he tried to get his left arm round his adversary's waist, but every feint was baffled by Piatte, who still remained on the defensive. Not a whisper could be heard, but only the loud breathing of the two wrestlers, and the sound of flesh striking flesh.

All of a sudden Jeannot sprang back, and immediately rushing once more upon his adversary, caught hold of him round the waist with his left arm, putting his right arm over Piatte's left shoulder. Piatte stood the shock without flinching, and with a rapid movement he brought Jeannot's right arm down, allowing him to pass it under his own arm so that Jeannot was grasping Piatte round the body, while Piatte was encircling him over the arms.

Under ordinary circumstances Piatte would have been at a disadvantage, but so powerful was his grasp that Jeannot, though the taller man, could not bend to catch his opponent round the waist, while Piatte fairly encircled his man—over the arms, it is true, but under the elbows. For a few seconds the two men held each other in a grip of iron, but I noticed that, while Jeannot was panting, Piatte did not seem out of breath. Then Piatte, with a tremendous effort, lifted Jeannot slightly from the ground; but, as he did so, Jeannot arched himself to regain his footing, and both men crashed heavily to the floor: they both fell on the side without loosening their grip, but Piatte quickly disengaged his left hand from under his adversary's body, with the evident intention of using his two hands to force his shoulders down. Taking advantage of the movement, Jeannot, arching himself on his head and feet, so that his two shoulders should not touch the ground, succeeded in turning Piatte a little round, and nearly managed to get on the top of him. Before he could do so, however, Piatte had slipped one hand on Jeannot's shoulder, and placed his other hand against his waist, thus pushing him away. Jeannot was still holding Piatte round the body, but the moment Piatte slipped his hand on to his shoulder he let go, and, with one hand on the ground, pushed himself away from Piatte, and the next instant both men were kneeling alongside each other. With a hand planted firmly on the ground, each one tried in turn to grasp the other by the waist, but in vain.

It was a fine sight to see these two powerful athletes rooted to the ground in grim silence, broken only by the impact of hands against muscular backs. At last Jeannot managed to encircle Piatte's waist, but, before he had succeeded in doing so, Piatte had caught him round the neck; for a second they were entangled, but Jeannot threw his legs up, and, turning a back somersault, slipped his hand from Piatte's arm and fell on his feet, standing in front of his adversary. Piatte had meanwhile remained on his knees, and, with tremendous efforts, Jeannot tried to move him, first by seizing him by the waist, then by the shoulders. But Piatte remained immovable as a rock. He told me afterwards that his chief object was to let Jeannot exhaust himself while he was saving his own wind.

This struggle lasted for a few minutes more, when Jeannot suddenly slipped on the damp cement floor, and, to save himself from being seized by Piatte, he flung himself away, and rolled behind his adversary. In an instant both men were on their legs once more, Piatte as cool as when he had first begun, Jeannot panting heavily. For a short time they both stood feinting, when Piatte, changing his tactics, made a rush at the Parisian giant, and, before the latter knew where he was, he had been lifted in the air and heavily thrown on his back with Piatte on the top of him. In order to well assert his victory, Piatte twice lifted Jeannot bodily, and made his two shoulders touch the ground. Then the victor stood up, greeted by our unanimous applause. Titi handed over to him a flask of brandy he had managed to smuggle in, and, after taking a long pull, Piatte wiped his mouth and, turning round, said, " Now it's your turn, Jeannot." It was only then that we noticed that Jeannot was lying where he had been felled, and we all feared that he might be seriously injured. Piatte hastened to his side, and was about to lift him when Jeannot opened his eyes and jumped up unaided. Turning towards Piatte, he extended his hand to him. " Shake hands," he said; " you are the first man who has ever felled Jeannot the butcher, but you're a good un; you fight square, and I like that; but you fairly took the wind out of me that last go. Now, boys," he went on, " to show you that I don't bear any grudge, I'll pay my footing, and I'll be as generous as that blasted millionnaire of a *Volontaire*. Here goes ' a hind wheel,' and good health to you all." So saying, he took a long pull at the flask which Titi had handed over to him. The combatants then wiped off the blood that ran from a good many scratches on their bodies, and donned their garments once more. In the excitement of the contest the fourth recruit was forgotten, and, as he hailed from Normandy (the Scotland of France), he kept cannily in the background, and so avoided paying his footing.

Titi then suggested that we should have a song or two, and it was fully midnight when, the candle having died out, we all tried to go to sleep. The night was bitterly cold, and as we had no blankets to cover ourselves with, we all slept huddled together like sardines in a tin.

Having been awake since 5 A.M., I was quite exhausted,

and soon dropped off to sleep, but only to wake up almost immediately with a horrid sensation that something had run over my face. I awoke my faithful Titi, who was sleeping beside me.

"Got any matches?" I asked hurriedly.

"Yes, why—want a smoke?" he replied, handing me a match.

Just as I was going to sit up to strike the match something else stirred my hair. When I had obtained a light I looked round, and to my disgust I saw half a dozen huge rats running about over my companions' bodies.

"Ah, it's the rats that worry you," said Titi; "you'll soon get accustomed to them—the place swarms with those fellows."

A nice prospect indeed! Every time I tried to go to sleep I was aroused by a rat cantering over my face, so at last I determined to sit up, gladly accepting Titi's offer of tobacco and cigarette-papers.

"The Sergeant of the Guard to-night is a good sort," Titi told me, "and he won't say anything if he smells a whiff of smoke."

At 2.30 A.M. the Sergeant turned up, and when he ordered us to get up and to clear out, I was already rejoicing at the idea that I should be able to spend a few hours in bed: but I was sorely disappointed when we were taken to the pump and ordered to fill the two huge tanks where the chargers had to be watered in the morning. The night—it was early in December—was a bitterly cold one, and the nipping wind pierced us to the bones in the intervals between our turns at the pump.

It was nearly five o'clock before we had concluded our work: I rushed to my bed, and when, a few minutes later, the Corporal called out for the names of the sick men who wanted to go to the medical visit, I put mine down, notwithstanding Titi's warning that if the Surgeon-major did not consider me ill, I should get an extra four days' *Salle de Police* for malingering.

At 6 A.M., after *réveille,* the Sergeant-major came to the room and called me.

"Look here," he said, "you are not going to begin these tricks with me—to report yourself sick just because you have slept in the *Salle de Police.*"

I assured him that I was really ill.

"So much the better for you, if you really are," he replied, "but mind you, I shall warn the Surgeon-major, and if he finds that you are shamming there'll be another eight days for you. And, by-the-by," he added, "I want to warn you that troopers who are punished with *Salle de Police* are not allowed to use the canteen, and if I find that you've set foot there—God help you! You will also, during the two hours of rest you get every day, have to do *corvées* (hard work, such as cleaning the cells, carrying *Jules* about, and doing any unpleasant jobs that have to be performed in the barracks)."

With this intimation he walked away.

Need I say that now I knew all that "*Salle de Police*" implied, it was not without dread that I looked forward to the seven days I had still to undergo.

Although the description of my adventures has been but just begun, enough has, perhaps, already been said to indicate that the military training which might be made of real educational value to French youngsters is but a sordid and degrading experience, to be remembered with loathing, or forgotten—if possible.

CHAPTER VI

AT 6.45 A.M. all the troopers who had had their names put down on the sick list were taken to the infirmary by the Corporal of the Week. We awaited the Surgeon-major's arrival in a corridor; that morning there were about fifty troopers on the sick list, and, to my great relief, I learned that the Assistant Surgeon-major was going to pay the medical visit. I had been specially recommended to this officer, and when I had previously called on him with my letter of introduction he had received me most kindly, and promised that if I ever wanted his services he would be glad to do anything he could for me. As soon as he arrived we were called into the consulting-room in batches, the troopers of each squadron going in together. The consulting-room was small, the only furniture consisting of a large table, on one side of which sat the doctor, with the infirmary Corporal opposite to him.

When the Corporals of the Week in each squadron brought the sick troopers to the infirmary, they handed over to the infirmary Corporal a book drawn up as shown in table on next page.

As the troopers came to be examined by the Surgeon-major, this book was placed by the infirmary Corporal before the doctor, who filled in the figures—these signifying the number of days during which each trooper was to be exempt from the work stated at the head of each column.

TROOPER 3809

NAMES.	EXEMPTIONS.				Remarks.
	Duty.	Boots.	Riding.	Dismounted Drill.	
Dupont, Sergeant . .	1	..	..	..	
Martin, Corporal . .	..	2	..	..	
Duval, Trooper . .	..	..	2	..	
Perrin, Trooper . .	..	..	..	4	
Bouchaud, Trooper .	..	..	..	..	Is able to do his work. 2 days' *Salle de Police* for having come to the medical visit with unwashed feet.

"Duty" means absolute exemption from all work, and if the trooper so exempted was under punishment in the *Salle de Police*, he was excused from sleeping in the cells.

"Boots" means that the trooper is excused from all exercises necessitating the use of boots—viz., mounted and dismounted drill, gymnastics, and *voltige*.

The two other columns need no explanation.

Whenever a trooper failed to be regarded as sick by the Surgeon-major, he was invariably punished with four days' *Salle de Police* by the Captain commanding the squadron. The Surgeon-major always refused to pass as "sick" troopers who were dirty, and I have seen poor fellows, with awful excoriations, sent back to their work *because* they were *dirty*.

A copy of the above-mentioned book was taken by the infirmary Corporal, who wrote down the surgeon's diagnosis of each case.

TROOPER 3809

That day the troopers of our squadron were called in first, and, as I was the sixth or seventh on the list, I watched the proceedings with keen interest.

The first trooper called up was suffering from a boil on the thigh. "What's the matter with you?" said the doctor.

"Well, sir," replied the trooper, a stupid recruit, "I have a sort of a red thing—you know, sir—just there," pointing to the place, "and it hurts me something awful when I ride."

"Well, show it," said the doctor.

The fellow tried to pull up his canvas trousers, but couldn't manage to get them up high enough.

"Why don't you take them off?" said the doctor impatiently.

The recruit hesitated, and the doctor, losing patience, ordered the Corporal to undress him; the boy thereupon, violently blushing, exposed his trouble. "Oh, a boil," said the doctor, handling him pretty roughly; and taking a lancet from his instrument case, he made a deep incision through the swelling. The recruit howled, but the doctor told him to shut up, adding that he would be "exempt from boots" for the next three days. "You will come back in three days' time," he added, and he then ordered the Corporal to give him a dose of sulphate of soda.

On the table stood four very dirty tin mugs; two of them contained a solution of sulphate of soda, and the others ipecacuanha and another emetic, mixed with water. The Corporal handed one of the tumblers to the trooper, and as he was going out with it the doctor cried, "No, no, my boy, you must drink it here." With a wry face the poor recruit swallowed the ghastly mixture, and the Corporal having ascertained that he had drained all the contents, gave the tumbler to a trooper who stood beside a cupboard containing medicines; without rinsing the tumbler, the latter trooper, who was attached to the infirmary, filled it up with another dose of sulphate of soda and replaced it on the table. In the meantime the man next on the list had been called. He was an *ancien* trooper (*i.e.*, one of more than one year's standing), and when asked what was the matter with him, he showed the doctor a huge sore on his heel, keeping the remainder of his foot inside his clog, which he held with one hand. "Take off that clog," said the Surgeon-major. The man hesitated to do so. "If you don't take it off at once," roared the doctor, "I'll send you back to your duty with four days' cells." The man obeyed, and the sight which he then displayed was too disgusting to be dwelt upon. Suffice it to say that his toes were encased in a cake of filth.

"Just what I expected," remarked the surgeon, "and still you're not ashamed of yourself," he went on, addressing the man; "go and wash yourself. The next time a trooper dares to come to me in such a state of filth I'll give him eight days." When my turn came the doctor told me to wait until the consultation was over, when he would see me privately. After me came a trooper who complained of pains in his back. "Oh, rheumatics," said the doctor; "ipecac." The man had to swallow the contents of one of the tumblers on the table, and rushed out very pale, in anticipation of what he knew would soon happen. He was exempted from drill on foot. Others were suffering from sores of various kinds, chiefly due to riding without being accustomed to it, and they were alternately ordered a dose of sulphate of soda or of ipecac.; indeed, these two medicines seemed to be considered a panacea in the French army.

One man, none other than Piatte, the hero of the previous night's contest, complained that he was not well, but the doctor could not elicit from him any particulars of his ailment.

"Have you any pain?" asked the doctor.

"Yes, sir, plenty of them," blandly replied Piatte.

"Where? In your stomach?"

"Oh, yes, sir, just so, in my stomach."

"Show me your tongue."

After examining this the doctor told him that his stomach could not be out of order, as his tongue was perfectly clean.

"Well, sir," said Piatte, "my stomach hurts me in just the same way that it does here," pointing to his back.

The doctor felt the place he had pointed out, and Piatte winced as though it caused him intense pain. "Have you lifted any heavy load lately?" good-naturedly said the doctor.

"Oh, yes, sir," innocently replied Piatte; "and you don't know, sir, what I've been suffering for these last four days. I didn't like to come to the medical visit, because I thought it would pass off, but really to-day, sir, it's more than I can bear." The doctor fully believed him, and exempted him from all duty for two days.

When Piatte walked out he winked at me. "Well, old chap," he whispered, "ain't that grand? We'll have a jolly good drunk to-day and to-morrow with yesterday's oof." If only the doctor had seen him wrestling the previous night, Piatte would not have fared so well.

The medical visit over, the Surgeon-major called me into his private office. "So," he said, "you've fallen out with your Sergeant-major. He sent me a note to warn me that you have been punished with eight days' *Salle de Police*, and he says that you are only shamming."

I told the doctor what had happened, and explained that

I was really feeling ill after the terrible night I had gone through.

"I can quite believe you," replied the doctor, "but I don't like to exempt you altogether from duty, as I do not want to show too openly the interest I take in you. I shall exempt you from 'boots' for a couple of days, however, so that you will be excused from mounted and dismounted drill, gymnastics, and *voltige;* in two days' time return here, and I will then exempt you from duty for two days, so that you will be able to have a good long rest in bed. If I don't come to pass a medical visit on that day I shall mention your case to my colleague, Surgeon-major Lesage, and he will do what I ask him."

I returned to the room, and as I was free until 11 o'clock, when I should have to go to the schoolroom, I hurried to my bed in order to get a refreshing sleep. De Lanoy soon turned up and asked me how I was. I told him I was dead beat, but he remarked that I had made a blunder in going to the medical visit. "It has," he said, "absolutely put the Sergeant-major's back up against you; he said to me just now that you are nothing but a lazy brute without two pennyworth of pluck." Although this rather upset me, I felt so exhausted that I dropped asleep before I could think the matter over. At 11 o'clock I turned up in the schoolroom, and Sergeant Legros ordered me to come and speak to him. "So, *Monsieur* Decle," he sarcastically remarked, "you've made the acquaintance of the *Boite*.* How do you like it?"

"Not at all, Sergeant," I answered.

"And therefore," he went on, "you thought that you would like a little rest to-day, didn't you?"

"No, Sergeant," I said, "I assure you I'm really ill."

---

* *Boite* (box): slang word for *Salle de Police.*

"Just so, just so," he went on. "But you'll soon get used to it, as I am afraid that I shall have to send you there *more often than your turn.*" (Another regimental expression in constant use in the French army.)

I returned to my table, and as the lesson we were told to learn that day dealt with hippology (the care and management of horses), a subject with which I was already conversant, I had soon learnt the page we had been given to study, and then joined my comrades in a game of baccarat, which a sporting member of our set had suggested. At first, as usual, we played for small stakes, but these were soon increased, banks being sold by auction and fetching as much as £10. In less than half an hour's time one of my comrades had won over £30, while I was a loser by nearly £12. These games of baccarat soon became an institution, but I am glad to say that I never "plunged," and never played beyond my means. One of the *Volontaires,* who did not belong to our set, asked as a favour to be permitted to join in our gambling, and having been allowed to do so plunged recklessly. Payments were made in I.O.U.'s, redeemable at the end of each month, but when the time came our plunger (whose losses were a good deal over £100) explained that he could not pay up just then as his allowance "hadn't yet arrived." Apparently that allowance never arrived; at all events, we never saw a penny of the money he owed us. As a matter of fact, we soon found out that his parents only allowed him £12 a month, a sum barely sufficient to cover the cost of his board at the canteen and the pay of the two troopers who fagged for him; so after paying certain necessary tips, he was, of course, left with hardly any pocket-money. While I am dealing with the money question, I may say that £300 was the minimum required to cover our necessary expenditure during our year's service in the cavalry, and a good many of us spent much more than that amount.

Being exempt from "boots," I was excused from attending gymnastics and *voltige*, and was therefore free from 12 till half-past 2, but of course, being under punishment, I could not go out of barracks. I proceeded therefore to hunt up the orderly of the *Capitaine d'habillement*, as I had heard from de Lanoy that his orderly had a room to himself, above the stores, and that, until de Lanoy was promoted to the rank of Sergeant, he used to arrange to keep a tub and all his washing things in that room, paying the man for the privilege 12s. a month. I found the fellow, but to my utter disgust he informed me that he had already arranged with three other *Volontaires* for the loan of his room (Walter being one of the lucky ones), and he absolutely declined to have another *Volontaire* using his apartment. "You see, old chap," he said to me, " if a lot of you fellows come to my room, I shall soon be found out, and not only shall I lose my billet as orderly to the Captain, but I shall be sent back to ordinary duty in the squadron, losing the comfortable little income I am now making, and I am not going to run the risk." I insisted earnestly, but without avail. I then inquired whether any other orderly had a room to himself, but found that he was the only one, and I was therefore reduced to the pump for my ablutions.

I explained just now that troopers who were punished with *Salle de Police* were prohibited from using the canteen, but I discovered that there existed, besides the two cavalry canteens, an infantry canteen where Dragoons could go; I therefore repaired there to have a meal, as I had been quite unable to swallow for *déjeûner* the repulsive mixture of bread and red beans cooked in stale fat, with a few pieces of bone and sundry bits of tendons

TROOPER 3809

served in a greasy tin pot, which formed the fare of the day. I found the canteen quite empty at this time of the day, and the cooking was decent; there was, besides, no chance of being discovered by any of the cavalry non-commissioned officers, for they all messed in a room set apart for them in each of the two cavalry canteens, while this one stood at the top of a portion of the building reserved for the line regiment. During the remainder of the time I served I never failed to use this canteen whenever I was punished, and the fact was never found out.

When I returned to my room, towards one o'clock, intending to lie down, a Corporal came to me and ordered me out for fatigue duty: I was to go and sweep the cells with the other troopers. I pointed out to the Corporal that I was sick and that I was exempt from "boots," so that I meant to have a rest while the other *Volontaires* were at *voltige*. "Yes, my boy," replied the Corporal, "I'm quite aware of that. But you're not exempt from clogs, and troopers exempt from 'boots' are not excused from fatigue duty. So, up you get, and come along." Reluctantly I followed. The Corporal presented me with a very dirty broom and accompanied by three other troopers I marched wearily towards the cells. First of all, I was told off to sweep the corridor, then the Sergeant of the Guard opened the doors of three of the cells used for solitary confinement. It was the first sight I had had of these cells, and I hoped that it would never fall to my lot to be incarcerated in one of them. Each was about twelve feet by six. On one side stood a wooden bed raised a couple of feet from the ground; and about seven feet long and two-and-a-half broad. A small shelf, a foot square, suspended against the wall by two strings, was meant for the prisoner's bread, so that the rats should not get at it.

TROOPER 3809

In a corner was a small "Jules," and alongside of it an earthenware water-jug with an iron beaker on the top of it; the only ventilation consisted in a small hole a foot square and strongly barred, opening above the door, so that when the latter was closed the prisoner found himself in almost complete darkness. While we were cleaning the cells the Sergeant of the Guard remained marching up and down the corridor, as there was a prisoner in one of them. His door was the last to be opened, and the Sergeant of the Guard ordered him to step out in the passage, while we were told off to clean his cell. The man looked the picture of misery. He had already been confined for five days, and during that time he had been able neither to wash nor to shave, and the short allowance of food had told heavily on him. Prisoners in cells are only allowed the ordinary trooper's ration every other day; during the intervening days they get one ration of soup without meat, their other meal consisting of dry bread and water. The prisoner asked the non-commissioned officer to have his water-jug emptied and refilled, as there was a drowned rat in it. I was told to hand over my broom to another trooper, and ordered with another man to catch hold of "*Jules*" and to go and empty it—a task, as you may imagine, I hardly relished. Fortunately for me, as I was crossing the yard I met my friend de Lanoy, who told me to put my odoriferous burden on the ground and to follow him. He then went to the cells and ordered the Corporal to send another man to relieve me, as he wanted me for special work. He then ordered me to go and wait for him outside his room while he remained behind. He soon joined me and told me to go and have a good wash and to return to his room. I went to the pump, and after indulging in a good scrubbing returned to de Lanoy's.

"What a filthy life this is!" I exclaimed, when I entered his quarters.

"Have you only just found that out?" he answered. "I have been serving two years and a half, and although I have been two years a non-commissioned officer, I am thoroughly disgusted with it. I heard the Corporal ordering you to follow him, and I might have told him to select another trooper for fatigue duty, but, you see, I have to be careful; if I showed you too much favour I couldn't help you as I may be able to under more serious circumstances. Now," he went on, "listen to my advice. Whenever a Corporal orders you for fatigue duty just call him aside and quietly tip him a couple of francs to drink your health with, asking him at the same time to allow you to find another man to do the work in your stead. You will never fail to find a trooper glad to take the job for a franc."

I followed his advice in the future, and it was only when no other trooper was handy that I ever did fatigue duty again.

That evening, at 7.45, I stood before the guard-room among the troopers punished with *Salle de Police*. The Sergeant of the Guard did not trouble to search us, but immediately marched us off to the lock-up. We were but six that evening; as usual, when the Sergeant had retired Titi lit his candle. After singing a few songs all the fellows dropped to sleep with the exception of Titi and myself.

"What a life!" said Titi to me. "I much prefer to be in quod—some of them ain't bad at all."

"What! Have you been in gaol?" I asked in astonishment.

"Have I been to goal! Heaps of times, old chappy!"

He was clearly not in the least ashamed to own it, but felt quite proud, and enjoyed my astonishment.

"What did you do before you joined the regiment?" I queried, in order to change the subject.

"*J' faisais la muche,*" he replied.

I did not understand what this meant, not being yet versed in low slang; and I imagined that it meant that—like many of the Parisians in our regiment—he had been a *vidangeur* (scavenger). I inquired what pay he used to draw.

"Oh," he said, "it depended; my last *marmite elle était rien épatante, mon vieux, elle faisait ses cinq roues de derrière tous les soirs!*"

He went on telling me a lot of stories on the subject, which cannot, unfortunately, be reproduced here, but which gave me a striking insight into the life of a French *maquereau* (a man who lives on unfortunates).

Seeing that he had absolutely no sense of shame, I ventured to ask him about his convictions. He became quite keen on the subject.

"Ah, my boy," he said, "don't think that it's only poor beggars like me who're sent to quod: I have seen there many a gentleman—yes, *gentleman,*" he repeated, as I was smiling—"gentlemen, like you, who drove in their own cart; but that's neither here nor there. There's one thing certain: *Y a pas d'justice en France, ma vieille!*" (There is no justice in France, old chap.) "One day, for instance," he went on, "I had been with some friends to the *Théâtre de la Vilette* (a small suburban theatre), and being a bit of an artist myself—I have been a super at the Porte St. Martin*—I became disgusted at the way

---

* The theatre of the Porte St. Martin was then the stage where historical melodrama was represented; it was associated with Frederick Lemaître and Melinge Taillhade.

one of the fellows played Taillhade's part. Instead of walking like a nobleman of the old times, and taking off his hat with a great sweep of the arm and bowing like a prince, that actor chap just walks in like if he had stepped into the café at the corner, and he takes his hat off like if it had been a billycock; I got that disgusted that I couldn't help shouting: '*Ah! malheur d'ous que tu sors?*' (Good gracious, where do you hail from?) Chambardeau, the grocer's assistant, then says to me: '*Tais donc ta sale gueule, Titi!*' (Shut up your ugly mug, Titi!) 'Ugly mug,' I says; 'what d'ye call that filthy beak of yours?' (*Ton sal museau.*) 'All right,' howls Chambardeau, 'I'll smash that phiz of yours * when we get out.' That was too much for me, so I jumps at him; all the people shout, 'Turn them out.' The police comes and chucks us out, and the other boys, guessing there'll be a row outside, follers us. Well, we first kick up a row to get our money returned; but it was no good, and the *sergots* † chucks us to the street: Chambardeau and me we goes into a side street to have it out. On the way Chambardeau pulls his knife out of his pocket. 'Knives?' I ask. 'Yes, knives,' he says. 'All right, *mon salop,*' ‡ I reply, 'I'll soon rip open your tripe-bag.' Some of the boys had joined us, and told us that the police were not likely to come, so Chambardeau he says: 'Are you ready?' 'Yes,' I says, and we close. Just then Mimi—she was the grocer's daughter, and she was sweet on me, you know—'twas that which made Chambardeau mad with me. Well, Mimi turns up. They'd gone and told her, some of the other chaps, and when she sees us going at it with knives she hollers, 'Murder! Murder! Police!'

* *La fichu tête a claques.*
† *Sergots:* slang for *sergeants de ville* (policemen).
‡ *Mon salop*=you piece of dirt; used as a term of comradeship.

The *sergots* come at a run, and just then Chambardeau he drops down. The *sergots* arrest me—the cowards! There was four of them. They knock me down and kick me all over, then they clasp the bracelets (handcuffs) on my wrists, while the others pick up Chambardeau. 'What's the row?' one of the *sergots* asks of him. 'Row?' he says; 'there's no row.' 'But,' says a *sergot*, 'you are wounded.' 'Am I?' says Chambardeau. 'I suppose that I fell on my open knife while I was playing with Titi.' He was a d—— sneak, Chambardeau was, but he never split on a pal. Well, they took us both to the police station and locked us up—me, Chambardeau, and Mimi. We had chucked our knives away, or else we should have had another round. 'It's a pity,' says Chambardeau, 'that the police came and spoiled the fun!' 'You bet, old chap,' I says. But then Mimi—she ought not to have been with us, but the cells for the women was full—she had been crying, and, as I was saying, she takes Chambardeau's hand. 'It was real good of you,' she says to him, 'not to have split on Titi.' 'I split on a pal!' he exclaims. '*Mimi, j'en ai soupé d'toi.** Ah,' he goes on, excited, 'I thought I'd make you love me; but it's no use, you must think me d—— low to imagine that I could split on a pal! Shake hands, Titi,' he then says, 'and keep her.' Just then his wound begins to hurt him. It was nothing—I'd only stuck him through the arm—but he was bleeding a lot, only he would not call out for a doctor for fear it might tell against me. So Mimi tears her apron and makes a bandage of it. The next morning we were all brought before the Commissary of Police; and although Chambardeau swore that it was all lies about our having been fighting, and my having stabbed him,

* I have done with you.

they sent us both to the *Dépôt* * in the *Panier à salade* †
(Black Maria). Two days later the *Juge d'instruction*‡
examined me. He knew me, that man; I had been twice
before him already.

"'So here you are again, Martin!' he says.

"'Yes, sir,' I answers.

"'Attempted murder this time,' he goes on, reading a
long report.

"'*Ah la bonne blague! C'est tout des menteries d'la
police.*' (Well, that's a good one! All lies from the
police.)

"'But,' he answers, 'you were caught in the act of
stabbing the man Chambardeau.'

"'Now, *Monsieur le Juge,*' I said, 'ask Chambardeau
himself, ask Mimi Robinson, the grocer's daughter:
they'll both tell you if I am not speaking God's own
truth.'

"'I have seen them both,' said the judge, 'and they
both accuse you.'

"Now you see, *mon vieux,*" went on Titi, waxing excited, and shaking me by the blouse, "you see I'd been
there before, and I knew that the judge was telling a lie
as big as himself. I had seen Chambardeau in the passage
at the *Dépôt,* and he had winked at me and telegraphed—
you know we had both been in quod before and had learned

---

* Central lock-up, where all persons who have been arrested the previous evening are sent in the morning. (Bailing out does not exist in France; but in case of arrest for slight reasons, such as making a disturbance, the Commissary of Police can release a prisoner after taking down his name and address. This is only done when the prisoner appears to be a gentleman.)

† "Salad basket": so called because prisoners are locked up in tight compartments, and are rudely shaken like salad in the baskets used by French cooks to shake the water off after washing it.

‡ *Juge d'instruction:* see Appendix B.

there how to telegraph with our hands—so he telegraphed: 'I have not been examined yet, and I'll swear we were playing, and I hurt myself; I won't split.' What's more, I had caught sight of Mimi in the witness room, and she would not have been left there if she had already been examined, so I knew it was all lies that the judge was telling just to make me confess. I didn't lose my head, but quite polite I replied:

"'I'm as innocent as an unborn baby, sir, and I only ask you to confront * me with Chambardeau and Mimi.'

"'That will come in due time,' said the judge; 'you are not going to teach me how to conduct my examination, are you?'

"'May the Lord Almighty preserve me from such a thought,' I replied, quite lamb-like, and to please him I added, '—a kind, considerate, and just magistrate like you, sir.'

"'That's enough, that's enough,' he says, but I could see that he was pleased.

"He then sent me back to gaol, and said he'd send for me next day. I heard afterwards that Chambardeau was examined after me: he swore on the head of his mother that he had hurt himself by falling with the knife, which he held open in his hand to peel an orange, and that while we were skylarking he slipped on a bit of orange-peel. But although the judge told him that he could not possibly have inflicted that wound of his on himself—and to prove it he read the doctor's report. Chambardeau replied that he had always been clumsy with knives, ever since he was two months old; but he overdid it, you know. I've always told him so—he overdid it when he showed the judge a scar on his right arm, and said he had cut himself there

* It is usual for accused and witnesses to be confronted before the *Juge a'instruction.*

while slicing bread when he was two years of age. The judge, of course, tried to make him believe that I had confessed, but Chambardeau, whose temper was rather quick, replied that he knew that was a d——d lie, and so the judge sent him back to gaol. Mimi was fine; she said she had seen nothing of a fight, but that we were skylarking, and that Chambardeau had slipped on some orange-peel and fell on his knife.

"I was examined three times that week, and once the next, and on the third week was 'confronted' with Chambardeau and Mimi. We all stuck to our story, swore that the *sergots* had told nothing but lies, and everything was going on beautifully until the judge picks up our knives that were lying on his table. One of them was still covered with dried-up blood: it was mine; so the judge says, 'Whose knife is that?' 'Hullo, they've found my knife,' Chambardeau says natural like. 'You are quite sure it belongs to you?' says the judge.

"'Sure!' answers Chambardeau; 'sure! a knife I've had for more than a year: I remember the day I bought it like if it was yesterday. It was a Monday, and it was raining hard, and it was just to get out of the rain that I went into the shop and bought it.'

"'*Greffier*,'* says the judge to his clerk, 'you have carefully taken down this deposition?'

"'Yes, sir,' answers the *greffier*.

"'And this knife?' asks the judge, taking another one from the table, 'is that yours?' I saw Chambardeau wink at me, but did not understand, so thinking it was Chambardeau's knife I said boldly, 'For sure it's my knife, sir.'

"'Look at it carefully,' the judge says, handing it over to me. I looked at it, and, without pretending to do so,

* Clerk.

looked at the maker's name. 'Of course it is my knife,' I again said, handing it back to the judge.

"'And where did you buy it?' he then asked.

"I thought that I had been jolly clever to look at the maker's name and address, but I thought I'd keep that for the last, so I said that I had bought it from a chap who had bought it from another chap. 'But,' I added, 'to show you that it's my knife and no mistake, I can tell you, sir, that it comes from Lebrun, rue de l'Arbre Sec.'

"The judge smiled in a way I didn't like, and, calling his clerk, he showed him the knife. 'Do you know that knife?' he said. 'Of course, sir,' replied the clerk; 'it is the knife you always keep on your desk!'

"The judge looked at me smiling, and did not say a word, but his silence went bang through me.

"I had put my foot in it, right up to the knee, so I pretended to gaze out of the window.

"'Chambardeau,' then said the judge, after a few minutes of uncomfortable silence, 'and you, fille * Robinson, you have both tried to obstruct the course of justice and to defeat its aim, but truth cannot be hidden from it.' He went on like that for ten minutes, old chap, and then he said to Chambardeau that, as there was nothing against him, he would be released, and then he went for me, calling me a sanguinary ruffian, one of those men who are a disgrace to society, and all sorts of tommy rot of the same kind. He concluded his little speech by saying that I would be sent for trial before the *Tribunal Correctionnel*,† where he hoped I would be made an example of, and then he dismissed us.

"Chambardeau and myself were taken back to gaol with

---

* *Fille:* woman, term applied to all persons of the gentler sex in all criminal proceedings.

† A kind of police-court. Only felonies are tried by jury in France.

TROOPER 3809

the *tourniquet* * on, held by a *Garde municipal*, and Mimi had just time to tell me that she would see about getting a good barrister to defend me. I told her to try and get a fellow called Lehautier, who had already got me off once: he could speak, that man, something grand. The last time he defended me, he told the judges that if I was before them it was because I was an orphan who had had no mother to look after my youth—the old lady was at the time doing five years under an *alias!*—and he talked them round so well that he actually drew tears from them, and I was acquitted.

"Chambardeau was released the following day, but it was not till a month later that I was tried. My counsel came to see me twice before the trial, and I did not like his ways. Mimi could not manage to secure Lehautier, who had become a great man, and wanted 300 francs (£12) to take my case up, so she got that little chap for 50 francs (£2). If you had seen the side he put on! 'Don't tell me that you are guilty,' he began. 'because, if you tell me so, my conscience '—*en va donc!* (get along) his conscience!—well, his conscience would not allow him to defend me. I told him, therefore, the story we had concocted, but he said that would never do, and advised me to say that it was true that I had stabbed Chambardeau, but that he had begun the row, and that I only acted in self-defence. And a jolly mess he made of it: he never told Chambardeau nor Mimi anything about what they had to swear; so they swore all wrong, and then the judge presiding over the court put me all sorts of questions about my previous convictions; and he then called me a de-

---

* *Tourniquet:* a piece of very flexible steel cord which is passed round the prisoner's wrist, or wrists, the two ends being held by the guard. The slightest twist causes such excruciating agony that no prisoner can escape.

moralised scoundrel and what not, and in the end I got two months! And," added Titi, violently shaking me by the blouse, "you call that justice! It was a fair fight, all fair and square, and I got two months for it. *Ah malheur!* That's what they call a Republic. If we had both been fine gentlemen, and fought a duel with swords, and, instead of bleeding Chambardeau a bit, I had stuck my sword right through his guts, every one would have said what a fine fellow I was. Instead of that, because I am only Martin, *alias* Titi de la Villette, I get two months, and they call me a scoundrel. *Ah malheur! malheur! malheur!* Liberté, Egalité, Fraternité.* That's all right for those who've got money, but the poor people, *on s'en fiche!* (Who cares about them?)"

I am bound to admit that Titi was right on some points; but, unfortunately, he did not realise to what depths of degradation he had fallen.

There is not the slightest doubt that, taken as a whole, the lowest classes in large towns, like Paris, Marseilles, Lyons, and others, are far more degraded than the people belonging to the same class of society in England, and the French military service, instead of raising these men to a higher plane, only brings down to their level those who belong to the better classes, such as peasants, small clerks, and so on. It is true that now men who have been convicted before serving their time are, as I have explained, sent to special battalions in Algeria; but still, even to this day, the three years every able-bodied Frenchman has to serve in the army are nothing but a period of ceaseless degradation for men possessing any self-respect. The system, one must acknowledge it, works better in Germany; and the British army cannot, of course, be com-

* The motto of the French Republic, which is painted on all French monuments.

pared to either of these armies in which every citizen has to serve; but I feel certain that had the troopers of my regiment been placed under the command of British officers, things would have been very different from what they were. Most of the troopers who were constantly punished would, with gentler treatment—and if the Sergeants and officers, instead of bullying them, had appealed to their sense of honour, and to their better feelings—have proved some of the smartest and most reliable troopers in the whole regiment. Instead of that they soon became discouraged, and ceased to care whether they were punished or not. When my Sergeant, after asking me how I liked the *Salle de Police,* added: " You will soon get accustomed to it," he condensed in those words all the reasons which make a blindly rigid system of discipline a complete failure.

CHAPTER VII

THE day following my second night in the *Salle de Police* was a Saturday, and inspection day. Our clothing was to be inspected on this occasion. Each trooper had to lay on his bed his various garments in such a way that the regimental numbers should be clearly displayed. The inspection took place at 2 P.M., but as early as 12.30 our respective Corporals compared the list in our *livret* with the clothes on our beds, counting our tunics, trousers, boots, underlinen, towels, and stable costume (canvas trousers and blouse), in order to ascertain whether any of our outfit was missing. All our underclothing had to be previously washed, as well as our stable uniform, so that troopers had to purchase secondhand canvas trousers and blouses to wear while the others were drying.

In order to avoid punishment in case any of my kit should be missing, I had, shortly after my arrival in the regiment, a complete duplicate set of outfit made to order by the regimental tailor, bootmaker, and armourer. The clothes were made of exactly the same pattern and cloth as those issued to us, but they were cut so that I could wear them without discomfort. I had regulation boots made in which I could walk with ease, and besides these I had several pairs made in Paris by my own bootmaker; in appearance these looked like regulation boots, but the toes were narrower and the heels lower, with box spurs, imitating the regulation spurs, screwed into the heels. These I used for drill on foot and on horseback. I had arranged to keep all my regulation outfit in a box which I left in the orderly's room which I have already mentioned. In this way I was always able to produce my regulation outfit in perfect order whenever a clothing inspection was held. That morning I sent Titi to fetch my clothes and regimental underlinen from their box, in which was also stored all my duplicate kit, as we were forbidden to keep on our shelves anything besides our regulation outfit, or to have even a locker under our beds. Under the previous Colonel troopers had been allowed to have a box in which they could lock up their private belongings, such as spare underclothing and letters, as well as any money they might possess. To be deprived of this convenience was hard on most of the troopers, as they had to carry their money day and night on their persons. It was even impossible to keep a book, as this was invariably "bagged" while its owner was at drill or stables. Petty thefts were of common occurrence, and it even happened several times to me to have loose cash stolen from under my bolster when I was asleep. To complain of a theft would only have made the complainant pass as a dirty sneak among his comrades, and would have exposed every man of his squadron to suspicion.

To return to the inspection: The Corporal having seen that each man's outfit was complete, the Sergeant came to inspect the troopers' clothes to make sure that they were in proper order, that no button was missing, and that all spots of grease or dirt had been properly removed. In case a trooper was short of some article of clothing, this was duly reported by the Corporal, the Sergeant making a note of it and reporting it in his turn to the Lieutenant. If there was time enough before the arrival of the officer, troopers who had sufficient money could go and purchase at the canteen any small articles which were needed to complete their kit (sponges and chamois leathers were especially apt to be stolen from *Volontaires,* as it was impossible to identify such articles). At five minutes to two we all had to be ready at the foot of our beds; and the Sergeant-major passed through the room to make sure that everything was in order, and every trooper properly attired. A quarter of an hour later the cry of " *Fire!* " (attention) was uttered by the trooper standing nearest to the door. This announced the arrival of an officer. The first to come was the Lieutenant of our *peloton,* a stout, middle-aged man, who spoke through his nose. He carefully turned over the clothes on each man's bed, distributing here and there a few days of *Salle de Police.* When my turn came he looked at me.

" So that's you? " he remarked.

" Yes, sir," I replied.

" Impertinent as usual," he went on. " How dare you answer me? "

" I beg your pardon, sir," I replied. " I thought you had questioned me."

" Oh, you did, did you? "

" Yes, sir."

" Well, don't think another time. I don't like troopers who think. You've got no business to think. D'ye hear? "

" Yes, sir."

" What? Don't you understand me? I tell you not to answer. Do you understand? "

Warned by what he had just told me, I shut up. Whereupon the Lieutenant, turning towards the Sergeant, remarked, " Sulky brute, that fellow."

" Are all your things there? " he then asked me.

" Yes, sir, I think so."

" You think! You always think. I told you not to think. You have no business to think. That's always the result of too much education. These lazy dogs of *Volontaires,* they are always thinking. Troopers have no business to think."

Continuing to mutter peevishly, the Lieutenant proceeded to overhaul my things while I stolidly stood at attention, at the foot of my bed.

"Look here, you—what's-your-name, what's the fellow's name?" he grumbled to himself, looking at the placard hanging at the head of my bed, on which my name and regimental number was written.

"Oh—Deele," he read aloud, holding a pair of eyeglasses in his hand—he seldom wore them on his nose. "Lionel," he went on, reading to himself, "too d——d aristocratic to have a Christian name like anybody else. Why is Lionel your Christian name?" he asked me; "will you tell me why you call yourself Lionel?" *

"Because my parents christened me so, sir," I replied.

"A fine reason!" he said. "But it doesn't matter. Don't you ever wear your clothes?" he added. "They are all new; they've never been worn!"

"No, sir," I said. "I bought duplicates so as to save those that were served out to me."

"Plenty of money to waste, eh? Regimentals not good enough for you? I suppose you would consider yourself degraded if you had to wear a regimental shirt? Linen's too coarse for a tender skin like yours, eh?"

I thought it as well to make no reply. Lifting up my blouse, the Lieutenant then looked at my shirt, and told me to unbutton it. I was wearing under my flannel shirt an undervest made of wool and spun silk.

"Ah! just what I thought," again remarked the Lieutenant. "The thing must wear flannel and silk like a

---

* As may have been noticed, my Christian name was a puzzle to every one.

Cocotte (a fast woman), and then calls itself a trooper. *I* don't wear any undervests, and yet I'm an officer! Well," he added, as he passed on to the next bed, " you've already found out that silk vests won't prevent you from going to the *Salle de Police*. You've got nothing missing to-day, but I'll soon catch you napping. You won't pass many inspections without having to send you to the *Boite*. Silk vests indeed!" he kept on muttering.

He then began to examine Titi's bed. After looking through his outfit he lifted up the mattress, and found underneath it a dirty pair of drawers and a newspaper. "Just as I expected," he remarked. "What's that?" he asked, showing the newspaper to Titi.

"Oh, it's an old newspaper, sir," blandly replied Titi, "that I put aside. I bought some things in the town and they were wrapped up in it."

The Lieutenant looked at the date of the paper; it was the previous day's number of a Radical journal.

"So, we read the paper here; the vilest rag, too, that was ever printed. Well, you will see what it will cost you, you dirty *Communard*. To begin with, you'll have eight days' *Salle de Police,* and I shall specially report you." So saying, the Lieutenant, holding the paper by the tips of his fingers, at arm's length, as if it had been something likely to contaminate him, handed it over to the Sergeant, de Lanoy, ordering him to go and throw that "vermin" on the dung-heap. "De Lanoy," he added, "on your way stop at the Sergeant-major's office and tell him to put you down for two days' *Salle de Police* for the disgusting state in which your *peloton* is kept."

As the Lieutenant was looking over the last trooper's outfit our Captain came into the room. The Lieutenant went and spoke to him, and they both returned towards Titi's bed.

"So, Martin," said the Captain in a great rage, "you dare to read papers in the barracks,* and as you are now undergoing eight days' *Salle de Police* you cannot possibly have brought it in yourself. I want to know from whom you got it?"

"I didn't get it from anybody, sir," replied Titi. "I found it in the courtyard of the infantry barracks."

"Don't tell me lies," said the Captain sternly, "or you'll be sorry for it. Tell me who gave you that paper."

"Nobody, sir."

"If you tell me," said the Captain, "I won't increase the punishment Lieutenant Pernod has given you. If you don't, I'll give you eight days' prison."

"I found it, sir," insisted Titi.

"Very well," said the Captain, "get your things ready to go to prison."

"Yes, sir," politely replied Titi.

"And if you go on much longer like that," said the Captain, in a voice shaking with rage, "you'll soon go to Biribi."†

The Captain walked out, accompanied by the Lieutenant, and soon afterwards two men from the guard, accompanied by a Corporal, came into the room with drawn swords, and Titi was marched away between them to the prison.

On inspection days we did squadron duty after "stables," having neither drill nor school, and those *Volontaires* who were not undergoing punishment were at liberty to go out of barracks until 8 P.M. The troopers who had twenty-four hours' leave were allowed to quit the barracks after evening stables and remain away until the

---

* It is strictly forbidden to read newspapers in French barracks and any infringement of this regulation is severely punished.

† *Biribi, Compagnies de Discipline*, see p. 32.

next Monday at 5 A.M. After stables the regimental orders for the day were, as usual, read out to us, as well as the punishments. Those were numerous, and included two days' confinement to the room, for a Lieutenant, for being out in civilian clothes the previous afternoon; *Salle de Police* for three Sergeants as a result of the inspection, while about twenty men were punished similarly, getting from two to eight days, their outfit having been found short, or their clothes soiled. Among the troopers punished with *Salle de Police* were three *Volontaires*, and, finally, came Titi's name, with a sentence of eight days' prison by the Captain " for having introduced a newspaper into barracks, and having obstinately refused to give the name of the trooper from whom he had obtained it."

That evening, I was, as usual, taken to the *Salle de Police,* where I was much astonished to find Titi lying on a straw mattress rolled up in a blanket. He called out to me as soon as the non-commissioned officer had locked us in, " Come here, old chap," he said ; " I'll make some room for you, old Decle, and we'll share my mattress and blanket."

Although a scoundrel, Titi was at the bottom of his heart a kind fellow, and I felt most grateful to him for sharing his rough bedding with me, especially when a little later on he produced his inevitable candle, and I saw that in order to let me lie down comfortably he was lying himself on the bare boards, his back only resting against the mattress.

I inquired from him how it was that he was undergoing his prison in the same lock-up as the one used for men punished with *Salle de Police,* and I expressed astonishment at his being privileged to enjoy a mattress and a blanket. He explained to me that the only difference between prison and *Salle de Police* was that the men punished with the former, instead of doing duty in the daytime remained in the *Salle de Police* day and night. They had, however, to do two hours' punishment drill in the morning and again in the evening, and during the remainder of the day they were employed on fatigue duty, having to carry water about, to make ditches and earthworks, and to do all the dirtiest work. On the other hand, they were allowed a straw mattress and one blanket, and were not called upon to work at the pump in the middle of the night. On the whole, it struck me that prison was a far milder punishment than *Salle de Police,* and I found this undoubtedly to be the case when later on I became personally acquainted with the former punishment.

CHAPTER VIII

ACCORDING to the doctor's orders I went to the medical visit in the morning. Being a Sunday, there were but a few men who had reported themselves, but besides myself there were two *Volontaires,* one of them being the poor fellow of whom I spoke when I described our first riding-lesson under Sergeant Legros; the inside of his knee had been so badly scraped that further riding had caused extensive inflammation, and he was ordered to the *Infirmerie* (a kind of hospital ward in the barracks, where sick soldiers who want special attention, but are not ill enough to go to hospital, are kept). As before, the doctor kept me waiting until he had disposed of the other cases, and then exempted me from duty for two days. I was thus excused from all work, and, what I still more appreciated, had not to sleep in the *Salle de Police.*

The doctor also inquired very kindly how we were treated by our Sergeant. I frankly told him the truth. " I am not astonished," he said; " I know the man and I pity you." He then went on to tell me how different had been the treatment of the *Volontaires* under the previous Colonel; my friend, de Lanoy, was then in charge of them, and none of the bullying we were subject to ever occurred, or would have been tolerated then. The doctor further allowed me to make use of the dispensary if I cared to read or write while off duty, and, as will be seen, I owe an immense debt of gratitude to him, as well as to the other Surgeon-major of my regiment, Dr. Lesage, who was

Surgeon-captain, Dr. Chatelain holding only the rank of Lieutenant.

In the afternoon I availed myself of the permission which had been granted me of using the dispensary, and I was sitting there sketching when Surgeon-major Lesage stepped into the room. He was a brisk and restless little man, very stern in appearance, but with the kindest of hearts.

"What the deuce are you doing there?" he asked, as I rose to salute him and stood at attention. I explained matters to him. "Yes," he said, "I know; Dr. Chatelain has spoken to me about you, but you're a bit of a *pricotteur*,* aren't you?"

"No, sir," I replied.

"Never mind, never mind," he said in his brusque way. "When you are ill, I'll look after you, but don't come to me when you aren't—I don't like it."

He hurried out of the room, and went to visit the troopers in the sick ward.

When I resumed work on the Tuesday it had been snowing hard during the night, and the cold was such that our fingers soon became benumbed through contact with our carbines. I have omitted to mention that in the cavalry white doeskin gloves are always worn at drill; and we were even allowed during the winter months to wear white woollen gloves. In the infantry the men drill without gloves, and only wear them on parade, or when they go out of barracks, their gloves being of white cotton.†

Before drilling us Sergeant Legros carefully examined our carbines, and gave *Salle de Police* "*à l'œil*" to three

---

* A fellow who shirks work.

† The regulation gloves for officers are brown driving-gloves, except on special occasions, such as reviews, official calls, &c., when white gloves have to be worn.

of us. As I have already explained, *à l'œil* means that the punishment is not reported to the officers, and therefore is not recorded. In my time this led to monstrous abuse, as neither the Captains nor the Colonel were aware of the number of men who were daily punished.

It was so cold that we felt quite delighted when we were commanded to start at *pas gymnastique* (a quick run), the Sergeant and the Corporal running with us for a couple of hundred yards, when they fell out. We soon, however, began to feel exhausted, but Legros noticing this called out to us: "You d—— lazy brutes, keep your distances, or I'll leave you on the run for half an hour longer." First one, then another, fell out, utterly unable to go on, each one of them being told that he would sleep in the *Salle de Police* that night; then came my turn, with the same result, but little did I care for the punishment, as I had to sleep in the den in any case. Altogether six of us were punished after we had been kept on the run for more than a quarter of an hour!

We were kept drilling on foot for half an hour longer, and during that time our Sergeant took a delight in making us "shoulder arms," "slope arms," "present arms," and leaving us in the same position for three or four minutes at a time, while if a single one of us wavered in the least he never failed to make us repeat the movement. Day after day the same thing occurred, until the two hours of foot drill became a daily terror to us.

Sergeant Legros took also special pleasure in the *voltige*. The few of us who, like myself, had soon learnt to run alongside the horse while cantering in a circle and to jump on his back facing the head or the tail, or to jump on the horse and then to alight by passing the leg over the neck, jumping up once more astride the animal, were seldom called. The Sergeant's delight was to get a *Volontaire* who could just manage to jump on the cantering horse, and then to order another clumsy chap to jump behind him: if the man succeeded in doing so without bringing the first rider to the ground, the Sergeant whipped the horse until both riders fell off, and in that case he usually gave each of them one or two days' *Salle de Police*.

Another trick he was particularly fond of making us perform was "the scissors." This was usually done on the circus saddle, although some of us could do it on the bareback horse with only a surcingle. It may be thus described:

Being on the horse you seize the iron handles fixed on each side in front of the saddle, then putting your weight on your wrists you throw your legs high up in the air, bending forward as much as you can; you then cross your legs, and letting the handles go you drop back into the saddle facing the horse's tail. To face once more the horse's head you repeat the movement, laying hold of two leather loops fixed at the back of the saddle, but you must be careful to bend your head downwards towards the outside of the circle described by the horse, or else instead of falling on the saddle you are violently jerked to the ground. A fairly good rider can soon learn to perform this trick bareback, throwing himself back with the aid of the handles fixed on to the surcingle, while to face once more the horse's head he pushes himself well forward towards the withers, and placing his hand on the animal's back he vaults with the weight of his body thrown well towards the inside of the circle.

Had we had a different Sergeant who, instead of having but one object in view—to punish us—had put us on our mettle and developed a spirit of emulation, we would have soon proved the pick of the regiment. One or two of the *Volontaires* were splendid athletes, two of us at least being able to jump over the whole length of a horse leap-frog fashion, leaping from behind and landing in front of the animal's head. Most of us could in the same way jump standing on to the horse's back, my friend Delbruck being among the best athletes of our lot. It is true that his mother was English and that he had received an English education.

That evening it was freezing so hard that we were allowed to take our great-coats to the *Salle de Police,* and the Sergeant of the Guard being a friend of de Lanoy's I was excused from pumping water, and sent to my bed at 3 A.M. The following day I was still more lucky, for de Lanoy having taken the guard, allowed me to sleep in the stables instead of the *Salle de Police.* I made myself snug alongside my mare, and the dear little beast cannot have moved for hours, for I slept beside her from 8.30 P.M. till 3 A.M. I was awakened by a great commotion: one of the chargers had kicked in such a way as to get astride the partition of his stall, where he got stuck. I arose to help the stable guard, and with the handle of a broom we managed after a good deal of trouble to unhook the partition, which fell to the ground, releasing the unfortunate horse.

I then returned to my own charger's stall, and passed a most comfortable night. I had once more to sleep in the *Salle de Police,* but, fortunately, that was my last day of it for the time being.

The frost was getting more intense every day, and it has, indeed, been recorded that the winter of 1879 was one of the severest within the memory of man. The cold at last was such that orders were given by various Captains that we should drill in the stables instead of out of doors; this at least saved us from having to run round a yard until we were completely exhausted.

TROOPER 3809

As we began to know Sergeant Legros better we were able to realise into what hands we had fallen: some days he was in a good humour and none of us would be punished; at other times he would only put in an appearance when we were assembled for drill on foot; but when he failed to appear at morning school, which in his absence was presided over by a Corporal, we were certain that it was a bad sign. The moment he appeared he looked sulky, with a heavy cloud over his face, and his first words to us usually were, " I am going to stick four of you in the *Salle de Police* to-night, so you had better look out." This promise he never failed to keep, and four of us invariably slept in the lock-up.

We were already in the middle of December, and Christmas was fast approaching, so that we all looked forward to the few days' leave we hoped to get at that festive season; but, alas, I little suspected what was about to befall me. The Colonel seemed to have taken an increased dislike to *Volontaires*. First came a regimental order by which the *Volontaires* were strictly forbidden to mess at the canteen. As, however, he could not stretch regulations far enough to prevent us from using the canteen, he worded the order thus: " In future," he said, " the *Volontaires* will have to go and fetch their rations from the kitchen like other troopers; Corporals are enjoined to report any *Volontaire* failing to obey this order." This was all very well, but he could not compel us to eat if we were not hungry. Still, the result of this order was great inconvenience to us, as it meant our being detained in the room until our *gamelle* had been brought by the orderly.

On the Sunday before Christmas I was expecting a party of friends who had promised to come and look me up, and had asked me to dinner. At afternoon " stables "

I therefore went to the officer of the week, and asked him for ten o'clock leave, as I said some members of my family were coming to see me. Immediately after "stables," donning one of the uniforms I had had specially made of better cloth, I went to the station to await my friends' arrival. They were artists, and were accompanied by two music-hall stars of the day. I waited for them on the platform, and when they alighted from their compartment, one of the ladies complained that an old gentleman, whom she pointed out to me, had been rubbing his foot against hers in so persistent and insulting a manner that she was compelled to request him to desist. I had a good stare at the old man, and made some uncomplimentary remark to the lady about him. We then proceeded to take our seats in a four-in-hand brake I had hired for the occasion, and drove off merrily to the forest, a few miles from the town. I was driving, and on the way I observed that we passed in one of the streets the old gentleman of the train. We spent a most pleasant afternoon, and were enjoying our dinner when my friend de Lanoy sent word that he wanted to speak to me. I asked him to join us, but he declined to do so, and insisted upon the waiter telling me that it was most important that I should come out to him at once. Accordingly I went, and, at de Lanoy's request, we adjourned to my room.

"What the deuce have you been doing, old chap?" he began; "Major Vian has just been to the barracks, fuming with rage, and ordered me to mount my horse and look for you all over the town, and when I had found you, I was to bring you back with me, and stick you straight off in prison."

I simply could not understand what it meant, and told him exactly how the case stood: that some friends, whose

TROOPER 3809

names I mentioned, as he knew them also, had come to spend the afternoon with me, and that before dinner we had driven in a brake to the forest. I asked de Lanoy whether by so doing I had in any way infringed the regulations; but he told me that he did not see anything irregular in my proceedings. He then inquired whether I had met the Major on the way and failed to salute him; but I was able to assure him that I was quite certain that I had duly saluted every officer I came across. "Well," he said, "I cannot understand it; but I will tell you what I will do for you: I will tell the Major that I couldn't find you; so go on with your dinner, and, as you have ten o'clock leave, enjoy yourself till then; but you must expect to be locked up the moment you return to barracks." De Lanoy then expressed his regret at being unable to join us, explaining that being on duty he could not possibly do so. This occurrence naturally marred the gaiety of the following proceedings, but my friends tried to cheer me up, and affected to treat the adventure as a joke. At ten o'clock I returned to barracks and reported myself to the Sergeant of the Guard. The Sergeant, a friend of mine, told me that "I had put my foot in it," and that he had strict orders to march me to the cells then and there. At the same time, with some curiosity, he asked me what I had been doing. I was as ignorant as he was of my supposed crime, and could supply him with no information. I handed my sword over to one of the troopers of the guard, and asked him to take it to my room with my helmet. I was then marched off to the cells. Between ten o'clock and midnight five more troopers were brought into the prison, all of them in full uniform, and in a disgusting state of drunkenness; of course they kicked up an awful row, and there was no sleep for me, as may well be imagined. At half-past twelve we heard a tremendous disturbance outside the cell door, and the moment it was opened a trooper, mad with drink, struggling, kicking, and swearing, was chucked inside. As soon as the door had been closed upon him he rushed to it, and for fully a quarter of an hour went on hammering and kicking at it like a maniac; realising then that his efforts were all in vain, he tottered towards the camp bed and threw himself bodily on two or three men who were lying on it. He was received with curses, and violently thrown off, dropping with a tremendous thud on to the pavement of the cell. He arose, however, madder than ever, and, with oaths and curses, declared that he was going to rip open the whole b—— lot of us.

Unfortunately at that moment one of the troopers struck a match and lit a candle. This only added to the fellow's drunken fury, and to our horror we saw him pull a huge clasp-knife from one of his pockets. We all sprang to our feet, but the drunken man, selecting a trooper against whom he evidently had a grudge, made a rush for him; at the same time the candle was upset, and in the dark we could hear the two men struggling and rushing about the cell. "Who has got a match?" I shouted. As ill luck would have it nobody could find one for the moment, so, unwilling to be ripped open in the dark, I groped my way towards a recess where "*Jules*" stood, and closed the door behind me. A few minutes, perhaps but a few seconds, later I heard Piatte's deep bass voice saying, " No you don't, my children, no you don't ! " I carefully peeped out, slightly opening the door. The candle had been relighted, and in the middle of the cells stood Piatte, in uniform, holding two men, one by his coat-collar, and the other by the wrist. It appears that Piatte had returned to barracks drunk that night, and had been taken to the lock-up, but, being in a very quiet mood when "boozed," he had merely gone to lie down in a corner. He had been aroused by the noise of the fight, and had immediately jumped up to separate the belligerents. It was dark when he first tackled them, and in the struggle he had been stabbed through the arm. In the meantime someone had found a match and re-lighted the candle just as I emerged from my place of safety. It was superb to see the Hercules Piatte holding these two men, absolutely frenzied as they were, as easily as if they had been mere babies. "Put down your knives, you beggars," he said to them, and as the man who had begun the row, and whose wrist he held, swore that he would do no such thing, but that he would soon have his knife through Piatte's digestive organs, the latter gave a wrench to his wrist which made the weapon drop to the ground. Some of us had in the meantime disarmed the other fellow, and Piatte then addressed them:

"Are you going to be quiet and go to sleep, you silly beggars?"

A torrent of abuse was the only reply, and the two combatants continued to swear they would have one another's blood.

"Very well!" said Piatte. "If you are so anxious to knock each other about here goes!" and so saying, he banged the two men one against the other half a dozen times as if they had been mere puppets. He then let them go. "Got enough of it, my boys?" he asked grimly.

They had apparently had quite enough of it, for they both went to lie down moaning heavily. Curiously enough, neither of them had been stabbed, and they had only received some insignificant scratches. Beckoning to Piatte to come to me, I examined his wound: luckily for him he was wearing his uniform coat, and the thickness of the cloth had partly stopped the knife, and it had only penetrated slightly into the flesh of his arm. It was with difficulty that I induced him to let me bind it up with my pocket handkerchief, a trifling service which the kind-hearted fellow never forgot, and which he repaid in more ways than one. When the Sergeant of the Guard came at 3 A.M. to take the men to the pump, I was ordered to stop in the cells, the Sergeant having received special instructions to keep me there until the Major turned up in the morning. There were two prisoners to keep me company, but dog-tired as I was, I soon dropped off to sleep, and did not awake till half-past six, when my friend de Lanoy came to look me up. He had tried to find out what I was charged with, but had failed to do so; he promised, however, to come and let me know as soon as he obtained any information, so that I should be prepared to face the Major, before whom I was to be brought at 10 A.M. De Lanoy also kindly suggested sending me my washing materials and a razor, in order that I should not look the disgraceful object I then did. Shortly afterwards the Corporal of the Guard brought me my things, as well as a bucket and a looking-glass, and while I was making my toilet he chattered with me about my case.

"You're in a nice hole, old boy," he said, "and I shouldn't like to stand in your shoes. What on earth have you been doing?"

I assured him that this was the very thing I did not know myself.

"Now that is all rot," he replied. "It must have been something, jolly serious, too, for when the Major came to the barracks yesterday he was in a greater rage than I have ever seen him in before. Yes," he went on, "I really thought he would have had a fit."

I once more renewed my assurance that I was absolutely unconscious of having done anything wrong.

"Get along with you," said the Corporal; "you won't get me to believe that, but if you choose to keep it to yourself, do so, by all means, I don't care." He then took my things away, and I was soon left to my own thoughts, the two prisoners being taken out to do work. At 9 o'clock de Lanoy returned, and told me that so far all he knew was that I had been given four days' *Salle de Police* by the Lieutenant who had given me 10 o'clock leave the previous day.

At 10.30 A.M. the door of the cells once more opened, and the Corporal of the Guard ordered me to step out, whereupon I was marched off between two of the troopers of the guard, who, with drawn swords, escorted me as far as the *Salle de Rapport.* The *Adjudant* soon came to the door and ordered me to walk in, stepping out himself at the same time, and closing the door behind him. The room was a spacious one, with a large table in the middle of it, at which a small bald-headed man sat signing documents; his back was turned to me whilst I stood near the door at attention. After a few minutes' silence, only interrupted by the grating of his pen upon the paper, the little man, without turning round, called out:

"Trooper Decle, come here."

I advanced, turned round to face him, and, as I saluted, what was my horror at discovering that the enterprising old gentleman whose foot had annoyed one of my lady friends in the train on the previous day, and about whom I had passed some rather uncivil remarks, was . . . my Major!! The reason I had not recognised him as an officer was that since I had joined the regiment he had been away on leave, and he had only just returned. I stood at "attention," my heart beating fast, but the old gentleman (his age was perhaps fifty-six or fifty-seven) did not speak a word, but stared at me from head to foot with a look that seemed to pierce me.

"So," he said, after a few minutes' time, "we are one of these *Volontaires,* one of these dashing *Volontaires,* who, although they wear a Dragoon uniform, are nothing after all but dirty *petits crevés.* We invite painted females, who are nothing but low *Cocottes,* to come and visit us, and we parade them about the streets in a four-horse brake when our officers are content to walk on foot! Trooper Decle," he proceeded in a stern voice, "you are a disgrace to the 50th Dragoons. You have disgraced your uniform by a contact with such creatures, you have disgraced yourself by passing uncalled-for remarks on your betters, and although you are a *Volontaire* you are a liar, and nothing but a b—— *maquereau.*"

I turned pale under the insult, but as I had determined to keep my temper, I made no reply. This seemed to excite the gradually rising fury of the Major, who had now risen from his chair and was pacing up and down the room livid with rage.

"Why don't you answer?" he cried; "what have you got to say, dirty swine that you are! I suppose you belong to the class of youngsters who are proud to be seen in the company of *Cocottes,* and afterwards leave those ladies to settle the bill for them."

This I confess was too much for me, but still determined to outwardly restrain my temper, I took two steps towards the Major, and crossing my arms on my chest, looked him straight in the eyes.

"I have let you insult me, sir," I said slowly, "in order to see how far you would go. The ladies of whom you have just spoken are, I know, far above your contempt, and it strikes me that if they had cared to accept your senile advances, you would probably have thought them most divine creatures. I need not defend them, they are too well known to require such defence," I continued, mentioning their names.

"As for myself," I went on, "you have accused me of playing the basest part a man can play in this world. It was not through respect for the gold stripes you wear on your sleeve that I kept silent, but through respect for your white hairs. In a few months' time I shall no longer be a Dragoon, and I hope that in a few years I shall be somebody, while you will be—yourself: nothing else but one of the mass of retired Majors whose intelligence and means will limit them to a glass of absinthe, and a game of dominoes before dinner, and the company of a local bailiff, or the constable of their native village. You called me a *maquereau* just now, and you seem to be so well acquainted with the habits of that class, that I can only conclude that you gained that knowledge personally at a time when nature made you more attractive than you are now."

The Major, who had been too dumfounded to answer a word so far, turned pale when I uttered those words, and, seizing his riding-whip, which lay on the table, lifted it as though about to strike me, shouting at the same time, in a voice choked with rage, "*Misérable!*" I wrenched the whip from his hands, and replacing it on the table stood once more at "attention."

"I will court-martial you," went on the Major; "you shall have ten years for this!"

"I may or may not, sir," I replied; "but supposing I am court-martialled, I shall bring witnesses to expose the way in which you behaved in the train yesterday, and you may regret the step you have taken. As to our present conversation there is only your word against mine, but I suppose that being only a trooper my word will stand for nothing, still, as I told you before, think well over the matter before you do anything rash."

The Major said nothing, but went on feverishly pacing up and down the room. He at last stopped, and sat down at the table.

"Decle," he said, "Lieutenant Riel has given you four days' *Salle de Police* for having told him a lie in asking for ten o'clock leave on the pretence that you were going to meet your family, and your punishment will be increased to fifteen days' *Salle de Police* for having been seen driving a four-in-hand through the town in fancy uniform. Now, go!"

I did not wait to ask for any further explanation, being only too glad to escape as I had. I must add that the Major was evidently persuaded that he had put himself in the wrong, for I was never afterwards punished by him, and in no case did he increase any punishment given to me. The whole thing was pretty rough on me, however, as those fifteen days meant my spending Christmas and New Year in the cells while all my comrades were enjoying a well-deserved leave. After the eight days' cells I had previously had, those fifteen days given to me within the first two months of my service branded me as a bad character, and I fully realised that in future punishments would be showered upon me.

CHAPTER IX

It will be readily understood that the end of that year was one of the most unpleasant times I ever went through. The cold was bitter, and we were pretty nearly frozen in the *Salle de Police*. Just before Christmas all my comrades went home with eight days' leave, and I was the only *Volontaire* left behind. There was one comfort, however, in the fact that, Sergeant Legros being also on leave, I escaped his daily bullying. By that time I had also learned how to avoid all fatigue duty, having found out that there was not a single one of our Corporals who was not open to a bribe; in fact, some of them knowing that I was pretty free with my money, openly came to me, saying, " I say, Decle, I am thirsty to-day; are you going to stand a bottle, or do you want to do fatigue duty?" Of course I immediately forked out a franc, and was thereupon left alone. I had also made friends with a good many of the Sergeants, and when any of those with whom I was friendly took the guard they invariably allowed me to sleep in the stables instead of the *Salle de Police*. The cold was so bitter just before Christmas that the Colonel issued an order allowing the troopers punished with *Salle de Police* to wear their second-best regimental trousers under their canvas ones, and to use their great-coats when sleeping in the cells.

On Christmas Day more than fifteen troopers were thrown into the *Salle de Police* during the night, all of them having returned to barracks in a state which an

English policeman would describe as "drunk and disorderly"; prominent among them were Titi and Piatte, both most gloriously drunk, but having just enough sense left to remember that their chum Decle was in durance vile. The moment they got in they called out for me, and on my answering them, they threatened every one with blue murder if a candle was not produced at once, as they wanted to see their dear Decle. I had smuggled in a candle as well as some matches, and thinking that it might keep them quiet, I lit it. The moment they saw me they rushed to me with demonstrations of affection with which I could well have dispensed, Piatte especially insisting on repeatedly embracing me, and, unconscious of his great strength, hugging me as tightly as a bear, until I feared he would crack my ribs. The boon companions then produced a miscellaneous collection of articles from their pockets—greasy papers containing sausages and *boudin* (a kind of sausage made of pig's blood with a lavish addition of garlic); mixed up with these were bits of cheese, cakes, and, last but not least, a pint of brandy.

"We brought you that, old chap," said Piatte, "because we didn't want an old chum to spend a miserable Christmas."

It must be remembered that Piatte was a Protestant from Lorraine, where Christmas is, I believe, religiously kept as the greatest festival of the year, while in other parts of France New Year's Day is considered far more important. To please the poor fellows, whose kindheartedness I fully appreciated, I partook sparingly of their victuals, although they were far from appetising. I pretended, too, to drink some of the vile brandy, but a sip of it was quite enough. The two men then sat down near me.

"Oh!" said Piatte, "we've had a grand time of it, a grand time, my boy!"

"Yes," interrupted Titi, who was a little muddled; "if you had seen that little infantryman flying out of the window you would have simply roared."

"Don't interrupt, Titi," screamed out Piatte, trying at the same time to give Titi a friendly buffet with his open palm; unfortunately, however, I sat between the two, and the badly aimed blow fell on my head and nearly knocked the senses out of me; seeing this, Piatte, to comfort me, hugged me once more in his powerful arms.

"Well," he resumed, "we started at three o'clock this afternoon, just after stables, and as we got outside Titi says to me, 'Got any oof, Piatte?' 'Oof,' I says, 'open your eyes well and look at that.' I had received, two days ago, a remittance from the old woman, my old granny—ten francs, *mon salop*. So Titi looks at it, and he says, 'Ah, ten francs; oh my, I'll show you something better than that,' and he pulls out of his pocket a 'gold un'—a whole twenty-franc piece. 'That's from my *Volontaire;* he's a rare un,' he says.

"That's you, you know," added Piatte, digging me in the ribs.

"That's God's truth," hiccoughed Titi.

"Shut your head, Titi—you're drunk. Isn't he drunk, that fellow? But, as I was telling you," Piatte went on, "we took the road past the railway, and came to that little pub 'The Three Jolly Comrades,' where there's a sign-board where they've painted a Dragoon, a Pioupiou,* and a Gunner walking arm-in-arm—you know the place, don't you?"

I didn't, but assured Piatte that I knew it well.

"'Let's go in,' says Titi: but I says, 'No.' Fancy go-

* A common slang expression for an infantryman.

ing into a place where they put a Dragoon arm-in-arm with a Piou-piou! But Titi, he says, 'Oh, never mind their bally sign-board if their wine's good,' and I says, 'There's sense in that,' so in we goes.

"There was a billiard-table in the place, so I says to Titi, 'After we have had a drink we will have a game, Titi.' We called for a drink, and a jolly nice girl comes to serve us. You should have seen her, old chap; she was a regular ripper—plenty of flesh and some to spare. I had taken her hand, and was telling her what a fine girl she was when half a dozen Piou-pious walked in the place. The girl tries to take her hand away and blushes, and I see one of the Piou-pious stare at me like mad. Well, I didn't say nothing, but I let go the girl's hand, and she brings us our wine and a flask of brandy; we finish our bottle, and just as we were drinking our last glass I see one of the Piou-pious take off his coat, and they all take billiard cues and calls out for balls; so I get up and I say, 'No, look here; 'tis our game and not yours.' One of them says, 'First come, first served.' I says, 'Just so; we came first, and first we play.' But the Piou-pious wouldn't give in, and the one that had stared at me, he calls the landlord. When the old man comes I say, civil like, 'Now, look here, landlord: I have come into your house, although I didn't like that 'ere board on the outside. How dare you call that "The Three Jolly Comrades," and put up a picture of a Dragoon walking arm-in-arm with a dirty mean bug of a Piou-piou, like if any Dragoon would lower himself in that way.'

"'Dirty mean bug!' shout all the Piou-pious together. 'You filthy *citrouille!*' (A nickname given to Dragoons, meaning "pumpkin.")

"This was too much for me, so I turns to Titi and I says, 'Did you hear that?'

TROOPER 3809

"'Didn't I?' he says. 'What shall we do—chuck all these dirty shrimps out of the window, eh?'

"'That's it,' I say, and I goes to open the window. I must tell you Titi and I had taken off our swords and put them in a corner when we came in. I had just opened the window when one of them takes his billiard cue by the tip and hits me with the thick part of it; but it just struck on my helmet, and you can see it hit hard. Look," added Piatte, picking up his helmet, which was quite bashed in. "Oh, then," he went on, "my blood was up and I went for that chap, and without more ceremony I take him by his coat-tails and his collar, and I send him, cue and all, right over the billiard-table, where he falls all of a heap and stops there. At the same time the four others had set on Titi, so I rushed to his help; he was down, and they were hammering at him like mad; so I hit one here, I hit another there, I gave the third a dig in the chest with my head, I sent the fourth against the billiard-table with a kick, and Titi gets on his legs. The others, except the one I had chucked over the billiard-table, had also got up, and we were fighting like mad when three other devils who were passing along the road stepped in and joined in the row. 'Oh,' I says, 'is that so? Helmets, then!' Titi understands me; we take our helmets off, and swinging them by the end of the horse-tail, we strike right in among them promiscuous like. My boy, if you had seen them: they drops one after the other; only three of them remained standing up, and while Titi was having it out in the corner with one of the chaps I stood facing the two others. One of them, the coward, draws his sword-bayonet, but with a swing of my helmet I knocks it out of his hand, and as the window stood open I chucked him out of it. The other one, in the meantime, had caught hold of me from behind, but

I soon shook him off, and lifting him from the ground—he was a miserable little cur—I shook him like a rat. I bang him against the wall, and at last he cries, 'Oh, don't, don't.' 'Going to beg pardon?' I asked. 'Oh, yes,' he says, 'I beg pardon.' 'Very well, then,' I says, sticking him on the ground, standing with his back to me, 'if you move God help you!' at the same time I holler, 'Prepare to receive cavalry!' and didn't he receive cavalry, just! With one kick in the back I sent him flying to join the others."

At the recollection of this Piatte burst into such a roar of laughter that it awoke Titi, who had fallen asleep on my shoulder, and he, too, began to guffaw idiotically.

"Shut up, Titi," yelled Piatte once more. "Where was I? Oh, I know," he went on. "Titi had by this time knocked his man down, and without asking for our bill, we pick up our swords and bolt like mad. As we get out, the chap I had chucked out of the window has just regained his feet, and he hollers 'Murder! Murder!' He was a Corporal, and 'twas a bad case. The landlord had been hollering 'Murder!' the whole time; but, d'ye see, the place stands all by itself, and only the three chaps I spoke of heard him. We hadn't gone a hundred yards before we see all the Piou-pious rush out of the pub and make for us like mad. We hadn't been such fools as to cut towards the town, so when we saw them after us we made off across country, and, as luck would have it, they didn't chivy us far. But we'd given them too good a dressing to be up to much. All the same, we ran for another mile, and then we sat down and had a good laugh. Then Titi, he says, 'It's all very fine, but I don't like it; that ere d——d Corporal'll be bad for our health: we must rig up an alleyby.' So to rig up his blooming alleyby, he says, 'Let's go down to the river, and first of all let's have a swill!'—we were pretty bloody and dirty, you bet—'and then we'll go to a bloke I know who's got a boat, and then we'll get back to the town, and make out as how we've come from the North Road, and we've been in the forest, and you got your helmet smashed bird's-nesting.' And so we did. By a roundabout way we got to the river and had a wash; we soon found Titi's bloke, and he took us over in his boat. 'Give us a hind-wheel,' says Titi, and he hands it over to the boat chap. 'Mind you,' says Titi, 'you've seen no Dragoons to-day.' 'Mum's the word,' he says back, and he pulls off and throws a line into the water quite innocent like. We ran towards the forest until we hit the road, and then we walked quietly down towards the town. On the way we meets Lieutenant Granford riding; he stops and says, 'What's the matter with your helmet?' 'Oh, sir,' I says, 'I tried to get a rook's nest, and nearly broke my neck.' 'Well,' says the Lieutenant—he's a good sort, you know—'you'll have to pay for it; but bird's-nesting is a better occupation than getting drunk.' 'Yes, sir,' says Titi, 'we don't mean to liquor any more!' 'I'm glad to hear it,' says the Lieutenant, and he canters off.

"'There's our alleyby,' says Titi, 'all cut and dried, and now for a bally good booze!' Ah! my boy, what a day we had of it! But unluckily we forgot the time. We'd only got ten o'clock leave, and as we were looking for another pub, to blow off our remaining four francs, we found one where the shutters were just being put up. 'By Jove!' says Titi, and asking the chap who was putting up the shutters what sort of time it was, we heard ''twas a quarter to twelve!' Off we cut to barracks, but on the way, just as we were getting round the corner, Titi didn't feel well, and he says, 'Hold hard a minute, old chap!' That's just what done it. Titi never can stand a drop of lush, and he began to be that sick, and made such a bally row, that the *Adjudant*, who was sneaking about the shop, he pounces on us, and wants our names. So long as we were walking it was all right; but the moment we had to stand at 'attention' things began to swim a bit. I see Titi isn't steady, so I catch hold of him to prop him up; but he clutches me, and we both sprawl on the ground. Well, that finished it. The *Adjudant* calls out to the sentry to send two men from the guard-room, and he orders them to march us up to the *Salle de Police*—and here we are. But we had a jolly good drunk," concluded Piatte, with a satisfied air; and extinguishing the candle we went to sleep.

The next day the two revellers had fifteen days' prison by the Colonel's orders. A complaint was lodged by the Colonel of the infantry regiment that an assault had been committed by Dragoons on one of his Corporals, and it appeared that two of the privates had also been seriously injured in the fray, and were lying in hospital. Fortunately for Piatte and Titi the injured Corporal and his comrades had reported that they were set upon by at least half-a-dozen Dragoons. The case was a serious one, however, and I feared that Piatte and Titi would be found out; this would mean a court-martial, and very likely they would be sentenced to death, a sentence invariably carried out in all cases when an inferior has been striking a superior. The following day the Corporal and two of the soldiers who had taken part in the fight were taken through our barracks. We were all mustered by squadrons in stable-dress, the prisoners among the others; the Corporal and the two infantry soldiers were marched along our ranks, and the Corporal soon pointed out a trooper as one of the offenders, while the two privates also declared that they recognised him. It fortunately turned out that the man was on guard duty the previous day; and on discovering this our Captain of the Week, who was in charge of the parade, immediately ordered the infantry soldiers to be taken back to their barracks, and to be sent straight off to prison; he also drew up a strong report against them, which was at once handed over to our Colonel, who demanded an exemplary punishment for the men from the Colonel commanding the infantry regiment. Doubtless these men merely made a mistake, for troopers look so different in stable-dress and in full uniform, that it is almost impossible to recognise them, unless you know them personally. Nevertheless, it was a narrow escape for Piatte and Titi. Our Captain gladly availed himself of the men's mistake to prevent further investigation, as the rivalry which exists between troopers and infantry soldiers extends to the officers, and in cases such as the one I have just described officers will generally try and screen their men. It is, indeed, very seldom that infantry officers are seen with cavalry officers, who generally look down upon the former with utter contempt.

Between Christmas and New Year we had hardly any drill, a large number of the troopers being away on leave, so that with the exception of stables we had scarcely any work, and I was able to rest in the day-time. At night I had, of course, to sleep in the *Salle de Police;* it was daily more loathsome a trial, as since the frost had set in the rats which infested the place were constantly coming to lie against us for the sake of heat. I devised an arrangement which proved most useful. I got a bag made of very thin india-rubber sheeting; it was about six feet long with a drawing-string at the top of it, so that when I had pulled it on I could fasten it round my neck, and it kept me as warm as if I had several blankets over me. When it was folded up I could wind it round my waist, where it looked like an ordinary belt. I also had the benefit of the mattresses Piatte and Titi were allowed as prisoners, and I soon got accustomed to the *Salle de Police* without suffering severely from it. There is no doubt, however, that it is a cruel and barbarous punishment, especially in the cavalry, as neither blankets nor straw mattresses are allowed to the troopers. In the infantry, soldiers punished with *Salle de Police* are allowed a straw mattress and a blanket, and have, moreover, no pumping to do in the middle of the night. It is scandalous, too, that troopers once in the *Salle de Police* should be isolated in such a way that in case of sickness or emergency they cannot possibly summon help. Many fatal cases have been the result of this practice. Some years ago a trooper was found in the morning frozen to death in the cells, and yet more serious tragedies have occurred. Since I served there was the case of a Zouave who was put in solitary confinement and forgotten there, his body being only found a week later; so great had been his pangs of hunger that it was found that he had been trying to eat the flesh of his arms and his hands, and when he was discovered the rats had themselves eaten a portion of his back and of his throat. I also remember another case of a man who was sent to the punishment battalions in Algeria; he was punished with two days in the *silos* and was forgotten there, and when he was discovered six days later he was still breathing, but the whole of his chest, on which he had been lying, was but a vast ulcer swarming with maggots. "How?" it will be asked, "can such a thing occur?" It may be explained in a few words.

Every morning before the guard is changed a list of all the men who are punished is drawn up by the *Adjudant's* clerk. In the columns standing opposite their names is written down the class of punishment which they are undergoing, with the number of days they have still to do, thus:

HOMMES PUNIS. (Men punished.)

Noms (Names).	Escadron (squadron).	Nature des Punitions. (Nature of Punishments.)			
		Consigne. (C.B.)	Salle de Police.	Prison.	Cellule (solitary confinement).
Martin	3	..	..	6	..
Piatte	3	..	..	5	..
Duval	2	..	..	..	3
Decle	3	..	12	..	..
&c. &c.					

As will be seen, the numbers in the various columns reserved for each punishment indicate how many more days of that class of punishment the soldier has to undergo, and this list is stuck on a board which is hung up in the room of the Sergeant of the Guard, a fresh list being made up every day. Supposing that by some mistake the *Adjudant's* clerk should, in making up his fresh list, put the figure belonging to Trooper Duval's name in the C.B. column instead of the cells, the Sergeant of the Guard would naturally conclude that there were no men in cells, and since in the case of certain barracks the cells are a few hundred yards away from the guard-room, the unfortunate fellow would be left in them without food, and might be unable to make himself heard. This was actually the case in the instance of the Zouave I have just mentioned. This arrangement turned out, however, to my benefit. One day, as I was complaining to de Lanoy of the hardship of having still ten days' *Salle de Police* before me, he suggested my making friends with the *Adjudant's* clerk, who would gradually leave out a few days in the punishment list; for instance, when I had still eleven days to do, he would mark nine days on his list, and at the end of a couple of days more, instead of marking seven days against my name he would put down five, and the following day mark me as having only three days more, so that in this way I should contrive to sleep in the *Salle de Police* for *seven* nights instead of twelve. De Lanoy added that this could never be found out, as the Sergeants of the Guard were daily replaced, and none of them saw anything but the fresh list. I immediately followed his advice, and found that a young fellow with whom I had become great friends had previously acted as *Adjudant's* clerk, and was on very good terms with the present occupant of the post. Both were fond of drawing, and as I did a little in that way myself, my friend suggested that he should take me to the clerk's office to show me his drawings. We adjourned there at once, and in the course of conversation my friend suggested to the clerk that he might as well strike off a few days from the remainder of my punishment. The latter readily agreed, and explained that it was especially easy to do so the following morning, as on that day the Week would be taken by the second *Adjudant*. He then asked me how many days I had still to do, and I told him that twelve days remained. " Oh, that will be all right," he said. " I'll put you down for seven, so that in case the *Adjudant,* who is just quitting duty to-morrow morning, should, when he takes back ' the week,' look through the list, he would again see your name on it. But it is very unlikely that he will see the list. He never calls for it."

This plan was duly carried out, with complete success,

though unfortunately it did not prevent my sleeping in the *Salle de Police* on New Year's Day.

I had purposely avoided going to the medical visit, as we had but little work in the daytime, and I did not like to pester the doctor or to take advantage of his kindness. I had cause to regret, however, not having done so on New Year's Day, as I spent a terrible night on that occasion. More than twenty-five troopers were thrown into the *Salle de Police*, and the disgraceful scenes I have previously described were renewed. Quarrels, fights, and fiendish uproar lasted throughout the night, so that I was unable to close my eyes. I was not, however, ejected from my resting-place, as I was lying between Piatte and Titi, who soon disposed of any man who tried to encroach on our domain. I fully expected that on the occasion of New Year's Day the Colonel would, in accordance with precedent, cancel all punishments. There was one man in solitary confinement, three in prison (viz., Piatte, Titi, and another trooper who had been absent without leave for five days), and about ten other troopers punished with *Salle de Police*, ranging from three to five days. On New Year's Eve the Colonel proclaimed in the Regimental Orders that all punishments would be cancelled, except in the case of troopers who were undergoing a punishment of more than eight days' *Salle de Police*. This, of course, was aimed at me, for the Colonel was fully aware that I was the only trooper who had lately been punished with fifteen days' *Boite*. As, however, I was free in the daytime, although I could not go out of barracks, I got a good dinner prepared at the infantry canteen, where I used to go and take my meals *sub rosa*. I also managed to bribe the Corporal of the Guard, and sent through him half a bottle of brandy, a bottle of wine, and a large meat pie to my two chums Titi and Piatte in prison. I need not say that my attention was greatly appreciated, and the two fellows heartily thanked me when I joined them in the evening.

On January 3 we resumed our work, under Sergeant Legros, who returned from his leave sulkier and more malicious than ever. Four of the *Volontaires* were sent to the *Salle de Police* that night, and the Sergeant threatened me with the same punishment because I was hoarse and was unable to command when ordered to do so.

I had now been sleeping for many nights in the lock-up and although I did not realise it at the time, the cold and dampness of the place had told heavily on me. I was so weak that I could hardly sit my horse, and I grew worse daily. On the Saturday (inspection day) we did our usual squadron duty, and after stables, as I was leading my charger to the watering-tanks, I felt hardly able to sit on her back. She was as usual prancing and plunging, and once or twice I had to cling to her mane so as not to drop off. As we were returning from the tanks towards the stables, the Lieutenant of the Week, who was also the Lieutenant of my *peloton,* shouted to me:

" Jump off your charger, and give it to another man."

I jumped off, and staggered towards the Lieutenant.

" You're drunk, you dirty pig ! " he screamed. " You shall have eight days' *Salle de Police* for drunkenness." Then turning towards the Sergeant, he went on, " Sergeant, can't you see that man is drunk ? Get him taken to the cells at once. Why couldn't you have seen before that he was drunk ? "

" I'll teach you, you blackguard ! " he added, turning to me.

I said : " Sir, I am not drunk, I am ill."

" And you dare reply ! " he again howled ; " you are

always answering back! We will see what that will cost you. Sergeant," he said to de Lanoy, " you will put down eight days' *Salle de Police* to this drunken swine for having come to stables helplessly intoxicated, and having made impertinent remarks to an officer."

I at once realised that if such a report reached the Colonel my punishment would be altered to at least fifteen days' prison, and seven days' cells, in solitary confinement, on bread-and-water, and that it would further mean a disgrace for me from which I should never recover. Fortunately, at that very moment, I caught sight in the distance of our regimental doctor, and without asking leave I ran to him for all I was worth.

" Sir," I said, " Lieutenant Pernot has just accused me of being drunk, and I implore you to examine me, as I am not drunk, but seriously ill."

The doctor told me to follow him to the dispensary, and as I was doing so Sergeant de Lanoy came hurrying along.

" Decle," he said, " Lieutenant Pernot has sent me to bring you back to him at once, and he threatens to have you court-martialled for having refused to obey his orders when you were told to go to the cells."

The Surgeon-major, who had caught the message, turned round to de Lanoy, " Go and tell Lieutenant Pernot," he said, " that Decle is coming to the dispensary with me by my orders, and there is an end of it."

De Lanoy returned to the Lieutenant, but before we had reached the staircase leading to the dispensary he returned once more, saying that the Lieutenant insisted on my going back to him, whether the Surgeon-major liked it or not.

The latter, whose temper was shortish, asked in a voice

shaking with rage whether de Lanoy was quite sure that he had exactly repeated the Lieutenant's words.

"Yes, sir," replied de Lanoy.

"Very well," said the Surgeon-major, "tell Lieutenant Pernot that I, Surgeon-major Lesage, holding the rank of Captain, order Lieutenant Pernot to come to me at once."

As de Lanoy hesitated, the Surgeon-major angrily added, "Do you hear me or not? You had better tell your Lieutenant to hurry up."

We did not wait long, for Lieutenant Pernot soon arrived, and had evidently been hurrying, as he was nearly breathless.

"What the deuce do you mean," said the surgeon, "by countermanding my orders?"

"Well," replied the Lieutenant, pointing to me, "that man is drunk."

"That remains to be seen," answered the surgeon, "and I am the best judge of that. I should strongly advise you not to interfere with my orders another time."

Thereupon he turned on his heel, and telling me to follow him, hurried up to the dispensary. There he laid me on a sofa, and asked me what was the matter. I told him that I had undergone fifteen days' *Salle de Police*, and felt perfectly worn out. He felt my pulse and took my temperature, which was very high.

"You are pretty bad, my boy," he said, "and I am going to send you to hospital."

I thanked him warmly, and told him how grateful I felt, pointing out that had it not been for him I might have been disgraced for ever in the regiment.

"Yes," he said, "I don't like the way they are treating you, and—I will tell you what—whenever you are bullied come to me, and I will excuse you from work. I respect you because you went through your last punishment without ever coming to the medical visit, and, in future, if you don't feel well, you have only got to come here and tell me what you don't feel fit for, and I will inform the Colonel." He added, " Troopers used to be punished only when they deserved it, but now the *Salle de Police* seems to have become a regular institution, and I don't like it—that is all I can say." He concluded by telling me that the dispensary Corporal would make out my *Billet de Hôpital,* and that he himself would come and see how I was that same evening.

CHAPTER X

It must not be imagined that a trooper can be sent to hospital without having to go through innumerable formalities, the French administrative system being so devised as to complicate the simplest matter. Before going to hospital, a full inventory of all the trooper's belongings has to be drawn up by the Sergeant *fourrier*, the trooper being allowed to retain only the undress uniform which he wears. The remainder of his kit, including his arms, are returned to the stores, where a fresh inventory is made, his saddle alone remaining in the squadron saddle-room. It would be tedious to describe the innumerable documents which have to be drawn up on the occasion. All these formalities having been at length completed, I was marched to the hospital by a Corporal and on arriving there, fresh ceremonials had to be gone through, after which I was handed over to the tender mercies of a Sister of Charity. She took me to the ward reserved for soldiers, the hospital being a mixed one, where civilians were also received. Our ward contained about twenty-four beds, and was spotlessly clean. The beds were excellent, and certainly far superior to those usually found in English hospitals. I then received my hospital kit, consisting of a huge night-shirt, a pair of dark blue flannel trousers, with a dressing-gown of the same material, a pair of woollen socks, slippers, and a *bonnet de coton*, a most extraordinary head-gear made of thick knitted cotton,

TROOPER 3809

finishing up in a point with a tassel sewn on to it. (Most of the French peasants still sleep in a similar night-cap, and, until thirty years ago, every Frenchman, even if belonging to the higher classes, used to wear this strange head-gear at night.) I was put to bed; my temperature was taken, and then I was left to my own thoughts. In the next bed to mine a poor fellow lay with typhoid fever, while in the bed on the other side lay an infantry soldier suffering from jaundice. The *personnel* of the hospital, or at least of the military wards, consisted of three Sisters of Mercy, with an old male nurse belonging to the Hospital Service Corps. The latter, however, was of little use, as he was usually drunk during three parts of the day. The Sisters, however, did not look harshly on this little vice of his, for the fellow was a most fervent Catholic, who never failed to go to Confession, and to High Mass every Sunday.

I had been about half an hour in my bed, when one of the Sisters brought me a cup of *tisane*, a kind of tea made of harmless herbs, which is always given in case of sickness, whatever may be the disease one may be suffering from. That Sister was a middle-aged woman, with hard, drawn features; the turned-down corners of her mouth expressed a violent temper, and a square chin showed indomitable energy. She sat down near me, and asked me if I was a Catholic. I replied that I had been baptized a Roman Catholic, but that I did not approve of the teachings of that religion, all my tendencies being Protestant. She expressed absolute horror at my being so plain-spoken, and told me that all the patients who were Roman Catholics were expected to go to Confession and Mass every Sunday. "If they don't," she added, "we can't compel them, and that is their own look out, but they do not usually stay here very long. You had better think the matter over, my lad," she added, as she arose from her chair. "I will send, in any case, the chaplain to talk to you of your spiritual state." I thanked her, but had no wish to discuss matters with her.

Later in the afternoon the head doctor of the hospital, who was Surgeon-major to the infantry regiment, and held the rank of Major, came on a visit of inspection. When he came to my bedside, he did not even give me a word of greeting, but looked at the board which hung at the head of my bed, and reading the diagnosis made by our regimental doctor shrugged his shoulders.

"Again a Dragoon," he said. "Why can't Dr. Lesage keep his patients in his own dispensary? Why did he send you here?" he went on, addressing me.

"I don't know, sir," I answered; "I suppose he found that I needed to be sent here."

"Well, let me see your throat."

He examined me, and remarked to the Sister that there was nothing much the matter with me, and that, although I might have a slight rise of temperature, every man had fever sometimes, adding that, if every Dragoon who had fever was to be sent to hospital, the place would soon be overflowing. He walked away with the Sister, and I could see that they were having an animated conversation. The doctor then came back to my bed:

"I hear," he said, "that you are a d——d heathen; is that so?"

"No, sir," I replied; "I told the Sister that I did not approve of the Roman Catholic religion, and that, although I had been baptized a Roman Catholic, I was a Protestant at heart."

"Oh," he said, "that is all the same; you are a heathen, and you ought to be ashamed of yourself. That is why, I suppose, Dr. Lesage sent you here. He likes heathens, and I don't. Well, he can look after you if he chooses." And, turning on his heel he walked off.

Later in the afternoon Dr. Lesage came to see me, and I told him what had taken place. He said that he was not in the least surprised, and that he was thoroughly disgusted with the bigotry of all the people connected with the place. He then called the Sister, and told her to show him the register where the head surgeon had written out his orders concerning my case. After looking through it, he told me that, just as he had expected, the head surgeon had put me on ordinary rations, but that he was not going to have it; and he immediately ordered that I should be put on a diet of chicken, eggs, and the like. He found my throat very bad, and said that I ought to have come to see him much sooner than I did. He also explained to me that he would give orders enabling me to get from outside whatever food I fancied, as well as books; he promised too to come and see me on the following day. I took advantage of his permission to send the hospital orderly to fetch me a stock of eatables, books, and some newspapers.

Our dinner was served at six o'clock, and I was much astonished when the Sister brought me a piece of beef which had been boiled to a rag to make soup. I reminded her that Dr. Lesage had put me on "fowl and egg diet."

"I know it," she said, "but, as there is none to be had to-night, you will have to put up with what there is."

I pointed out to her that rations of fowl had been served to at least six of the other patients.

"Well," she said, "the fact is, there is none left."

Upon this I declared that, unless I had a portion immediately brought to me, I would forthwith send a letter to Dr. Lesage to explain how matters stood.

"Oh," she said, "please don't trouble yourself, and I'll go to the kitchen, and see if there is some remaining."

Ten minutes later she returned with the wing of a fowl, and when I had finished it she brought me an omelet. I mention this incident to show the gross partiality which is usually displayed by Sisters of Mercy in French hospitals. Most of the patients, who belong to the humbler classes, are afraid to complain, and I have constantly seen patients who make a display of deep religious zeal treated with the utmost attention, receiving the best of fare, while others who were lax in the practice of religion, or who had the misfortune to be Protestants, were given the commonest food, even if the doctor had ordered special delicacies for them. The Sisters of Mercy have absolutely no training in nursing, and an English nurse, after a year's hospital work, is far more efficient than Sisters of Mercy who have spent years in the wards. I do not mean to say that there are not to be found among the Sisters touching examples of disinterested devotion to their fellow-creatures, but, taking them as a class, their employment in hospitals is not calculated to benefit the patients, and they are far inferior to English trained nurses in education, manners, and skill. They have no fear of dismissal, as, in case of their failing to do their duty, they are merely removed to the headquarters of their order. It is true that it would be most difficult to replace them in French hospitals, as there exists in France no body of trained nurses like those in this country. The French lay nurses are almost invariably middle-aged women of the charwoman type, who have had no practical training, and are usually addicted to drink. In the largest hospitals the administration of drugs and the dressing of wounds devolves entirely on the medical students, and nurses, whether Sisters of Mercy or lay, merely stand in the wards to watch the patients, and in case of need they have to go and summon a student. While I was in the hospital, I witnessed some shocking examples of the way in which sufferers were treated. I remember one night when a patient, who was suffering from a most serious attack of jaundice, cried out to the Sister on duty for a basin. The Sister, who was counting her beads and muttering prayers in a half-dozing state, merely lifted her eyes dreamily towards the patient, but took no notice. The poor fellow called her again and again, and, seeing how matters stood, I got out of bed, and, going to the Sister, called her attention to the patient. "Go to bed," she said to me: "it is no business of yours. The female attendant has gone out; it is her work, and not mine, to carry basins about." I thereupon went to fetch what was needed myself, and rendered what help I could to my sick comrade. Facts such as these help to explain why the poor in France have a greater dread of the hospital than many people have of the workhouse in England.

It took me a few minutes to find a basin that night, and while I looked about I must have caught a chill, for the following day I had a relapse. I had been rather upset, too, by the death of the typhoid patient in the bed next to mine. His old mother came with his father that afternoon, and their distress was heart-rending to witness.

"They have taken my boy, they have killed him," the poor mother kept repeating; complaining bitterly that she had not been informed of his illness till too late.

Two days later, early in the morning, as luck would have it, none other than Piatte was brought into the hospital; he was carried on a stretcher, and carefully laid in the vacant bed next to mine.

"You see, old chap," he said, "I would not leave my chum Decle, so here I am."

"What is the matter with you?" I asked.

"Oh, broken leg, that is all."

The two cavalry and infantry doctors then arrived, and Piatte was questioned as to the way in which the accident occurred.

"It's a beast of a charger that's kicked me in the stables," he told the doctor.

He was carefully examined, and the doctors found that he had broken his leg below the knee. The limb was set, and although the poor fellow must have suffered dreadfully, beads of perspiration running down his face during the process, he did not utter a single complaint. Dr. Lesage remained near him after the others had retired, and told him that he would soon be all right.

"Ah, that's nothing, sir," said Piatte; "but look here, sir, I'll tell you what: if you would like to do me a great favour you would come and look after me yourself. *You can do anything you like to me*, but I do not want that other infantry doctor to mess about with me."

Dr. Lesage promised that he would attend him, and before retiring held out his hand to the injured man. This evidently went to the poor chap's heart, and his eyes moistened.

"Thank you, sir," he said; "thank you. It is good of you to shake hands with me—a bad character as they make me out. If the officers were all like you, why I would jump into the fire for them—and mind you, sir, I won't forget it."

Dr. Lesage retired, more moved than he liked to show. When he had gone, I asked Piatte how he felt.

"A bit queer," he said; "but you don't know, old chap, how well I worked it. I thought I had killed myself, you know."

"Weren't you kicked?" I queried.

TROOPER 3809

"Kicked," he said; "well, it wasn't a horse that kicked me. I'll tell you how it all happened. When I got out of prison yesterday, I said to myself, I must have a spree, so, after 'Lights out,' I got over the wall. You see, my old granny had sent me another ten francs for the New Year, but, of course, being in prison, I only got my money when I came out, so then I jumped over the wall, and, my boy, I can tell you I had a grand booze. At two o'clock this morning I said to myself, 'It is time to go back.' So I got into the little lane at the back of our stable, you know. The wall there on the top side of the lane is only six feet high, so I easily got on top of it, but on the other side there is a drop of at least thirty feet, you know, alongside our stable. I had often done it, and it was only thirty yards along the wall to get to the back door of the barracks, where you can get down quite easy. But last night it had been raining, and freezing afterwards, so that the wall was that slippery that I had to walk on all fours to keep my balance. I was a bit on, I suppose, and I don't know how it happened, but just as I was getting near the end of the wall I slipped, and down I went. Oh, my boy, what a drop it was! I came down flop, and when I tried to rise it was no go; one of my legs felt like cotton-wool. I knew that if I called for help I should be nabbed, so I crept on all fours as far as the room. I then went to wake up Titi; he took off my clothes and laid me on my bed. By jove! didn't it hurt me. Titi says to me, 'Let me go and call for help, you can say that you have fallen down stairs.' But I say, 'No, that's no go, and it won't wash.' So we arranged with Titi, that just before *réveille* he would take me down to the stables, which he did. By God, you don't know what it meant to go to the stables: I felt my heart in my mouth the whole way; to come down the stairs I sat down, and holding on to Titi's neck, I let myself slide, and then to cross the yard I tried to stand on my other leg, but it was all numb; so I sent Titi to fetch Monard, and between them they carried me to the stables and lay me behind your kicking mare, as she's known as a kicker. As soon as the others come down to clean the stables, I shout, 'Ah, murder, murder!' One of them goes and fetches the Sergeant, and I tell him how, passing behind your mare's heels, I got kicked. Titi, in the meantime, had gone to fetch me a stiff glass of brandy, as I felt pretty queer. The Sergeant then sent for a stretcher, and they carried me to the dispensary. When the doctor came I told him I had been kicked, and when he looks at my leg, he says: 'It's jolly funny that it should have got swollen up so quickly.' Of course I told him that I have got a queer constitution, and he says, 'Yes, a queer constitution indeed,' and then he tells the Corporal that I must be taken to the hospital at once, and he sends everybody out of the room, and he says to me:

"'It was not a horse that kicked you, eh, Piatte?'

"'Well, sir,' I says, 'if you ask me, not as an officer, but as the gentleman that you are, I will tell you the truth.'

"'Go on,' he says, ''tis not as an officer that I am asking you.'

"'Oh, then,' says I, 'that mare, sir, that kicked me, 'twas a paving-stone.' And I tell him the whole story, from beginning to end, and then he got very wild, and asked why I hadn't sent for him at once, and he also asked whether I supposed that he would give me away.

"My boy," concluded Piatte, "he is a ripper, that man.

"I remember one day—it was two years ago—I went to

the medical visit, and he says, 'What is the matter with you?' so I replied, 'I rather tell you privately, sir,' and he says, 'Very well.' After the medical visit he calls me to his room. 'Well?' he says. I then told him what was the matter with me, and as it is the rule, you know, that men suffering with that complaint are punished with thirty days' confinement to barracks, I asked him if he would mind keeping it dark. 'Of course,' he said, and he sent me to the dispensary for a fortnight for rheumatism. Now don't you think that he was a brick?"

I quite agreed with him. This matter is one which has given rise to many discussions in Parliament, and in the English Press, especially with regard to the British troops in India. The French system appears to me one of the chief causes of depopulation in France, when one considers that nine-tenths of the male population have to pass through the ranks of the army. The fear of punishment prevents most soldiers from attending the medical visit when they suffer from complaints of this kind, and the consequence is that in most cases they wait until the disease has made such progress that the doctors are unable to cope successfully with it.

The day Piatte was brought to hospital the Roman Catholic chaplain came to see me. I told him exactly what my religious views were, but far from showing himself offended, he showed me the utmost kindness, and asked me to go and visit him when I was able to leave my bed. I did so, and found him a most enlightened man. I frankly explained to him my views, and although we could not, of course, agree, our discussion was carried on in the most courteous terms, and he told me that although he regretted that he was unable to convince me, he should always be glad to see me, placing at the same time his fine library at my disposal. He was a man well versed in science, and, although a fervent Catholic, did not consider those whose opinions differed from his as black sheep, and he had the utmost respect for sincere religion of every kind.

I stopped a week longer in hospital, and felt rather glad of Piatte's companionship, as I had taken quite a liking for this poor fellow, who interested me. I asked him many a time why he did not give up drink, which meant his ruin.

"Give up drink, old fellow," he invariably replied, "why should I? It is the only thing which makes a man forget. Don't imagine that I was a drunkard before I came to the regiment; but they've driven me to it. During my first year's service I was keen on doing my best, and I hoped to be promoted to the rank of Corporal. I had got through the exams. all right, and had been actually nominated for promotion after the manœuvres we were in the thick of were over, when the crash came. One night, when three other troopers and myself had made ourselves comfortable in a barn full of straw, in comes a Corporal with a pipe in his mouth. Just then he hears a step outside, and suspecting that it is an officer, he shouts out:

"'Who's been smoking here? Now look sharp—are you going to tell or not?'

"I wasn't asleep, and I saw through his dirty trick in an instant. The other fellows were soon aroused, and confusedly asked what was the matter. The Corporal repeats his question, but of course there was no culprit to answer it. Then in comes the officer—for the Corporal's suspicion was right enough.

"'Go and fetch a lantern,' says he.

"Off goes the Corporal and gets one.

"Then the officer says:

TROOPER 3809

"'Someone has been smoking here, let the man come forward.'

"Of course nobody moves because nobody has done it, for 'twas the Corporal all along.

"'Very well,' the officer says; 'let's have your numbers,' and he tells the Corporal to put them down.

"Mine was the highest as it happened, and on finding this out the officer says:

"'You put eight days' *Salle de Police* to that trooper.'

"When the officer has gone I go out to the Corporal—he was a Hussar chap, and so was the officer—and I tell him that it's not right what he's done, and that he knows well enough that it's him that had been smoking, so he turns savage on me, and he says:

"'You'll have two days more for insulting me.'

"The next day I tell what's happened to my Lieutenant, and he says that he will speak to the Hussar officer; but my Lieutenant comes back, and he says that the officer doesn't mind cancelling my punishment, but that the Corporal insists on letting his two days stand as they are, and that he won't cancel them. All that makes a shindy between the younger officers of our regiment and those of the Hussars, and the General hears of it, because two of them officers actually applied for leave to fight a duel. The General sends for me—he was just mad because during the past fortnight two other barns had been set on fire—and he tells me I am a scoundrel to have smoked in the barn; but I tell him how things happened, and that 'twas the Corporal himself who'd been smoking. The Colonel of the Hussars, who just happened to be coming for some report to the General, says:

"'Ah, that's the swine who nearly set a barn on fire last night, and now he tries to take away the character of one of my Corporals!'

"This makes the General quite mad, and he gives me fifteen days' prison. Yes, old chap, fifteen days' prison, when I'd done nothing. It fairly turned my blood, and I went away hardly knowing what I was doing. I passed a pub and went in. I called for absinthe and brandy and the Lord knows what else. The more I drunk the more I wanted, and I was that mad that when two Hussars walked into the pub I sprang on them, and if others hadn't come to their rescue 'twould have been a case of murder, I think. They had to tie me up, and by Gad it took eight of them to do it. To my first punishment, fifteen days' prison, and fifteen days' solitary confinement in cells, were added, and when, two days later, the manœuvres ended, I was marched back to barracks—a prisoner. Of course any question of promotion was at an end—to think of it after I had worked so hard to become a Corporal! When I came out of prison I no longer cared a b—— d—— what happened to me. I drank whenever I had money, and if I hadn't, Decle, my boy, I would have shot myself. How I have got through these last three years I don't know. They threatened more than once to send me to Biribi. What did I care? If it hadn't been for our late Colonel—he understood me, that man—I should have done something desperate; but since he is dead—ah, *malheur!* The new Colonel calls me a disgrace to the regiment, and a disgrace to the French army: but what do I care? But then when a chap like our doctor doesn't feel ashamed to hold out his hand to me—well, my boy, it goes to my heart. You, too, old Decle, although we are both mere troopers, you are a gentleman, while I am but a labourer and a low blackguardly drunkard; and yet you treat me as a friend. Give me your hand, old boy."

I gave it to him, and he pressed it between his two enormous palms, and then, in a husky voice, he added,

"Ah! it's long since I have felt so happy," and with the back of his hand he wiped off a tear.

"Forgive me, old chap," he said, "I know I'm making a fool of myself!"

For answer I could only squeeze his hand, and I turned round to hide a tear of my own—a tear of pity for the poor fellow whose feelings I could now understand so well.

During the long days we spent together Piatte delighted to speak of his home; he belonged to the country, where he drove a diligence: he loved horses and animals, and he was still full of old and quaint superstitions. "I was seventeen," he once said to me, "when I drove a coach for the first time, and I shall never forget that night. I had never driven the coach except to bring it round from the stables to the inn, when one night the Governor orders the diligence to be got ready for a foreign gentleman who wanted to catch a train twenty miles from our place. All the other carriages were out, and the diligence alone was available. When Jean-Paul, the usual driver, hears of it he says that he will not drive it for all the money in the world, it being a Friday night in the month of January. 'Why?' I asked him. He told me that at one place where the road meets the Strasbourg road there was a ghost which always came out from behind a tree when the diligence passed along at night on a Friday in January: 'his grandfather, his father, and him too had seen it, and he did not want to see it no more.' I didn't believe much in ghosts, so I offered to drive, and my governor, to whom the coach belonged, let me go. The horses were fresh, the carriage light, and we were rattling along at a good pace when all of a sudden I see a woman dressed in white jump from behind a tree and stand in the middle of the road. 'Hi! hi! look out!' I shout, but she did not seem to heed me, and before I could pull up the leaders were on her. They shied and reared, but there she rises between the two of them and seems to jump over the wheelers, and for a second or two she flitters in front of me like a huge bat. As I looked round I saw that we were just at the spot which Jean-Paul had told me was haunted. I felt my heart in my mouth, and lashing the horses put them at a gallop—and they didn't want no urging either; but the ghost seemed to fly in the air alongside the coach for a distance of about a hundred yards, when she disappeared in a bush."

I told Piatte that it was the effect of his imagination, but he was positive about it; according to him the ghost had the face of a young girl with very dark hair, and was draped in white garments with a kind of hood over her head.

Soon after his first adventure he became the regular driver of the diligence, the former driver having been upset with the coach and killed on the spot. During the year previous to his military service he had worked in some large engineering works, and he always swore to me that until he was first punished he had never been drunk, adding at the same time that during the fourteen months he had still to serve he meant to drink whenever he could get a chance. I thoroughly believe that if he had become a Corporal he would have been one of the best men in the regiment, and there is no doubt that it was the injustice with which he had been treated which led him to drink and degradation.

At the end of ten days I left hospital, and, on my return to barracks, was kept for three days in the dispensary as a convalescent. During the whole time I had been in hospital I had been unable to get a bath, and when I suggested taking one the doctor laughed at me, and the

TROOPER 3809

Sisters considered me a kind of lunatic to want a bath when I had a sore throat. It was therefore with great relief that, on my return to barracks, I was allowed by our doctor to go out to the town to have the wash of which I was naturally in great need.

CHAPTER XI

AT the end of January we passed our first examination. Each one of us had to command in turn the various kinds of drill we had been taught so far—viz. drill on foot without arms, carbine and sword drill, as well as mounted drill in the riding-school. We were also examined on hippology and the first principles of topography, and were questioned on that portion of the regulations which referred to the duties of Corporals, and we were further examined as to our individual proficiency in *Voltige* and gymnastics. There was not a single one of us who hadn't received by that time a more complete military education than any of the Corporals in the regiment, but although troopers can, according to the regulations, be promoted to the rank of Corporal at the end of three months' service, none of us received any promotion. I was the fifth by marks out of the fourteen of us. After this examination the order of our day's work was altered, and mounted drill, instead of taking place in the riding-school, was carried out on the manœuvring ground, about three miles outside the town. This was a vast area of loose sand, a certain portion of which was prepared for different exercises. There were jumps too of various kinds, but none of them above three feet high. The most peculiar arrangement was what we call the "crater," a huge hole about thirty yards in diameter, and from ten to twelve feet in depth, shaped like a crater, and tapering at the bottom. There was also a narrow defile some hundred feet long, just broad enough to allow the passage of four riders abreast. For the present, however, no use was made of these obstacles, but we went on drilling as we had done in the riding-school. Squares were marked out with huge poles, and we rode in Indian file around them. Half-an-hour before the time fixed for mounted drill four of us were sent out under the command of a Corporal to mark the squares. We were all very keen to be selected for this work, for having to carry the poles we were allowed to ride with stirrups, and when we had marked the squares, we always had ten minutes or a quarter of an hour to spare, during which time we used to jump our horses and canter round the manœuvring ground. We also began mounted drill with arms—viz. carbine and sword. In my time swords were not fixed to the saddle as they are now, and we invariably carried our carbines slung over our backs, the boot never being used. Most cavalry officers considered the carrying of the carbine in the boot a most dangerous plan, likely to break the trooper's leg in case of a fall. The carrying of the carbine across the back, on the other hand, was a most cruel torture, especially as we were never allowed to use our stirrups. The French cavalry carbines are much heavier and longer than those in use in the English cavalry. (We had, of course, the Gras pattern in my time.) On Saturdays, besides undergoing the weekly inspection, we had to prepare a number of horses for the infantry officers. The Captains in command of infantry companies being mounted, Lieutenants and sub-lieutenants had to be taught riding, and few of them had any idea of what riding a horse meant, their only knowledge of such animals being derived from seeing them in the streets. Of course the Sergeants who had drawn up the lists of the horses to be used by the infantry officers took a secret pleasure in selecting the hardest trotters as well as the most vicious chargers in each squadron, so that my little mare was invariably chosen. The costumes donned by the infantry officers for this riding lesson were rather peculiar. Most of them wore patent leather gaiters over their trousers, while a few appeared in tightly-fitting grey breeches. As we brought our chargers to them the timid learners always carefully inquired about the special vice of each.

I well remember the appearance one day of a young infantry Lieutenant putting any amount of " side " on, and adorned by a resplendent pair of patent leather top-boots.

" I say, Dragoon," he said quietly, slipping a two-franc piece into my hand, " that looks rather a nice little horse your're holding there."

" It isn't a horse, sir," I replied.

He looked much astonished, and said : " What ! You don't call it a mule, I suppose ? "

" No, sir," I replied ; " I call it a mare."

" Oh—ah—yes ! " he said. " A mare, of course. Fact is, I'd hardly looked at her. Is she lively ? " he added. " I don't like a beast with the paces of a donkey ! "

" Yes, sir,'" I said ; " you'll find her quite lively enough."

" But she's not vicious—not vicious ? " he asked anxiously.

" Vice ! " I replied. " She doesn't know what vice means. She likes to show off a bit, that's all."

" Just what I like," said the Lieutenant. He asked me to get on her back, and after I had made her prance about a bit, I dropped the reins on her neck, and pulling a bit of sugar from my pocket I made her turn her head to eat it from my hand—a trick I had taught her.

"What a jolly little beast!" said the Lieutenant, as I dismounted; "mind," he added, "that you do not let anybody else ride her." "No fear, sir," I answered, upon which he tipped me another franc. I was careful to bring the mare last of all into the riding-school, having purposely put the stirrup-straps three holes too long for my man. The Lieutenant walked up to me. He looked at the girths as if he knew everything about a saddle, and then measured the stirrups, asking me if I thought they were right. "It's not for me, sir," I replied, "to presume to advise a gentleman like you, who probably has horses of his own." "Of course—of course," he replied, highly flattered. "I should say you're a rare un with horses," I again said. "How do you know?" he asked proudly. "I can tell a gentleman when I see one," I answered. "Just so," he went on patronisingly. "I suppose you've been in good houses before?" "That's just it, sir," I innocently replied. Just then our *Capitaine Instructeur*, who gave the lesson to the infantry officers, rode into the riding-school and ordered the officers to mount. We had to hold our charger's head and the off-stirrup, and the Lieutenant having got on to the mare remarked that the stirrups were rather long. "How many holes, sir?" "Just shorten those two holes," he said. Purposely I went on slowly shortening one of the stirrups, holding the mare's head at the same time, and, as I fully expected, before I had time to touch the second stirrup our Captain commanded the Lieutenants to fall in, and I let go at once the mare's head, and she began to prance about. Her rider, who knew nothing of riding, foolishly pulled on the bit and pressed his legs to keep his equilibrium. My mare, greatly resenting such treatment, darted forward into the middle of the riding-school, plunging and rearing. In a second or two the officer was landed on the ground, while our Captain coolly asked him what he was doing there? He replied that it all had happened because his stirrups were not right. In the meantime I had rushed to catch the mare, and as the Lieutenant came to remount, our Captain told me to put the stirrups to their proper length. While I was doing so the poor young Lieutenant whispered to me: "Mais c'est une bête terrible que cet animal." * I advised him not to use the curb, and not to touch her with his heels, as she did not like it. "It is very difficult not to use the heels," he replied, with dismay, "I wish I had never seen that beast."

The poor fellow knew even less about riding than I had thought, and I soon regretted having recommended him to take my mare, as twice more she landed him in the middle of the school, and ultimately the Captain commanding the lesson made him change horses with one of his colleagues.

To return to our own work. Shortly after we had started drilling on the manœuvring ground we began to drill by *pelotons* on foot. The cavalry drill on foot is essentially different from the infantry drill, as all the movements are performed in the same way as the mounted drill; for instance, the troopers being dressed on two ranks, to break off by fours they swing on a pivot as if they were mounted, and the drill on foot is, indeed, especially intended as a preparation for the mounted drill. Our work in the field, however, consisted of two distinct rôles: we had to act as cavalry and at the same time as mounted infantry, although we were absolutely unfit for the latter work. I have often discussed with French officers the question why mounted infantry have never been tried in France, but all the French officers seem to believe them to be practically useless. They point out

* It is a terrible beast, this animal.

that all the French cavalry being drilled and armed in such a way as to be able to act as mounted infantry, there is no necessity for the latter. This is all very well in theory, but it is out of the question in practice. All the trooper is fit for when dismounted is to defend himself, but the moment he is sent forward on foot, his heavy, cumbersome trousers, his boots with spurs nailed on to them, and fitting as loosely as they always do, are a terrible burden to him. More than once when we were sent out as sharpshooters through heavy ground, we had not gone 200 yards before our boots came off our feet; in this respect it may therefore be safely said that, whatever their other qualities may be, the French are very inferior to the English or German cavalry.

Too much time is wasted in educating the troopers to drill on foot, and nothing is done to develop individual initiative in the field. There were not ten of the troopers in my regiment who could have been trusted alone as scouts, and even among the *Volontaires*, men who had all received a good education, not one half of them at the end of the year's training thoroughly understood the use of a map, and with the exception of Delbruck and myself not one could have made a sketch-plan, however rough, of the ground we had been over. Another of the great mistakes made throughout the whole of the French army is the tendency to overburden soldiers as well as horses. Cavalry horses have to carry in the field a kit which, including the rider, amounts to an average of 22 stone, in the light cavalry the kit is, it is true, a little lighter, but there is hardly a stone and a half difference. The light cavalry horses are small, few of them being over 15 hands, while many are under. In the heavy cavalry there is hardly a horse standing 16 hands high, and the average size ranges between 15.1 and 15.2. In the infantry, soldiers have to carry in the field, cartridges included, an average of over 80 lbs. During the Madagascar war this enormous burden was not even reduced, and naturally 50 per cent. of the men died within five months of the beginning of the campaign. Another great fault of the French system is that too much is expected of the troopers, instead of their being regarded exclusively as mounted men.

Their uniform is not only grotesque, but is quite unsuitable for riding. I have often heard it said that the introduction of top-boots and breeches would entail too heavy an expenditure—but the Germans have them, and their cavalry is not inferior in numbers to the French. But this is a digression.

Our Sergeant Legros was as great a bully as ever; *Volontaires* were constantly being punished, and never a week elapsed without my being sent to the *Salle de Police;* in fact, Legros got so accustomed to punishing me that many a time he used to say to me in the morning, " I am in a bad temper to-day, and you'll get two days' *Salle de Police*— you'll find out why later on." At other times he used to tell us that he meant to stick four of the *Volontaires* in the lock-up that day, and, true to his word, he always found some cause for punishing exactly four of us during the day. I had become so used to punishment by that time that it had grown quite indifferent to me, and I became a mere dare-devil.

One day having been sent to the lock-up *à l'œil,* I found that the Sergeant of the Guard was my friend de Lanoy, and he told me that I could go and sleep in my own bed. As my punishment had not been reported, he ran no risk, but unfortunately for me that night I made a fool of myself. Titi, whom I had told that de Lanoy had excused me from sleeping in the *Salle de Police,* came to tell me a long story of how his brother had come to see him on most important business, and how he could not get leave to go out to him, adding that he was sure I would help him. I told him that I would willingly do so if I could, and he then unfolded his plan to me. "You see," he went on, "when the Sergeant of the Week comes for the roll-call at eight o'clock, the Corporal will report you as being in the *Salle de Police*, but what you will really do will be to get into my bed and cover your head well up, so that your face can't be seen, and then they will think that it is me. In the meantime I shall have got out, letting myself down from the window into the street with my forage rope." Foolishly enough, I agreed to the plan. At a quarter to eight Piatte, who had long left the hospital, helped me to let Titi down through the window, and as soon as he had landed safely in the street I went and wrapped myself up in Titi's bed. Piatte, I must say, tried to dissuade me, but having promised Titi, I said I would certainly keep my word. I covered up my head, and soon after, the Sergeant of the Week walked round the room to make the evening call. When he passed in front of my bed he walked straight up to me and pulled the blankets off. "What are you doing here?" he cried. "Sergeant," I replied, "Sergeant de Lanoy has allowed me to sleep here instead of in the lock-up." "And this is why," he said, "you sleep in another man's bed, after you have helped him to get out through the window. You will have four days' *Salle de Police*. And now," he added, "off you go to the cells." The Sergeant was a new one who had exchanged into the regiment a few days previously, so he was a stranger to me, and though immediately after the call I rushed after him, he had already walked into the Sergeant-major's office and reported the matter to him. When he came out I asked him to cancel my punishment, not so much for my sake, as for de Lanoy's, who might be severely punished for having excused me from sleeping in the cells. The Sergeant expressed his regret, but told me it was too late, as he had already reported the matter to the Sergeant-major, adding that he was absolutely unconscious that by so doing he might bring one of his comrades into trouble. I advised him to go and see Sergeant Legros at once, in order to urge him not to lodge a complaint against de Lanoy, adding that I wished to take the whole blame upon myself.

I was very glad to find the following day that de Lanoy had not been embroiled in the business. I did not fare so well. The four days the Sergeant had given me were altered to eight by our Captain, and the Colonel added four more to the total, so that I had twelve days in all. I can honestly say that this was the only punishment I fully deserved among all those which were bestowed on me. Titi also got fifteen days, so that we were once more companions in misfortune. It was during that time that our Sergeant-major suddenly altered his behaviour towards me. I had been about three days in the lock-up when one afternoon he called me into his office and locked the door. He looked much embarrassed, but asked me to sit down, and offered me a cigarette and a glass of beer. This seemed a very extraordinary proceeding on his part, but I accepted the proffered hospitality and waited for him to open the conversation. "I am sorry, Decle," he said, "that you should have been once more punished, but I'll try to make your punishment as light as possible, and I have already given instructions that you are not to sleep in the *Salle* to-night, as I am acting *Adjudant* to-day." I thanked him, and silence followed. "By the way," he said, "I have also sent for you to ask your advice. You are a gentleman and a man of the world, and

I want some information, but before I consult you I want your word of honour that you will not mention to a living soul what I am going to tell you." I assured him that he could make his mind easy on this point and reckon on my silence. "Well, it is just this," he began: "I am in a fix, and I want to borrow five hundred francs (£20), and unless I get the money within a fortnight I shall be a disgraced man. You know how strict the Colonel is, and how severely he punishes non-commissioned officers who are in debt. Now don't you know a Jew who would lend me the money?"

I replied that I was not acquainted with money-lenders, but that in any case I was quite certain that none of the fraternity would advance him the money unless he could give some substantial security. "I could give my pay," he replied; "wouldn't that be sufficient security?" I fairly laughed in his face. "Your pay," I said; "why, it does not amount to twenty pounds a year; that would be no security at all." The man must have been in a fix indeed, for he grew pale and trembled visibly. Once more he told me that unless he had the money his creditor would apply to the Colonel, and that would mean the ruin of his military career. "I tell you what," I then said; "why should you go to money-lenders? Let me lend you the money, and you can repay me whenever you like." He protested that he could not possibly accept money from me, but I assured him that I could well afford it, and at last he said that he accepted my offer, but that he did not know how to express his gratitude. I knew perfectly well that from the outset he had meant to get the money out of me, but I was not going to let him off so easily as he imagined. I therefore told him that although I would be very glad to let him have the money, I could not give it to him in a lump sum, as my allowance was only paid to me monthly, and I added that my money being in Paris, I should have to go there to fetch it, and that having eleven more days' *Salle de Police* to undergo, I should have to wait until I had finished my punishment, and until I got leave. "Oh," he replied, "I will arrange that for you. To-day is Monday, and I'll see that your punishment is put down as finishing on Saturday morning, and then I'll give you leave to go to Paris from Saturday night till Monday night. You see," he went on, "I am acting as *Adjudant* during the whole of this week, and I need not report you missing, so nobody will be the wiser."

I thanked him, but he replied most courteously that it was from himself that the thanks were due, and he added that he was very sorry he had hitherto misunderstood me, but that in future he would be delighted to do anything he could on my behalf. I retired, feeling much pleased with myself, as I knew that in future I should have a devoted friend in my Sergeant-major, whose power was far greater than that of any of the officers of our squadron. For instance, no officer, with the exception of the Captain commanding the squadron, would dare take upon himself to grant a trooper twenty-four hours' leave *sub rosâ*, while the Sergeant-major could do this easily, merely by not reporting the trooper as missing from the calls, and even should an officer inquire where the trooper was, the Sergeant-major could always reply that he had given the man leave not to attend the "stables," which he was entitled to do; moreover, as no officer was ever present at the night-call, the Sergeant-major could deal with that roll exactly as he liked. On the Saturday my Sergeant-major kept his promise, and told me to get dressed immediately after "stables." He advised me, however, to go to my rooms in the town to change my uniform for civilian clothes, as that week the platoon at the station was supplied by the infantry. I should explain here that soldiers on leave who are allowed to leave their garrison town are supplied with a paper stating that they are permitted to go to a specified place outside the garrison. In order to prevent soldiers leaving the garrison without leave, a non-commissioned officer is sent every Saturday and Sunday to the railway-station, and makes the soldiers show him their written leave before they are allowed to take their ticket.

When I was dressed to go out my Sergeant-major accompanied me as far as the hotel, and we had a chat while I was changing my clothes. He told me incidentally that he had re-enlisted one year before, and that he hoped to be sent to the school of Saumur within the next two years, which would enable him to become an officer in three years' time, and he again insisted on the fact that if the Colonel found out that he was in debt he would lose all chance of going to Saumur, and might even be reduced to the rank of ordinary Sergeant.

I promised faithfully that I would bring back at least 100 francs from Paris, and I then jumped into a brougham and ordered the blinds to be carefully drawn down, as the fact of being seen in civilian attire would have meant imprisonment at least. In order to avoid meeting any of my officers, I had timed myself to go by a slow train; but before I got out of the carriage I carefully peeped round, and did not get out until I had made certain there were no cavalry officers about. The traffic superintendent was a personal friend of my family, and he had given me a card specially recommending me to all the stationmasters of the line, and allowing me to use any train I chose, even goods trains. Privates are not as a rule allowed to ride in first-class carriages, and non-commissioned officers are also debarred from this privilege, so that the traffic superintendent's card was doubly useful to me, enabling me as it did to travel by express trains which only contained first-class carriages. Upon entering the station the stationmaster allowed me to stop in his office until the last minute, and sent for my ticket, thus reducing the chances of detection to a minimum. I reached Paris safely, and when I returned the next evening my Sergeant-major was waiting for me at the hotel, in order to take me back into barracks without my name being taken down by the Sergeant of the Guard, who has to report the names of all troopers who come in after evening call, the exact time at which they return being entered against their names. I told my Sergeant-major that I had been able to get 100 francs only, but that I would get a further sum if I went to Paris the following Sunday. He thanked me profusely, and told me that he would arrange that I should go to Paris on the following Saturday. It soon became an understood thing that when I wanted to go to Paris without leave, I was to ask him to arrange it for me, while on my return I duly handed him from fifty to a hundred francs. Before my first year's service was over the Sergeant-major had been enabled to repay considerably more than twenty pounds he owed to his obdurate creditor, but he still maintained the fiction, and whenever I handed him over the price of my journey to Paris, he thanked me warmly, invariably adding, "Ah! I am so glad, I shall be able to take that to my creditors to-morrow!" In this way the Sergeant certainly received between fifty and sixty pounds from me in all.

CHAPTER XII

ALTHOUGH my Sergeant-major had altered his behaviour towards me, he could only help me in the squadron, having no power over the *Volontaires,* who were under the absolute command of Sergeant Legros. Captain Hermann, who was nominally our chief, and who was supposed to give us lectures twice a week, never took the trouble to do so, and we scarcely ever saw him for more than a few minutes at a time. He left, in fact, the whole of our instruction in Legros's hands, and the latter's powers seemed to become greater every week.

Hitherto, whenever we had wanted to apply for leave we used to send our application through the usual channel, handing it over to our Sergeant-major, who transmitted it to the Captain; but the Colonel issued a regimental order to the effect that in future any *Volontaire* wishing to get leave would have to apply for it through Sergeant Legros. Our Captain also strictly forbade us to apply for ten o'clock or midnight leave from the officer of the week (to whom all such demands were made by the other troopers), and told us that in future we should have to apply on the Saturday to Sergeant Legros for any leave we might wish to obtain. He added that any *Volontaire* who applied for leave to the Lieutenant of his company, or to the Sergeant-major, would be punished with eight days' *Salle de Police* for having done so. It is needless to say that I never obtained a single day's regular leave after that; but I cared little, as my Sergeant-major had become so friendly to me that he used to give me whatever leave I wanted.

It was about this time that I met with rather a serious accident. I was leading my mare and two other chargers to the watering-tank, when one of the chargers was bitten by the other, and rearing straight up in the air, came down on my mare, who fell down on the top of me. I was much bruised and nearly stunned, but fortunately, no bones were broken. I was led to the dispensary, and, after examining me, the doctor ordered that I should be detained there. I have already explained that there was a ward in the place where sick troopers who were not ill enough to be sent to hospital were placed under medical treatment. The ward contained twelve beds, and adjoining it were two rooms for non-commissioned officers. The beds were of the usual military type, and the sick troopers were only allowed the ordinary rations: those who could afford it, however, being at liberty to send for extra food from the canteen. There were no nurses attached to the dispensary, and it was superintended by a Corporal assisted by one trooper. I confess that I far preferred being there to going to the hospital. During the ten days I passed in the dispensary I made great friends with the Sergeant, who was himself sick. He had enlisted before his time for conscription was due, and his aim was to work his way up to a commission from the ranks; but although he had served already three years, he was thoroughly disgusted with military service, and had made up his mind to leave it at the end of his five years' engagement. He explained to me that he stood absolutely no chance of being sent to the Saumur school, as only three Sergeants were selected every year, and, although he had passed the examination some time previously, he was only fourth on the list. He ought by rights to have been the second, but the two candidates who were classed second and third had taken that rank through their fathers' influence, one of them being the son of an ex-Minister of State and the other of an influential Senator. The Sergeant had but one more chance, and he felt sure that another job would be perpetrated, as among the next candidates stood the Colonel's nephew and two sons of Generals. He added that his only chance would be to re-enlist for another five years, but he was not inclined to do this. He was a thorough gentleman, and had had an excellent education, and he naturally hated the life he led among ignorant comrades —men who had no idea of common decency, and who were addicted to the grossest immorality.*

As *Volontaires* had only to serve for one year instead of for the five during which the other troopers had to be under the flag, military instruction had to be carried out a good deal more rapidly than in the case of the ordinary recruits. As soon, therefore, as we had become proficient in the use of our arms on horseback, and showed that we understood thoroughly drilling on foot by *peloton*, we were put through mounted drill by *peloton*. We were taught to walk, trot, and gallop in two ranks, to

* The picture he drew of the average Sergeant was not an inviting one, but all he told me was quite in accord with the description given in a book published later on—"Sous-Offs," by Lucien Descares. This book was written by a *Volontaire* who had served at Evreux in the Duc de Chartres' regiment, both under the Duke himself and under the Colonel who had replaced the former when he was expelled from the French army. The latter officer was so furious with the work when it appeared that he ordered it to be burnt on a dung-hill, and promised thirty days in prison to any trooper found reading it. The book presents a vivid picture of the life of sergeants in a cavalry regiment; but to appreciate it the reader must have served in the French army himself, as it teems with military slang; I may add that the details given are so gross that its pages cannot be perused without disgust.

wheel to the right and to the left, to break off by fours and by twos, and then to form again into line, each one of us having to act in turn as commander of the company. At first we had to execute all these movements without stirrups, and a good deal of time was also devoted to the improvement of our riding capacities. In this respect our instruction was first-rate. We were first taken over jumps singly, being taught to trot our chargers until we got within twelve to fifteen feet of the jump, when we had to let go the reins and get over the jump with our hands behind our backs. We also had to do the same with drawn swords, and without holding the reins, the same movements being repeated with the carbine held on the leg. Then we had to repeat the exercises by twos and by fours, and after some time we were taken over the jumps in two ranks. We were also taught to pass through the *défilé*, a most difficult manœuvre.

In order to complete the regulation number of thirty troopers which form a *peloton,* some old troopers were added to our ranks. We were then started at a gallop, wheeled round, and brought in front of the *défilé*. This, as I explained before, consisted of a narrow lane between two high hurdles, and was just broad enough to allow four troopers to ride abreast. When we got within twenty yards of the *défilé*, we had to form fours, and the moment we had gone through it we had to form once more in line. The passage through the crater at full gallop was also a most exciting exercise. The two troopers riding in the centre of the line had to pass down the bottom of the crater while the others rode on the slope; the centre of the front had to increase his pace so as to keep our lines perfectly straight, and as we came out of the crater our two lines had to be unbroken.

I was much astonished at the manner in which we were

taught to charge. Instead of charging in serried ranks, the moment the command "Charge!" was given, every trooper had to force his horse forward as hard as he could go, without troubling to keep in line; in fact, it resembled a race rather than the onset of a compact mass. The troopers of the front rank charged with the points of their swords held forward, while those of the second rank held their swords high up, ready to cut down their men, and as soon as the command had been given every trooper had to shout at the top of his voice three times, "Charge! Charge! Charge!" This, with the clattering of the scabbards against our spurs, drove the chargers to the highest pitch of excitement, and every one of them went for all he was worth. We were also taught to charge in serried ranks, but it was explained to us that in case of war this mode of charging would hardly ever be used, as it would enable modern artillery to destroy whole regiments before they had been able to reach the enemy. The charge over the bugle sounded "Assembly" (*Ralliement*), and at this command we had to reform our line.

At the beginning of April we underwent a second examination before a board consisting of the Captain and the Commander of the *Volontaires*, the *Capitaine Instructeur*, and one of the Majors. The three *Volontaires* who obtained the first places were nominated Corporals after the examination. One of them certainly fully deserved his promotion, but the two others only obtained it through interest; one of them in particular, who is now Duc de * * * *, ought by rights to have been classed among the two last, but his family was able to put great pressure on our Colonel, and one of our Lieutenants who was his first cousin helped him to obtain a place on the list to which he was in no way entitled. The same thing happens in the case of the promotion of officers in France, and in some cases undeserved favour is shown in an absolutely shameful way. I am well aware that in all countries of the world family interest goes a long way—in this country it is hard to get on without it—but at least it may be said that the recipients of special favours have always something to show to their credit, while this is far from being the case under the French Republic.

After we had passed our half-yearly examination we began our duty as trained soldiers in earnest, and besides company drill we were taken to the shooting-range once a week, one day being also devoted to service in the field. Our shooting, I confess, was very poor, but this was chiefly due to the bad sighting of our carbines, none of which were true. They were theoretically sighted up to a thousand yards, but could not be relied on above three hundred. The range was in the middle of the forest, in an opening among stately trees, and the target stood at the foot of a small hill. While firing was going on two of us were sent to patrol the approaches on each side of the targets, as quite a number of poor people used, at the risk of their lives, to lurk behind the targets in order to pick up the bullets. The patrols had strict orders to prevent any one from approaching within two hundred yards of the butts, and we had to keep a very sharp look-out, for these bullet-collectors were up to many dodges to evade us. All of a sudden, for instance, a couple of them showed themselves on the road leading to the open space between the troopers and the target, and although we shouted hard to warn them off, they pretended to be deaf and not to hear us. We had, of course, therefore, to gallop towards them, and as we came up to them they pretended to be wood-gatherers on their way home. Meanwhile, half-a-dozen others had crawled under the bushes a couple of hundred yards behind the targets, and we had thus to start off once more at full gallop to clear the place of the new intruders, as the shooting had to be interrupted the moment they came in view. It was for that reason that the best riders, mounted on the fastest chargers, were usually selected for this patrol work, and I usually managed to be sent out. I thoroughly enjoyed the work, as it gave me the chance of a good gallop over rough ground, and more than once we had quite exciting chases across country after the most obdurate of the law-breakers. I say "we," as after a short time it became necessary to post two troopers on each side of the targets, this decision having been come to on account of an accident which happened while the infantry were practising. An old woman had managed to creep, unseen by the sentry, right across the line of fire, and just then a volley was fired and she received two bullets in her body.

I cannot speak at all highly of the way in which we were taught field service. We were supposed to learn how to direct ourselves, how to reach a specified point with the help of a map, and how to report on the country we had been across. The explanations given to us by our Sergeant showed that he knew very little about the subject himself, and I am certain that none of us ever understood a word of his explanations. I was perhaps the only trooper who knew anything technically about topography, having begun at a very early age to go in for mountain-climbing; and as this became a regular hobby with me I had studied map-making, and had learnt not only to read the smallest details of the map, but also to find my way among the greatest difficulties, a detailed map representing to me not only the roads, but also the whole contour of the country, and the nature of its surface. During the few years preceding my service I had also explored the French Alps, forming the frontier between France and Italy, of which no map had then been published, and I had never failed to make rough surveys and triangulations with the help of the prismatic compass, an instrument of which I suppose our Sergeant had never even heard. It was a great pity that we were never accompanied by an officer on these field days; but I do not remember our Captain turning up more than once during the three months this part of our education lasted. We were also taught, after a fashion, how to take to pieces and to lay down a railway line, and two or three times we were shown how to use dynamite.

Such was our work during April and May; it could certainly have been made most interesting but for the terror we always stood in of being punished. So far as I was concerned, I do not remember a fortnight elapsing without my being sent to the *Salle de Police*, usually for the most absurd reasons. Another great mistake which was committed was that of never allowing us any personal initiative; and we did not even dare to ask for any explanations. One or two of the *Volontaires* having ventured to do so met with a rebuff, accompanied by a punishment.

Shortly after the half-yearly examination we were also told off to take the guard according to the roll in our different squadrons. As our regiment had only the barrack guard to supply, an individual trooper's turn only came about once a month. Ordinary troopers were allowed to get a comrade to take their turn for them, but the Colonel issued an order to the effect that no *Volontaire* would be allowed to be replaced when his turn for taking the guard came round. The troopers told off to

TROOPER 3809

take the barrack guard numbered six, besides a trumpeter and two stable guards, and were commanded by a Sergeant and a Corporal—all of them selected from the same squadron. Besides these troopers, two stable guards from each one of the other squadrons had to be supplied at a few minutes before 8 A.M. The troopers nominated for guard duty met in the yard at some distance from the guard-room, and the Sergeant in command carefully examined each man to ascertain that his equipment was in good order. The officer of the week of the squadron who supplied the guard also inspects the troopers' equipment, and the *Adjudant* of the Week stands by, and at eight o'clock sharp marches the in-coming guard past the Captain of the Week, halting the men in front of the guard-room. He then gives the word, "Front!" and a fresh inspection of each trooper is made by the Captain of the Week. At the same time the out-going guard has been formed up by a Sergeant, and is marched away under the orders of the outgoing Sergeant, who soon dismisses his men, and returns with the Corporal to hand the service over to the Sergeant who replaces him. He has also to make his report to the Captain of the Week, or to the *Adjudant* in the absence of the former. The sentries are then relieved by the incoming Corporal and sent back to their rooms. All the troopers who have been on guard the previous day are excused from duty for four-and-twenty hours. The first time I took the guard, the Captain of the Week was an old Captain who was a perfect disgrace to the regiment. He was constantly drunk, and while at one time he would abuse the troopers in the vilest fashion, at another he would display a familiarity which was most embarrassing. That morning, being in one of his furious moods, he found something to say about the equipment of every one of us, called us a set of dirty pigs, and told our Sergeant that he was a worse pig than any of us.

"When I was a youngster," he added, "things were different. Then we had soldiers—then we had an Emperor; but now that is the lot of swine one has to command," pointing to us. "Look here," he went on, "they have given me the Legion of Honor, but I am ashamed of it; and you see," pointing to the decoration on his breast, "their d—— Republic; I've put the head the other way, so that it should not be seen!"

He then ordered the *Adjudant* to dismiss us. He walked into the guard-room, where a wooden camp-bed, similar to the one in the *Salle de Police,* occupied the whole length of the room, while a few forms, on which we could sit, were scattered about. In a tiny recess adjoining this room was a table. This was the portion of the guard-room reserved for the Sergeant. We only had to supply two sentries, one in front of the barrack gate and the other near the entrance of the forage-store in a small side-street some two hundred yards from the barracks. Our Corporal made out the list of the sentries and stuck on the wall a bit of paper on which he had written our rotation. We had to be twenty-four hours on guard duty, so that each one of us had to be on sentry-go four times, doing two hours at a time, and with an interval of four hours before his turn came round again. I was put on the second turn, from 10 A.M. to noon, 4 to 6 P.M., 10 to 12 P.M., and 4 to 6 A.M. The Sergeant and Corporal were both on friendly terms with me, so that I did not have too bad a time of it. I took a great deal of interest in the duties of the Sergeant, and he explained to me what an awkward task his was. Of course I was supposed to have learned before all the routine of a Sergeant of the Guard, but merely hearing a description read out gives one but a poor idea of what things are in practice.

The Sergeant of the Guard is of course responsible for the relieving of sentries (though the actual duty is left to the Corporal); he has besides to see that the trumpeter is punctual in the various calls, he is responsible for the cleanliness of the various barrack-yards, and of the cells, and the *Salle de Police,* and for all the sanitary arrangements of the barracks. Whenever he requires troopers for fatigue duty he gets the trumpeter to call the various Corporals of the Week belonging to his squadron and tells them how many men he requires. He has the right to call the troopers who are punished with *Salle de Police* or confinement to barracks, and order them for fatigue duty.

He has to examine every Sergeant, Corporal, and trooper who goes out of barracks, and has power to prevent their going out in the event of their outfit not being in proper order. He has also to see that no strangers come into the barracks without proper leave. After the night-call he sees that the doors of the barracks are closed, visits the stables to ascertain that no horses are loose, and that the stable guards are at their posts. He has also during the night to make rounds outside the barracks, and in case a horse or a trooper is taken sick and requires urgent help, he has to send round to call either the Vet. or the doctor as the case may be. The regulations on this subject are rather amusing, special stress being laid on the fact that the Sergeant of the Guard must only send on such an errand an *intelligent* trooper. There is no doubt that a Sergeant taking the guard gets very little opportunity for rest during the continuous twenty-four hours he is on duty, especially if he is under the orders of a strict *Adjudant,* or of an erratic Captain of the Week, such as Captain des Tourelles, who was on duty the first time I took the guard.

When I took my first turn as sentry I was put outside the barrack gates, my instructions being as follows:

In case any officer up to the rank of Captain passed me I was to shoulder arms, and if the officer was a Major or Lieutenant-colonel I had to present arms; in case of our Colonel coming to the barracks I was to present arms, shouting at the same time, " Aux armes," all the troopers in the guard-room having to turn out and to render him military honours. I had to prevent strangers from going out of barracks with a parcel, and was not to let any Corporal or trooper out of barracks if they carried a parcel or a carbine, unless the Sergeant of the Guard gave me orders to the contrary. When I took my third turn (from ten to twelve) I was placed as sentry before the forage-store, and my orders were of the strictest—I had to challenge anybody passing within ten yards of me, and in case no reply was given to my challenge, I was to arrest the offender and to call out for help. This last order was well meant, but the guard-room being over three hundred yards away, I did not see how the others could possibly hear me. I was also ordered to prevent any one from approaching the wall of the store, and in case the offender did not move away after being challenged three times I had to fire on him. I had not, however, to salute any officers, such honours being dispensed with after evening call. For the first hour nobody passed through the street, but towards half-past eleven I noticed Captain des Tourelles coming along; he was rather unsteady in his gait, and had to help himself by holding on to the wall. When he came within the regulation distance I challenged him, whereupon he leant against the wall of the store and said: "That's all ri', my boy, it's all ri', it's me."

I walked up to him and respectfully told him that my orders were to allow nobody to come near the wall of the forage-store.

"It's all right," he said, "it's me."

I expostulated with him, but I could not get him to budge, and I hardly knew what to do, when he pulled a cigarette out of his pocket and asked me for a match. I was well aware that if I allowed him to smoke near the forage-store I became liable to be court-martialled, but, on the other hand, if I laid hands on an officer I should also be court-martialled, so while he was fumbling in his pocket for a match I said to him, "Look here, sir, this is the forage-store, and you know that I can't let you smoke here."

"The forage-store," he replied, "the forage-store—shpose can't smoke—here, you smoke it for me, my boy," he added, handing the cigarette over to me.

I stuck it in my pocket and again asked him to move on.

"Yes, move on," he said; "it's all very fine to say move on, but I sh'ld like to know first where my house is. Now where is my house?"

I knew that he lived opposite the stores, and pointed out his house to him.

"Oh," he said, "that's my house? Funny my house getting so big all of a sudden. Why, it's all over windows—why's that, now tell me why d' I see so many windows?"

"It's rather foggy, sir," I replied, "that is what makes you think so. It is your house all right, and there are only four windows to it."

"Contr'dict me," he said, "and you contr'dict your

superior officer. You will have four days' *Salle de Police*, you understan'—four days' *Salle de Police* for contr'dicting your superior officer. Now—just hold on to me."

I noticed that he was ready to collapse, and putting my carbine against the wall I held him up. After a few minutes his attack was over, and it evidently did him good, for he seemed much steadier on his legs, and proceeded to walk with some accuracy in the direction of his house. He had just reached the middle of the road when he stopped and called out to me, "Dragoon!" he said, "you are a nice old Dragoon, and there's for you." Thereupon he handed over to me a 50-centime piece, and then reached the door of his house with my help. I suggested his handing me over his key, and having opened the door for him I stuck the key in his pocket and closed the door upon him. Soon after the Corporal came to relieve me, and I returned to the barracks.

When I reached the guard-room I went to the Sergeant's room, and told him what had happened, but we both agreed that it would never do to report the matter, as it never paid to "give away" an officer. I had to be once more on sentry-go (from 4 to 6 A.M.), but I tipped one of the troopers, who agreed to take my turn, and to remain four hours instead of two at his post. At half-past twelve, as I was disposing myself to lie down for a good sleep, Captain des Tourelles turned up again. All the other troops were lying down, and I had just left the Sergeant's office, so the Captain pounced on me. "Trooper," he said, "catch hold of a lantern. I want to go for a round," and at the same time he shouted for the Sergeant and Corporal of the Guard; noticing through the open door the Sergeant, who had begun to doze with his head resting on his arms. As soon, however, as the

Captain called out to him he jumped up and stood at attention.

"*Nom de Dieu de fainéant!* (You d—— lazy beast "!) he cried out in a drunken voice. "There, I catch you asleep."

The Sergeant tried to excuse himself, but the Captain told him to shut up.

"I am going with this Dragoon," he said, pointing to me, "to see whether everything is in order, and if everything is not in order *je t'en ficherai de dormir*. Come on," he added, turning to me, "walk in front of me."

I prepared to do so, and asked the Captain where he wished to go.

"To the *Adjudant's* room, of course," he replied. "Why d'you stick the light of that lantern in my eyes? Come on, walk alongside of me, and give me your arm: you know that I am a father to all my Dragoons, and I don't know where I have seen your face, but I like you— yes, I like you," he went on repeating.

As we got to the staircase leading to the *Adjudant's* room the Captain stopped, and told me he was not going up all those stairs, and he ordered me to go and rouse the *Adjudant*, and to tell him that if he did not come sharp he would be sorry for it. The *Adjudant*, who had been a gendarme, and was an old soldier of many years' standing, having only a few months to wait to get his pension, cursed and swore when I explained matters to him. I abstained from telling him that the Captain was drunk, but he evidently knew the old fellow's failing, for he muttered, as he got out of bed, "Drunk again, the old beast!" I did not wait for him, but returned to the Captain. I found him sitting at the bottom of the stairs dropping off into a doze; but as soon as he heard my steps, and saw the light of my lantern, he tried to get up, but was quite unable to do so until I helped him. He looked at me in a stupid way, and muttered, "What do you want?" I reminded him that he had sent me to call the *Adjudant*.

"The *Adjudant?* oh yes, the *Adjudant*. Why isn't he here?"

"He is dressing, sir, and coming at once," I answered.

"Dressing?" he said. "What business has he to be undressed? I'm not undressed."

Thereupon the *Adjudant,* who had donned his uniform in a remarkably short time, came down the stairs.

He saluted, and said: "You have sent for me, sir?"

"Sent for you," slowly replied the Captain. "Oh yes—I sent for you; why the devil didn't you come at once?"

"I was in bed, sir, and had to dress."

"Well," replied the Captain, "you had better go and undress and get back to bed; I don't want you. I've got a Dragoon, and I have got a lantern, and do you imagine that I want any one to show me what is wrong? Don't stare at me like that," he added. "Go to bed, I tell you."

The *Adjudant* saluted, and quietly returned to his room, evidently well accustomed to such scenes.

"Come on, my Dragoon," said the Captain, taking hold of my arm, and dragging me towards the kitchen. When we got to the door I told him where we were.

"That is just it," he says; "it's the kitchen I want to see;" and as we stepped in, he slipped on the dirty floor, and before I could stop him he was sitting down besmeared with grease. He laughed, but the fall appeared to have done him good, and to have partly recalled him to his senses. I helped him to rise, and as he did so he turned to me, and ordered me to light up the stove with my lantern. "That's all right," he said, "I only wanted to see in what state the cooks had left the kitchen. I'll give them four days' cells to-morrow for having left their floor in such a disgraceful condition. And now I'll go home."

According to his orders I walked ahead, and, pulling himself together, he followed me; he told me to lead him as far as the gate of the infantry barracks, thus saving himself a détour of at least 300 yards. When he got to the gate he had so far recovered that he was able to order the infantry Sergeant to open it for him, and he walked straight out, the Sergeant never suspecting for a moment the state he was in. I returned to the guard-room and reported matters to the Sergeant, who asked me to keep the matter quite dark for the sake of the honour of the regiment.

I do not mean to suggest that the picture I have just drawn is meant to represent the average French officer. Captain des Tourelles was, like Lieutenant Pernot whom I have previously mentioned, one of those officers who had gained their commission during the Franco-Prussian War; and who but for an accident would never have held the rank of an officer in the French cavalry. They were therefore men of an exceptional class no longer to be found in the French army. Most of the cavalry officers nowadays are gentlemen, and this remark even applies to the majority of those who have gained their commission through the ranks, since the examinations for the admission of cavalry Sergeants to the school of Saumur can only be passed by men who have received a superior education, and, as I have already stated, the Cadets of the St. Cyr who are allowed to serve in the cavalry are selected from amongst the most able of the candidates. I should not like to give so high a character to the French infantry officers. From my personal experience, as well as from all I have heard, I should say that very few of them are gentlemen. There are, of course, exceptions, but, taken as a class, they are certainly below the average British Sergeant in education, manners, and military training. I am speaking here of the subalterns, as those who reach a higher rank are either men belonging to the middle classes, whose contact with gentlemen has improved their manners, or men who belong to good families but have been unable to secure the highest places as Cadets at St. Cyr.

Such then was my experience of the first guard I took. Twenty-four hours on duty seems a long time, but after all, troopers enjoy a great deal of rest between the intervals of sentry-go, and " Taking the guard " is really more of a hardship to Sergeants and Corporals than to the troopers themselves. Where it becomes a real burden is in Paris, or other great towns where the various regiments have to supply a considerable number of men for different guards, so that the Sergeants may be called upon to take the guard as often as twice a week, and even the troopers cannot expect more than a week's immunity.

CHAPTER XIII

IN June we began "squadron school," and were drilled on the manœuvring ground with our respective squadrons. It was only then that all the officers attended the drill, for the training of the *peloton* had been left almost entirely to the Sergeants. By this time we might be regarded as trained troopers, and, indeed, in time of war the *Volontaires* would have been quite fit to act as Sergeants, although it did not seem to be the aim of the French military authorities to use the *Volontaires* as such, in the reserve, in case of war. All the reserve men had their own Sergeants already, and it was therefore difficult to understand why so much of our time was wasted in giving us a military education far superior to that of the average non-commissioned officer.

Since we had begun to see less of Sergeant Legros I had not been incessantly punished as I had been when we were constantly under his orders, and I almost dared to hope that I should be able to finish my time without getting further acquainted with the *Salle de Police*. However, it was not so to be. One Sunday morning at 6 o'clock a Corporal, who was on weekly duty, came to me and asked me to let him have five francs, adding that if I gave him the money he would not send me down to clean the stables. I gave him the money, but half an hour later he came and asked me for more. He had no time to press me hard, as he was called away by the Sergeant, but, as soon as the latter had done with him, he came back just as I was going down to stables. He was already drunk, and said he wanted another five francs. I absolutely declined to give him the money, pointing out that as he was on duty that day he would be severely punished for getting drunk, and I might also get punished for having supplied him with money. This put him in a frightful rage, and he asked me if I took him for a fool. I told him that it didn't matter whether I took him for a fool or not, but that he knew perfectly well that he made a fool of himself when he was drunk.

"All right," he said; "you will have two days' *Salle de Police* for having called me a fool. By the way," he added, "Lemaire is sick, and you will have to take the guard for him."

I remonstrated, explaining that I had taken the guard the previous week, and that it could not therefore be my turn to take the guard, even to replace a sick man.

"You refuse to obey the orders of the Corporals?"

"Of course I don't refuse," I said, knowing well that in his state of mind he might, upon the least provocation, report me as having refused to obey orders, and this would have meant a court-martial, and most likely a sentence of several years' hard labour.

"Well, get ready then," said the Corporal.

"I want to go and talk to the Sergeant-major first," I replied.

"No you don't," he said, standing in front of me.

Of course I could not lay hands on him, for, as I have already explained, the slightest assault on any man holding a rank superior to one's own was invariably punished with *death*. I therefore proceeded to get my things ready, well knowing, however, that it was physically impossible for me to get my kit into proper order for parade upon so short a notice. Soon after, the Corporal having reeled away, I went to the Sergeant-major's room, but there I found only his orderly, who told me to my utter dismay that the Sergeant-major had gone the previous evening on twenty-four hours' leave. I therefore walked down to the stables in order to find the Sergeant of the Week. On my way, however, I fell foul of the Corporal, who asked me where I was going.

"I am going to speak to the Sergeant of the Week," I said.

"No you don't," he replied; "you just walk back with me."

"I am going to the Sergeant of the Week," I repeated.

"You refuse to obey orders then?" asked the Corporal.

"No, but I am going to the Sergeant of the Week."

"By God," he said, "if you don't follow me to the room at once I will go straight to the Captain of the Week and report you for having refused to obey orders."

Of course I had no alternative but to follow the Corporal, and I had to dress anyhow in order to be ready in time for the parade of the guard. The leather tops of my trousers were not properly polished, my sword and carbine were not spick and span as they ought to have been for parade, and the brass work of my helmet was a trifle tarnished, for it had not been cleaned since the previous afternoon. As it was, I had to run to join the other troopers on parade, and when I got there the command "Attention" had already been given. Captain des Tourelles was Captain of the Week, and the moment he caught sight of me he ordered me to come to him.

"You are late," he said.

"Captain," I replied, "the reason of it is——"

"Shut up!" he interrupted; "don't answer me—you are filthy, you dirty beast!" He then began to examine my buttons, my sword, my helmet, my carbine, muttering the whole time, "Swine, swine. You are a *Volontaire*, I think, and you come here late, and as filthy as a pig! You shall have four days' *Salle de Police.*"

"But—sir—" I ejaculated.

"You dare answer me! You shall have four days more. Step back into the ranks!"

After we had been paraded and dismissed to the guard-room, I went to the Sergeant of the Guard to explain my case. This man was of low extraction, a peasant, in fact, who had been promoted to the rank of Sergeant merely on account of his undoubted severity. (He had once sent a man before the court-martial for refusing to obey him, and the poor trooper was sentenced to two years' hard labour.) This would seem to constitute a poor qualification for promotion, but, in many French regiments, it is notorious that a Corporal who sends a man before a court-martial is almost certain to be rewarded for his harshness. The Sergeant took very little interest in what I told him, and said it was no business of his, and that I had better speak to the Sergeant-major about it. The following day, when I left the guard, I went to see my Sergeant-major, but, unfortunately for me, he had obtained a two days' extension of leave, and the Sergeant *fourrier*, who was acting in his stead, told me that my punishment had already appeared on the report, and had been forwarded to the Colonel.

"Very well then," I said, losing my temper, "I shall go and complain to the Colonel," and I asked him to transmit my application to see that officer. He strongly urged me not to do so, assuring me that I should get no redress, but I was obstinate, and my demand was duly forwarded through the usual channels.

At noon the Sergeant *fourrier* showed me a copy of the Colonel's orders for the day. "You have got it pretty hot," he said, and he showed me the passage of the Colonel's decision referring to my case. To my dismay I read the following:

"The punishments inflicted on Trooper Decle by Corporal Armand and by Captain des Tourelles are altered to twenty days' *Salle de Police.*"

I had, therefore, to sleep in the cells that night, and the Sergeant told me that the answer to my application to see the Colonel would probably appear in the following day's regimental orders. I did not see Sergeant Legros until the following day, for, as I have explained before, troopers who have taken the guard are exempt from duty for four and twenty hours. The next morning, however, when we went to schoolroom, Legros called me.

"So you have been at your tricks once more, eh Decle?" he said.

I told him exactly what had occurred, but he only shrugged his shoulders.

"Serves you right!" he said. "You *Volontaires* get into the habit of throwing your money right and left, and if you hadn't begun by tipping the Corporal all this wouldn't have happened."

In the regimental orders of the day the Colonel stated that the application of Trooper Decle to see him was granted, and that the said Trooper Decle would have to be at his house at 1 P.M. the next day. I therefore got Titi and my other orderly to clean my clothes and my equipment with the utmost care, and at one o'clock sharp I proceeded to the Colonel's house. I was received by one of his orderlies, who took me to the kitchen. He went to inform the Colonel that I was there, and returned saying that the Colonel had sent word that I must wait. The cook very graciously offered me a cup of coffee, and during the good three-quarters of an hour that I had to wait she related to me the details of her family history, telling me that she had already saved £20, which would make a nice little dowry when she got married, and also suggesting that I should take her out for a walk next Sunday. (I could only politely express my regret at being unable to do this, as I was undergoing punishment.) She further told me that she did not care much for her place, as "*la Colonelle*" * was too close-fisted, and there was not enough *grattage* (perquisites) in the place. At the end of three-quarters of an hour the Colonel's orderly told me to walk upstairs, and showed me into a study where the Colonel was writing at a desk, in regimental trousers, a pair of slippers, and a black alpaca coat. He did not turn round, and I stood, helmet in hand, near the door. I had quite forgotten the regulations, and, finding myself in polite society, I had instinctively uncovered. Just as I remembered that I ought to keep my helmet on, and was replacing it, the Colonel, hearing me move, turned his head round.

"What are you fiddling about with your helmet for?" he asked. "Stand still, will you?" and he went on writing. Ten minutes later he ordered me to come forward. I saluted and stood at attention.

"Take off your helmet," said the Colonel.

I took it off.

"Your hair is too long, you will have to get it cut; and you will soon get a court-martial if you go on like that. Put on your helmet. What do you want?"

"Sir," I began, "I have been punished——"

"Punished!" he exclaimed. "Yes, you are always

---

* It is customary in France to designate the wives of superior officers and officials by their husband's titles; even in good society people will speak of La Generale, La Colonelle, La Commandante, La Prefete, La Sous-prefete, and so on.

punished. You are the worst trooper in my regiment. We don't want men like you in the French army. What do you want?"

"Sir," I once more began, "I have been punished by Corporal——"

"I know it," he replied, waxing quite angry. "I told you so before, you are always punished—always punished. If it is to tell me that that you have come here, you might have stopped at the barracks. Why the deuce don't you tell me what you want? Do you think I am standing here at your orders?"

"If you will allow me to explain, sir," I replied, "I will tell you why and how I have been punished."

"I don't want to know anything about it," said the Colonel, in an angry voice. "Let me see, how many days have you got?"

"Twenty days, sir," I said.

"Have you finished your punishment?"

"No, sir, I have only done two days so far."

"And you dare to come and complain to me! But I ought not to be astonished—for cool cheek and impudence you haven't your equal. Go back to barracks and tell the *Adjudant* to put you down ten days more for having made an unjustified complaint. That's all—look sharp!"

I saluted, and as I was walking towards the door the Colonel added: "I will teach you not to come and bother me in future." On my way to barracks I thought of the advice the Sergeant *fourrier* had given me, and I felt distinctly sorry that I had not followed it.

At the end of ten days I began to be so exhausted by sleepless nights and the hard physical work we had now to do that I began to feel seriously ill. I also had a relapse of sore throat accompanied with fever, undoubtedly due to all lack of sanitary precautions in the *Salle de*

Police. Since the warm weather had come, to the other horrors of the place another was added. Fleas and lice came through the boards by thousands, and our rooms were infested with vermin. I went to the medical visit, and the doctor found me so seriously ill that he had to send me to the hospital, promising at the same time that he would do his best to try and get me invalided. A fortnight later he proposed me for *invalidation,* but the Special Commission before whom I was examined refused to invalid me, but consented to allow me two months' sick leave. I was kept a week longer in hospital, and at the end of that time left the regiment for two months. This interval of respite I spent in Switzerland, where I did a good deal of mountain climbing.

I can hardly describe my feelings when I had to return to my regiment, and to go back to slavery. When I rejoined my corps I found but a few men in barracks, as the regiment was away at the manœuvres. The fifth squadron alone, which forms the depôt, was left in barracks, and there also remained a few troopers in each squadron, mostly sick men, who were to look after the chargers which had been left behind as unfit for hard work in the field. I tried my best to get permission to join my regiment, but this was not granted me; on the other hand, the Major in command of the depôt, who was acting as Colonel in the absence of the regiment, selected me to train some of the young horses which had proved refractory. This is the only good time I had as a trooper. I was particularly fond of the work, being allowed to ride whenever I liked, and having permission to use my own hunting-saddle. I had six horses to train, so that I was in the saddle almost the whole day, and had no one to bully me.

When the regiment returned, the *Volontaires* were once

more put together, and prepared for their final examination, which was to take place in the middle of October. On their return from the manœuvres the troopers who had completed their five years' service left for their homes amidst great rejoicings. Shortly after the departure of the time-expired men (*la classe*), a good many of those who had remained behind broke away from the regiment, but most of them returned before the expiration of six days, the law being that after six days' time a trooper absent without leave becomes a deserter, and is tried by court-martial, the sentence passed on him ranging from one to three years' hard labour. Those who absented themselves for less than six days were punished with fifteen days' prison by the Colonel, but after some time so many troopers absconded in that way, that, in order to put a stop to the practice, the Colonel promised that any man absenting himself without leave in future would get thirty days' prison, and that all the troopers belonging to his company would be confined to barracks for thirty days also. Notwithstanding this, one trooper, who had twice absconded within the last four months, ran away once more, and the troopers of his company were duly consigned to barracks during thirty days. When the fellow returned at the end of the fifth day, his comrades, infuriated by the punishment they had received through his misconduct, determined to punish him on their own account, and the Lieutenant in command of the *peloton*, when he heard of this, secretly consented to the plan. When the trooper returned, the Lieutenant ordered that before he was taken to prison he was to be sent to the room " to change his clothes." The moment he entered he was seized by the other troopers, tied face downwards on to a table, and every one of the twenty-four troopers of the company filed past him, each one dealing him a sharp blow with the buckle end of his charger's girth. He was then untied, and led to the riding-school, where a blanket was in readiness. In this blanket were placed sundry wooden clogs, besides platters and a scabbard or two. The blanket was then held all round by the defaulter's comrades, and he was chucked into it, and sent flying high up into the air perhaps a dozen times. I witnessed the punishment, and wondered how the poor fellow after being sent flying more than fifteen feet into the air, and then dropping amidst a shower of scabbards, clogs, and platters, back into the blanket, was not killed outright. When the punishment had come to an end the trooper was marched to the prison, or, rather, supported thither. On the way he met his Lieutenant and complained bitterly of the treatment he had received, but the officer merely told him that he had fully deserved all he had got. The following day he was so bruised and shaken that he could not rise, and he asked for a doctor. The latter went to see him, but declined to do anything for him, merely relieving him from punishment drill during the next couple of days.

At that time there were from twelve to fourteen troopers in prison, so that a *peloton de chasse* (punishment company) was organised, under the orders of a certain Sergeant de Cormet, who enjoyed the reputation of being the most severe Sergeant of the whole regiment. An episode which occurred during the previous winter may be quoted as an example of his method. It was bitterly cold, and he was drilling the prisoners, making them do the sword exercise and keeping the troopers for five or ten minutes in the same position. He had ordered the second position of the *coup de sabre vers la droite,* which consists in holding the sword extended to the right at arm's length; at the end of a few minutes the troopers became so tired that none of them were able to hold their bodies straight, and had to put their left shoulders down, and let the points of their swords drop. De Cornet as usual walked behind them coolly saying, " Trooper Gabier, four days more for not holding yourself straight; Trooper Chirac, your sword is not straight, you will have two days more," and so on. All of a sudden one of the prisoners, a poor weak fellow, said to him:

" Sergeant, my hands are frozen; will you allow me to blow in them for one minute? I can't hold my sword any longer."

" Four days for speaking in the ranks," answered de Cornet, in his monotonous voice.

The trooper's fingers were as white as wax, and he soon repeated his request with a similar result. At last, unable to stand the pain any longer, the trooper put his sword under his arm and blew on his fingers.

" Hold your sword in position at once," said the Sergeant; " I shall report you to the Colonel."

" But, Sergeant, I can't," cried the trooper.

" You refuse to obey? " said the Sergeant.

" I can't, I can't," said the trooper, sobbing with pain, and at the same time trying to grasp his sword, but finding himself unable to close his benumbed fingers.

Again the Sergeant ordered him to hold his sword out, but the man burst into tears, and once more sobbed, " I can't, I can't!" Thereupon the Sergeant commanded another prisoner to carry the sword, and calling out to one of the troopers on guard, ordered him to fetch the Corporal, and when the latter came he had the poor fellow conveyed to the cells, and reported him for refusal to obey orders. The trooper was therefore tried by court-martial, and sentenced to *two years' hard labour!* I little dreamt at the time that the day would come when, as will be seen

TROOPER 3809

presently, I would have the misfortune to be placed in the power of this fiend.

As the day fixed for our final examination approached we were all busy looking through our various books in order to be well up to the subjects in which we were to be examined. Our Sergeant chiefly made us practise to give the word of command; and when one of us was placed in command of the company, he had, before ordering any movement, to explain fully the way in which such movement ought to be executed. In fact, we were taught to act as Sergeants. At last the great day came. The subjects on which we were to be examined were these:

Dismounted drill, and command.
Hippology.
Voltige.
Gymnastics.
Topography.
Knowledge of regulations in barracks and in the field.
Riding.
Mounted drill, and command.

The maximum number of marks which could be gained for each subject was twenty. We were examined by a Board of Officers, consisting of a Major, the Captain *instructeur,* our own Captain, and one Lieutenant. The order in which we were called was settled according to the numbers under which we had been enrolled, so that I came third on the list of troopers; the three *Volontaires* who had been made Corporals coming of course before the others. The first subject on which we were examined was dismounted drill. (The Corporals could select their own subject, so that their examination was merely nominal.) The two *Volontaires* who were examined before me were told to explain the mere rudiments of the subject, but when my turn came I was ordered to explain and command the most difficult manœuvres. I did this with credit to myself, and I was further ordered to command sword drill; this I also did well, and I was then sent back to the ranks. With the exception of three or four of the *Volontaires*, who bungled most frightfully in explaining the simplest movements, all of us knew our work thoroughly well. We were then taken to the riding-school and examined on Hippology; only four or five of us knew anything about this, and d'Alvarez, who was a Corporal, knew so little about the subject that the Lieutenant had to prompt all his answers.

We were then dismissed for breakfast, and were told to return at eleven o'clock to the riding-school to be examined on *voltige* and gymnastics. We were hardly given a chance to show what we could do, however, as the officers were anxious to go and have luncheon. When they returned at 3 P.M. we were taken to the schoolroom, where our proficiency in topography was put to the test. I have never seen anything more ridiculous than this part of the examination, for with the exception of the Captain *Instructeur*, the officers seemed to know very little about the subject, and most of the *Volontaires* knew still less. We were closely examined on all questions dealing with the duties of Sergeants and Corporals, in barracks and in the field, and, although the officers who examined us tried their best to put me wrong, I showed myself quite proficient, which evidently disconcerted the officers, as I heard them whispering, "We must give him good marks, but it's a nuisance, you know."

"We shall find a way," replied my Captain. I did not realise then what this meant, but I understood it quite soon enough.

TROOPER 3809

This part of the examination over, we were dismissed for the day, and ordered to be ready for mounted drill, with full kit, the next morning at 8 A.M. At the appointed time, the officers who had examined us the previous day turned up at the barracks, and accompanied by a trumpeter we started for the manœuvring ground.

We had first to ride individually at various paces, and were then ordered to go over the jumps. Very little notice was taken of our riding, and while this went on the officers chatted together, hardly bestowing a glance on us.

After this we had, each in turn, to take command of the *peloton*, and to explain and command various evolutions according to the officer's orders. I was successful in all the various manœuvres I was ordered to command; but many of the others made a sad mess of it, especially when they had to wheel their company round, take it at a gallop to a certain point, and then return so as to march past in fours before the Major. Miscalculation of distances was the commonest source of error. The examination over, we were marched back to barracks, and in the evening my Sergeant-major told me that he had seen the marks, and that I was among the first half. I expressed my delight, but he said warmly:

"Don't crow yet, my boy; they mean to keep you a second year, and they will find a way to do it."

I was thunderstruck, for I never thought, for an instant, of such a contingency. I told the Sergeant-major that it would be monstrous, considering that I had proved my proficiency.

"Take my warning," he said, "and don't be astonished if they keep you another year."

De Lanoy, to whom I went, then said that he did not think that the Colonel could possibly keep me, as he would have to keep a good many others who were below me in proficiency if he did so.

It was, therefore, with a beating heart that, on the following day, I stood on parade, awaiting the result of the examination, which was to be proclaimed to us by our Captain, who had prepared a little speech for the occasion.

"I have to congratulate you," he said, "on your proficiency, which is due to the untiring efforts of Sergeant Legros, whom I hope soon to see duly rewarded. With the exception of two or three of you, I have never had a better or more intelligent set of troopers under my orders. Now I will, before reading out to you the result of the examination, explain how it has been arrived at. The maximum of marks allotted for each subject is twenty, and the number of marks gained by each candidate is multiplied by a coefficient fixed according to the relative importance of the subject." He then read out to us the various coefficients (which will be found farther on). "In your previous examinations," he went on, "we did not reckon good conduct, but this being a final examination, and the submission of each trooper to discipline being a matter of such paramount importance, the Colonel has decided to give it due prominence, and has, therefore, fixed the coefficient at the figure of fifty, which makes altogether the maximum number of marks to be gained 2000. I am glad to add that many of you have obtained more than the three quarters of the possible number of marks, and this, I say once more, is entirely due to the efforts of your able Sergeant."

The Captain then read out the list. At the head of it stood the names of the three *Volontaires* who had been previously appointed Corporals, the first being d'Alvarez. This made us smile, for, though we all liked him, we knew perfectly well, that if it had not been for the influence of his family, he would have ranked near the end of the list. The two other Corporals had worked hard since their promotion, and fully deserved their position. The Captain, however, continued to read out name after name, and yet mine had not been reached. I became more and more alarmed, and I turned cold when it came at last, at the very end of the list, with 633 marks only, while the man before me, one of the most vulgar, ignorant, and stupid fellows I ever met, had 1027. All the others looked at me, and felt in their hearts that a gross injustice had been committed.

I was aroused from my thoughts by the Captain's voice:

"Decle," he said, "I am sorry to have to communicate bad news to you; but the Colonel, after due consideration, has decided that, having regard to the too small amount of marks you have obtained—you see you are the only one who has less than half of the possible maximum—the Colonel, I repeat, has decided that you shall be kept back to complete your military education. I am sorry for you, but it cannot be helped. As to the others, those who are already Corporals will be promoted to the rank of Sergeant, and the next three on the list are promoted to the rank of Corporal."

Thereupon he dismissed us. I went to him, and begged and implored him to ask the Colonel to reconsider his decision, but he replied that I was merely wasting my time and his.

The blow had fallen, and I felt like a madman! The first thing I did was to obtain a copy of the list, which was posted up in the schoolroom. I then saw how the trick had been played. A few words of explanation will make the device clear.

TROOPER 3809

The result of the examination, so far as I was concerned, was as follows:

	Co-efficients.	My marks.	Totals.
Dismounted drill and command	8	13	104
Hippology	5	16	80
Voltige	6	12	72
Gymnastics	5	10	50
Topography	5	9	45
Knowledge of regulations	6	10	60
Riding	7	18	126
Mounted drill and command	8	12	96
Grand total			633

The highest marks obtained out of a possible 1000 were 816, the lowest marks (given to the *Volontaire* next to me on the list) were 177. By the actual marks obtained I ought to have been classed the fifth out of fourteen, but as the examiners were determined that I should be the last on the list, the following plan was devised:—

"Good conduct" was added to the other items, and a coefficient of no less than fifty was allotted to it. With the exception of two other *Volontaires* besides myself twenty marks were given to every one for good conduct, thus increasing their totals by *one thousand!* The *Volontaire* who was last but one was given seventeen marks for good conduct, and this, multiplied by fifty, made 850 to be added on to his beggarly 177, giving him a total of 1027 marks. I was given nothing for good conduct, so that I remained with my original 633 marks, and was thus classed last. The regulations stated that *Volontaires*, who at the end of the year had failed to show a proficiency sufficient to enable them to obtain a number of marks at least equal to half the possible maximum at the final examination might be detained for a second year —I was therefore detained *according to the regulations!*

It was with an almost broken heart that I bade goodbye to all my comrades, and when I watched the train which took them away disappearing in the distance, I felt like a marooned stowaway who watches the departing ship sink below the horizon. When they had gone I went to my room at the hotel, seriously debating whether I should desert or else shoot myself. That I did neither remains a source of wonder to me.

CHAPTER XIV

I DO not intend to enter into many of the details of my second year's service, as this was a mere repetition of what I had already gone through, and I will therefore confine myself to a brief description of that portion of my adventures which may offer some special points of interest.

Some time elapsed before the arrival of the new *Volontaires,* and during this period we had practically no work to do with the exception of " stables." All the Sergeants of my squadron, and many of those belonging to other squadrons, had made friends with me, and they all pitied me for the cruel position I was placed in. Meanwhile the senior *Adjudant* retired with a pension, and my Sergeant-major was appointed in his stead, while Sergeant *fourrier* Vaillant became Sergeant-major. Vaillant was a particular friend of mine, so that with his help, and the support I knew the *Adjudant* would give me, I hoped that if a decent Sergeant was put in charge of the *Volontaires* I should soon obtain my discharge. There was no chance of our being entrusted again to the tender mercies of Legros, as he had also been appointed Sergeant-major.

A number of *Volontaires* were drafted into our regiment that year—I believe there were nearly thirty of them. Socially and intellectually they were very inferior to my previous comrades. There never existed between them that spirit of comradeship which was so great among the little set to which I belonged. Shortly after their arrival a trooper from the first squadron came to tell me that Sergeant de Cormet wanted to speak to me, and that I was to go to his room at once. I could not imagine what he wanted with me, as I did not belong to his squadron, and I had never had anything to do with the man. I went, however, and when I reached his room I asked him whether it was true that he had sent for me.

"Yes," he said, " I want to speak to you. I have just heard that I am going to be put in charge of the *Volontaires,* and as it appears that nobody has yet been able to break you in, I merely wanted to warn you that I mean to succeed. If ordinary means are not successful, I'll stand no nonsense, and I'll find some way to get you court-martialled. A few years in a gaol would do a lot of good to a swine of your class."

I had so far made no reply, but stood with my arms folded on my chest. My face must have expressed my stifled anger, I suppose, for when I took two steps forward the Sergeant retreated towards the window. "Don't be afraid," I said, " I am not going to touch you —you are not worth it; but now that you have told me what you mean to do, I will also tell you what *I* mean to do. Remember this—you may find a way to get me court-martialled, though I doubt it, but if you do—when I come out, be it in ten years', in fifteen years', or even twenty years' time—I shall kill you."

"You dare to threaten me—me a Sergeant!" he said.

"Don't get my blood up; you had better not," I replied; " remember that there are no witnesses here, and if you rouse me I might cause you bodily harm. I am a good deal stronger than you. But I think that this conversation has lasted long enough, and I will only add a few words to what I told you before. I warned you what I would do if you got me court-martialled, but I further warn you that if you bully me while I am under your orders I will punish you when I am no longer a soldier. And now that we quite understand each other I will say good afternoon, only mind," I added, " if you report me for what has taken place here I will deny everything; you have no means of proving your word, and you would not have dared to tell me what you did in presence of witnesses."

I returned to my room fairly heart-broken at the idea that I was going to be under the orders of the most cowardly brute in the whole regiment; I had seen the fellow at work when he was drilling the prisoners, and I knew that if I had had a bad time of it while I served under Sergeant Legros, it would be ten times worse under Sergeant de Cornet. Shortly afterwards the *Volontaires* and the recruits of the year arrived, and being a trooper of a year's standing I was allotted a recruit to whom I was supposed to teach his work. I almost despaired of ever doing anything with the fellow, and in vain I tried to prevent his being bullied, but the stupid chap seemed to do all he could to invite it.

" I say, you chaps," he said to the troopers on his arrival, " I am a Parisian, you know, and I am not going to stand any nonsense. I have been in a grocer's shop, and I am not a greenhorn. Besides, my cousin Beaujean has been in a Dragoon regiment, and he has told me all about it, so no bullying please, or else you will have to do with Jossier—that's my name."

I need not say that after this little speech of his, Jossier became the butt of all the practical jokers in the room. The scenes I described at the beginning of this book were of course once more renewed, but one of the jokes which were played on my *bleu* (recruit) was quaint enough to be related. He was in the habit of wearing at night a *bonnet de coton*, similar to the head-gear which was given to us at hospital, but much more bulky. When drawn out to its full length it was fully two feet long, and when he had it on his head the peak stood some eight inches above his head, with an enormous tassel fixed on to it. One evening, after he had gone to sleep, a practical joker set the tassel alight, and being of cotton it began to burn merrily. Nearly all the men in the room collected round his bed to see the fun, and hearing a noise he sat up in bed and looked at us in a bewildered way. By this time the tassel was burnt down, and the other part of the head-gear was smouldering away.

"Well," he said, "you are a nice lot of fools to stand there staring round my bed like a lot of idiots. It's very funny to look at a man, isn't it?"

We were all laughing, as he had not yet noticed that his head-gear was on fire; but all of a sudden his speech was interrupted, as he felt an uncomfortable heat near the crown of his head, and having impulsively put his hand to his head he realised what was the matter, and chucked away his *bonnet de coton*.

"Ah, you swine," he exclaimed, "I'll teach you," and he jumped out of his bed, making a dash for us. Unluckily for him, the first man on whom he jumped was Piatte, to whom he dealt a blow on the chest. Piatte caught hold of him by the arms and legs, and shouted, laughing, "I say, boys, I've caught a flea; let's make it jump!" Immediately a blanket was produced, and the recruit tossed up, and when they put him once more on his legs he did not complain, but quietly sneaked into his bed.

During the fortnight which elapsed until the *Volontaires* were put together, I was told off by my Sergeant-major to drill half a dozen recruits, and at the end of the week I had already got more out of my recruits than any of the Corporals who were in charge of the others. The method I employed was to promise my men a bottle of wine if they drilled well, and of course they all did their utmost to gain that reward. Captain Hermann, who, as the reader will remember, was in command of our squadron, and had been in charge of the *Volontaires,* was evidently pleased with me, and actually came to congratulate me. This state of affairs unfortunately lasted only for a fortnight, and at the end of that time the new *Volontaires* were formed into a separate *peloton,* and on account of their number two officers were placed in command of them—Captain Hermann and Lieutenant Amy. Two Sergeants were also detached for this service—Sergeant de Cormet and Sergeant Cordier. The latter was a personal friend of mine, and I knew that he would counteract de Cormet's bad intentions towards me. No Corporal had yet been selected by the Colonel, and therefore when the *Volontaires* were assembled for the first time, I took my position to the left of the company, the Corporal's place, which, by rights, belonged to me as the senior trooper. The previous year when we were formed into a separate *peloton* there was among us a *Volontaire* who had been detained and who belonged to the lot who had served before us, and Legros had always made him do Corporal's duty. But evidently de Cormet did not mean to treat me in that way, for he ordered me to take my place in the ranks among the others, and he made me go through all the rudiments of the instruction, as if I had been a raw recruit. The other Sergeant treated me very differently, and when he took the service the following day he ordered me to act as Corporal. Lieutenant Amy, however, turned up in the middle of the drill and sharply reprimanded the Sergeant, ordering that I should be put through the rudiments of the drill absolutely as if I had been a raw recruit. To make things worse, Sergeant Cordier was taken with typhoid fever a few days after he took charge of us, and having had a relapse during his convalescence he was sent home on six months' sick-leave.

Early in December two Corporals were appointed to help de Cormet: one of them, Lormand, was a schoolfellow of mine, who had enlisted three months before, and had just been promoted to the rank of Corporal.

I had been doing work with the new *Volontaires* for a fortnight, and Sergeant de Cormet hadn't yet found it possible to punish me, for Lieutenant Amy was always present when we drilled, and de Cormet himself spent very little time in the schoolroom, leaving one of the Corporals in charge of it. As, however, the previous year's regulations as to leave were still in force, de Cormet had always refused to let me apply for leave. A few months before, I had attained my majority, and at the beginning of December my solicitors wrote me a most urgent letter pressing me to come to Paris without delay, to settle some important matters. I showed this letter to de Cormet, but he absolutely declined to grant me leave, and the Captain to whom I then went was equally emphatic in his refusal, adding that I should only get leave for the New Year provided I was not punished in the interval. As it was most necessary that I should go to Paris that week, I went to see the *Adjudant*, Bernard, my former Sergeant-major, and asked him to let me go to Paris from Saturday afternoon after "stables" until Monday morning. He at once promised not to report me missing, and told me to go and settle matters with my Sergeant-major. The latter readily acquiesced, and suggested a plan which would enable me to reach Paris before the offices were closed. "Stables" being over at 4 o'clock, I could by catching the 4.30 train reach Paris at 5.30, and as the offices do not close till 6 o'clock (Saturday half-holidays are unknown in France), I should be in time to transact my business. My Sergeant-major, however, remarked that if I wanted to catch the 4.30 train I would have no time to go to the hotel to change my regimentals for civilian attire, and therefore suggested that I should dress in civilian clothes in his room and leave barracks by the infantry gate. I had made it a rule whenever I went to Paris without leave to wear over my clothes a long blue blouse falling below the knees, with a silk cap (the costume of the lower classes in the North of France), and I also wore a false beard and blue spectacles. I donned this attire in the Sergeant-major's room, and in order that I should have no difficulty at the gate he accompanied me there, and told the Sergeant that I was a friend of his who was in a hurry to catch his train, and I was thus allowed to pass. I reached the station only just in time, and the train was already moving, so that I had to jump into the carriage nearest at hand, and received a severe shock at finding myself in company with two officers of my regiment. Having a newspaper in my pocket, however, I opened it, and held it in front of my face. My disguise was so good that the officers had not recognised me when I jumped into the carriage, but I was afraid that they might become suspicious if I held a newspaper in front of my face during the whole journey. I therefore got out of the carriage at the following station, where I had just time to jump into a second-class compartment. Here, to my astonishment, I found my school-fellow, Corporal Lormand, also in civilian attire; I knew that he had no leave, and as we had been great chums at school, I did not hesitate to remove my false beard and blue spectacles, which were a great discomfort to me.

"Well I never!" exclaimed Lormand when he recognised me. "Your disguise is so good," he added, "that I should never have known you. But how is it that you are going to Paris without leave?"

"I might put the same question to you," I replied, "as we seem to be both in the same boat."

We chatted pleasantly until we reached Paris, where we parted company—not, however, without having arranged to lunch together the next day.

I returned to my garrison town by the last Sunday train and found the *Adjudant,* to whom I had wired, waiting for me outside the barracks, so that I should walk in unquestioned. He told me that everything was all right, and that nobody had noticed my absence, so I went to my Sergeant-major's room to change my clothes.

The next morning, as we were assembled for dismounted drill, de Cormet called me to him.

"You went to Paris yesterday without leave," he said.

"No, Sergeant," I replied.

"I tell you that you went to Paris yesterday without leave, and what's more, in civilian attire."

"You are making a mistake, Sergeant," I again said.

"Didn't you see Decle?" he then asked, turning to Corporal Lormand.

"Yes, Sergeant, I saw him," replied the latter.

"What have you to say to that?" asked de Cormet.

"Nothing, Sergeant."

"Very well," he went on, "I will send you to the prison at once;" and forthwith he had me marched off by the Corporal of the Guard.

I need not say that Sergeant de Cormet had absolutely

no right to send me to prison, but knowing that the Captain would always endorse whatever he did, he never hesitated to give us punishments far in excess of those he was entitled to inflict. At breakfast time, after he had dismissed the *Volontaires,* he came to the prison, where he found me alone.

"Now I have come to speak to you, Decle," he said. "I have not yet reported the matter either to the Lieutenant or to the Captain, and if you will tell me the truth I promise you that you shall not be punished. I am fully aware that you went to Paris in civilian attire, with leave from your Sergeant-major, and I believe with the *Adjudant's* knowledge, but we shall leave the latter out of the question. Now if you will make a declaration in the presence of the Captain and another witness, saying that you have been to Paris with leave from your Sergeant-major, you shall not be punished."

"Will you allow me to think over your offer, Sergeant?" I asked.

"Yes," he said; "I will release you now, and give you till eleven o'clock to make up your mind. You will then come to my room and tell me what you have decided."

I was accordingly let out of prison, and pretended to go to my room, but the moment de Cormet had disappeared, I rushed to the *Adjudant's* room and told him how matters stood.

"What do you mean to do?" he asked me.

"You need not put such a question to me," I replied. "You ought to know that I would rather get sixty days' prison than give you and my Sergeant-major away; what we must do," I added, "is to discuss the situation with Sergeant-major Vaillant, so that he may be fully aware of what I mean to say, and act accordingly." The *Adjudant* dispatched a trooper to call the Sergeant-major.

When the latter turned up he was greatly concerned to hear what had happened, but I assured him that he need have no fear, and explained my plan to him. I would say that I left barracks on the Saturday evening after arranging my bed so that it appeared as if I were sleeping in it when the Sergeant of the Week passed through the room to call the evening roll. I would also say that the Sergeant-major gave me leave not to attend stables on the Sunday (which he had a perfect right to do), and that I returned to barracks on Sunday night by getting over the wall. I would also explain that I was not reported missing at the Sunday evening roll-call, one of my comrades having prepared my bed as I had on the previous night, so that the Sergeant of the Week did not notice my absence. Sergeant-major Vaillant remarked that if I told that story I should be punished with special severity, but I said I did not mind in the least so long as I did not get him into trouble. He thanked me profusely. " In the state of mind the Colonel is in," he added, " if he found out that I had given you leave he would be certain to reduce me in rank." The *Adjudant* remarked that de Cormet's motive was plain, for being first on the list of the Sergeants proposed for promotion to Sergeant-major's rank, he wanted to avail himself of the chance of getting Vaillant reduced to secure his place.

At eleven o'clock sharp I went to de Cormet's room and found him in the most amiable frame of mind.

" Well," he said, " I suppose that you have made up your mind to tell the whole truth ? "

" Certainly, Sergeant," I replied ; " I see no good in shrinking from it, and I will tell you exactly what happened." I then told him the story I had concocted with the Sergeant-major and the *Adjudant*.

" You are telling me lies," he angrily exclaimed. " I

can't understand your doing your best to get an exemplary punishment when you can so easily get off scot-free. Why don't you confess purely and simply that you had your leave from your Sergeant-major?"

"I will tell you why, Sergeant," I then replied, "and the best of reasons is that I had not his leave, and as there are no witnesses here, you can't use what I am going to say against me. You want me to accuse my Sergeant-major so as to get him reduced in rank, because you hope to be appointed in his stead. None but a man as mean as you are would try that sort of game. You can do what you like, but I shall merely repeat what I told you just now, and I once more want you to understand that I had no leave whatever, and that my Sergeant-major knew nothing about my going to Paris. Now do your worst."

"Oh," he said, "I wanted to do you a good turn, and that's how you take it. You will see what it will cost you! I shall report the matter at once to the Captain."

He was as good as his word, and in the afternoon the Captain turned up at the barracks and sent for me.

"I thought some time ago, Decle," he said, "when you were doing your work with the squadron, that you were really trying to turn over a new leaf. I find, however, that, on the contrary, you are doing your best to get yourself sent to Biribi. What is the meaning of this story that I hear from de Cormet about your having gone to Paris in ridiculous civilian attire, and with the complicity of your Sergeant-major? I have spoken to the latter, who is naturally most indignant, and I am not sure that I shall not have you court-martialled for having basely made a false accusation against one of your superiors."

"I have not accused my Sergeant-major, sir," I indignantly replied, "though I was asked to do so by the Sergeant——"

"No further accusations!" interrupted the Captain with severity.

"Sir," I continued, "I do not know what Sergeant de Cormet may have told you; but, if you will allow me, I will repeat to you what I told him, and freely confess all that I have done."

I thereupon once more repeated the story we had concocted.

"But," cried the Captain, "Sergeant de Cormet distinctly told me that you had tried to exculpate yourself by asserting that you went to Paris with your Sergeant-major's leave!"

"I swear to you upon my honour that I never said so, sir!" I replied.

The Captain then sent for de Cormet, and told him that I denied having tried to excuse myself by alleging that I had permission from the Sergeant-major.

"Didn't you tell me," said de Cormet, "that you were not reported missing on the Sunday because you had leave from your Sergeant-major?"

"Certainly," I replied; "I was excused by him from attending stables, but I distinctly told you that I had no other leave: you know it quite well, Sergeant, as you——"

"Oh," quickly interrupted de Cormet, addressing the Captain, "I suppose, sir, that I misunderstood what Decle told me."

"But didn't he tell you," replied the Captain, "how he deceived the Sergeant of the Week by making a sham figure in his bed?"

"Yes, sir, I remember now," said de Cormet quietly.

"I am afraid that you were too kind to Decle," said the Captain, "and that you wanted to save him from a severe punishment, and it did not strike you that if I had found out that Sergeant-major Vaillant had given him leave I would unhesitatingly have asked the Colonel to reduce him to the rank of Sergeant. As to Decle, I will begin by giving him four days' prison, and I will draw up a report at once, which you will take to the Colonel."

I had to hand the whole of my kit to the Sergeant *fourrier*, and was then led to the prison. The *Adjudant* came to inform me, later on, that the Colonel had altered my punishment to eight days' prison and eight days' cells in solitary confinement. All punishments have to be accompanied by an explanation, showing the reasons why the punishment has been inflicted, and in all cases involving prison the punishment has to be reported to the Major-general in command of the brigade to which the regiment belongs. Here are the reasons for my punishment as they appeared in the Regimental Orders of the day:—

" The trooper Decle," said the Colonel in the Regimental Orders, " will be punished with eight days' prison, and eight days' cells, for having infamously deceived the Sergeant of the Week by making a dummy in his bed— for having gone to Paris without leave in civilian clothes and in disguise—and for having, notwithstanding the orders previously issued, applied to his Sergeant-major for leave not to attend stables instead of demanding such leave from the Sergeant in charge of the *Volontaires;* for having further deceived the Sergeant of the Week in getting another trooper to make a dummy in his bed, and for having returned to barracks over the wall. This trooper is warned that unless he amends soon his conduct the Colonel will be under the painful necessity of sending him before a *Conseil de discipline.*" (See p. 32.)

TROOPER 3809

When the *Adjudant* came to communicate this order to me he promised that he would not let me be put in solitary confinement, but that I should spend the fortnight over which my punishment extended in the common prison. He also promised to give orders that a steak should be brought to me from the canteen and placed on the top of my daily rations. He added that as he was being relieved from duty that day he would recommend me to the other *Adjudants*, and that my punishment would begin with prison, so that when he took " the week " again on the next Monday he could see about arranging that I should not be put in solitary confinement. The worst consequence of the punishment I had just received was that it prevented me from entertaining any hope of being released from active military service after the first examination of the *Volontaires*, and I knew that in future I should be treated still more harshly than before.

I was chiefly indignant with Corporal Lormand. To think that a schoolfellow of mine, who professed to be my friend, who had accepted luncheon from me the previous day, could have been mean enough to denounce me! To think that, although he had gone to Paris without leave, in civilian attire, like myself, he was not punished, but congratulated by the Captain for having " given me away "! All this made me ask myself whether such a thing as common justice existed in the French army.

I have seen a great deal of the world since. Years have elapsed since all this happened, but from all I have heard from young fellows who have served their time but recently, the system is still just the same. The bullying of privates by Corporals and Sergeants is as bad as in my time, the officers are jealous of each other, and, instead of encouraging privates so as to make them love their *metier,* they plot and scheme to get promotion, while the Corporals and Sergeants chiefly strive to find or manufacture defaulters, well knowing that by so doing they will attract their chiefs' attention, and thus get advancement.

CHAPTER XV

WHEN I was sent to prison there were four other troopers undergoing a similar punishment, but I did not see anything of them until the call for "Soup," as they were kept out all day on fatigue duty and punishment drill. Before they returned the *Adjudant* came again to see me, and advised me to go to the medical visit the following morning. He told me that he had seen the doctor, and laid my case before him, and that the doctor had promised to exempt me from punishment drill and from fatigue duty. He sent me too, at my request, some paper and ink, and all the books we had to study for our examinations. I had also smuggled into the prison Conway's admirable little guide-book to the highest peaks of the chain of Monte Rosa, which I meant to translate into French to while away the time. I also went with the Corporal of the Guard to fetch a straw mattress and a blanket, to which, as previously explained, a prisoner is entitled. In the evening I asked the Corporal of the Guard to put my name down for the medical visit of the next morning.

When the other prisoners returned for their dinner, they were much astonished to find a *Volontaire* as their companion. Most of them were undergoing prison for having *tiré une bordée* (having been absent without leave during five days, and having remained away up to the very last limit they could reach without being proclaimed deserters). These men were thoroughly bad characters, and very different from Titi and Piatte, who were mere dare-devils; for Titi himself, though he had been in prison several times before he joined the regiment, had never been convicted for anything worse than street broils. The awful life of immorality he had led before coming to the regiment was due chiefly to the surroundings among which he had been brought up, but notwithstanding his failings, the fellow would never have committed a theft, and I would not have hesitated to trust him with any amount of money. My present prison companions, however, were of a very different type. None of them, it is true, had been convicted before joining the army, but I soon gathered from their conversation that it was through sheer luck that they had escaped so far. Of course, as I was a common trooper like them, and in prison, they spoke quite openly of their past life before me, and even bragged of their misdeeds *pour m'épater*. One of them, the fellow who had received so severe a punishment from his comrades when he was thrashed and tossed in a blanket in the riding-school, had never ceased to speak of the treatment he had received, and he used to swear that if, when his time was out, he ever came across one of his assailants, he would put a knife into him.

While we were eating our food he returned once more to the subject, and when I told him not to brag so much about what he would do, he got quite indignant.

"You don't believe me, old chap," he exclaimed; "why, don't imagine that it would be the first time! Many are the times when I have *chouriné* (stabbed) a bloke. Me and two others we were for a long time in *les boulevards extérieurs* (a part of Paris which at that time was still most dangerous), and a pretty good haul we sometimes made. I remember once an old woman was going home late at night—we knew her well—she owned a good lot of property, and she had been to collect her rents that day. One of us followed her the whole day, and in the evening he came to tell us that she had gone to dinner with her daughter. You bet, we kept a lookout for her. At ten o'clock, sure enough, there she comes. The *sergots* had just turned up a side-street to make their rounds, and we knew that the coast would be clear for at least a quarter of an hour. We hid in a doorway, and as she passed us Bibi le Mufle jumps on her from behind, while the other chap who was with me lands her one in the mouth. We laid her on the ground, and I was searching her pocket when she begins to kick up the devil's own row, and shouts ' Murder! Police! ' I couldn't find anything in her pockets, and just then a bloke who had heard her giving tongue comes along, and he begins shouting ' Police! Murder! ' ' Oh,' I says, ' I'll soon give him murder.' What does a bloke deserve who comes and interferes with gentlemen at their business? So I rush at him and I soon stopped his howling with a jab from my *Eustace* (slang word used for big knife). The others, who were busy searching the old woman, never noticed the police who had come round, and although I shouted to warn them that ' *les pantes* ' (the police) were coming, they couldn't make tracks in time. Bibi le Mufle tried to run away, but unfortunately he fell over my bloke, and they collared him there. They accused him of having done for the chap, but he swore that it wasn't true. The old woman recovered, and so did the bloke, and you'd never guess what that man did. He swore that it was Bibi le Mufle who had stabbed him. And the old woman, who was stupid-like when she recovered, swore that only two chaps had attacked her. The others behaved like bricks, they never gave me away, and so I got up a collection to get them a good counsel, and they only got three years; so you see, old chap, I am not afraid to use my knife, and I swear to God that some day or other I'll have the life of one of them chaps who knocked me about as they have, and, what's more," he concluded, "*j'en ai soupé du régiment* (I am sick of the regiment), and I mean to make a clean bolt of it the moment I get out of prison."

It will be seen that my prison companions were not very desirable acquaintances.

When I went to the medical visit the following morning, the doctor took me apart, and asked me to tell him exactly what I had done to be treated with such extreme severity. I began to tell him the same story as I had told my Captain, but he stopped me.

"I know," he said, "that you are humbugging me. I heard part of the truth from your Sergeant-major, and you may trust to my word that whatever you tell me will go no further."

I therefore told him exactly what had happened, and the part Sergeant de Cormet had played.

The doctor replied that it looked as if my Sergeant meant to drive me to do something desperate, and he added that he was determined to put a stop to it. He had already given special orders excusing me from fatigue duty and punishment drill, and at my request he also ordered that an extra blanket should be given me. He added that he was disgusted at the way in which I was being treated, that my constitution was being ruined by the harsh treatment I was subjected to, and that he considered that I was unfit for service under such conditions.

When I returned to prison my fellow-prisoners were doing punishment drill in the barrack-yard, and I felt glad to be rid of their company for the time being. I was busy all day translating Conway's book, and the time passed almost pleasantly, as I had at least nobody to bully me. The following day was Sunday, and my fellow-prisoners were only taken out in the morning, so that their society was inflicted upon me the whole day. De Lanoy, who was on guard that day, came to pay me a visit, and took me into the corridor leading into the prison to have a chat with me. I heard some startling news from him—how two Sergeants who had just re-enlisted and received their premium of £24 had deserted, as also had two or three troopers. He brought me a novel, and advised me to cut off the strings of the binding and to hide the bulk of it inside a loaf of bread, keeping out only a dozen pages at a time, so that in case the Captain of the Week should visit the prison I could hide these pages inside my shirt, and should they be discovered by the officer I could say that it was waste paper. His advice proved excellent, as that very afternoon the Major came to visit the prison. He inquired what all the books I had were, and I replied that they were the regulation books we had to study, and that I had been allowed to bring them into prison so as not to waste my time. I had carefully hidden in a dark corner Conway's little book and inserted the pages of my translation into my blotting-pad, so that I was not found out. The Major felt me all over, and made me produce the paper inside my shirt, but seeing only a few loose leaves he did not take any more notice of it.

During the night Piatte and Titi were marched into the place. When the door had been closed upon them a candle was lit, and Titi embraced me with transports of joy, being evidently in high spirits.

"Ah, what fun, old fellow!" he cried out. "It's too funny, you know."

"What have you been up to again?" I asked.

Piatte, who was also roaring with laughter, said, "I'll

show you." He was in full uniform, and proceeded to take off his tunic, an example which was followed by Titi. When they had removed their garments I saw to my amazement that they were both dressed in acrobatic fleshings.

I could not help laughing, and asked what on earth it meant.

"Well," said Titi, "we both got midnight leave, and as a fair was going on we thought we would go and have a look round. We soon came across a big tent. 'Twas the wrestlers' place, and so I says to Piatte, 'Let's go in.' It only cost 50 centimes for the first rows, and in we went. They were not a grand lot, you know, these chaps, and Piatte says to me, 'Why, I could knock any one of them down with one hand.' 'Oh,' I says, 'I don't say that I would do it with one hand, but I would jolly well manage to bowl over any one of the boiling.' Just then the boss steps into the middle of the ring and says, holding a basket full of five-franc pieces, 'Now, gentlemen, if there is any one among you who would like to back himself against me, I'll undertake, if he manages to down me, to hand over to him the contents of this here basket —one hundred francs!' . . . Nobody moved, so I says to Piatte, 'Shall we have a go?' But Piatte, he says, 'Oh, we can't go in uniform.' So I says, 'I'll soon settle that,' and I went behind the tent, and I tell one of the chaps to call the Guv'nor. 'Look here,' I said, 'did you mean what you said just now?' 'I did,' says the boss. 'Well, then, there's my chum and me, we'd both like to have a try, but you see this is how things stand—we can't wrestle in uniform, but if you will lend us a costume we are game.'

"'Oh,' says the Guv'nor, 'I can do that, but if so, I can only give you twenty-five francs if you downs me, and in case you don't, you will have to deposit five francs for the loan of the costume.'

"Piatte says he is quite game, but the Guv'nor must make it five francs for the two. He agrees to this, and he takes us to his caravan, where we change our things. While we are doing this, the Guv'nor he had gone back to the ring, and announced that two distinguished ammytoors had accepted the challenge, he also goes to the outside of his shanty and shouts out, 'There's going to be a grand match of ammytoors *versus* professionals!'

"At the end of a few minutes he comes and calls us. 'Of course,' he says, 'you can't both come on at the same time—which one of you will come first?'

"'I'll go first,' Piatte says.

"'By gad,' the Guv'nor then exclaims, as Piatte got up from the corner where he was sitting. 'By gad, you ain't much of a show in uniform, but you are a strappin' un in fleshings. Too heavy a bit, and clumsy-like, but you are the kind of chap I like to measure myself with.' So they goes to the ring, and the Guv'nor presents Piatte as the distinguished ammytoor who is going to have a go. Piatte makes his bow to the spectators, and the fun begins. I watched it from a chink in the tent. At first I didn't like the look of things. He was a fine chap the Guv'nor, and he was on his mettle; he had got scientific ways too, which told heavily on Piatte, but for all that he did not last long, and Piatte felled his man. The crowd got mad like at seeing the Guv'nor fairly beaten, and they gave Piatte a real ovation. Piatte, business-like, he catches hold of a hat, and makes a collection among the spectators. He got fifteen francs, my boy, and with the twenty-five francs he had won, that made forty. Now came my turn, but when I was brought into the ring and presented to the ladies and gentlemen, I noticed two of our Lieutenants and a Captain who marches in just then. I couldn't go away, but I says to myself that they will never recognise me, and we begin to wrestle. The Guv'nor was tired, and he matched me with another chap. My boy, 'twas a fight! It lasted more than twenty minutes, but at last I downed my man, downed him straight and square, and laid him on the two shoulders. When he gets up, the Guv'nor, who felt sick like at having lost his money, shouts 'Foul!' All the spectators took my part, and the officers got quite excited, and said he would have to pay the money whether he liked or not. Piatte, whose blood was up, he jumped into the ring and threatened to go for the Guv'nor if he didn't fork out at once. Seeing how things stood, the Guv'nor says as he'll abide by the decision of the officers, so they jump into the ring. They hadn't recognised me or Piatte up to then, and it was only when one of them comes near me to tell me that I'm in the right, that he stops suddenly, and stares at me, and cries, 'Why! you're a Dragoon!'

" I was so taken aback that at first I didn't know what to say, but seeing that none of the officers belonged to our squadron, I said at last, quite bold like, 'Dragoon! sir! You're making a mistake.'

" The officer, a Lieutenant, then turns to the Captain and the other Lieutenant, and says, 'Why, look, this chap's a Dragoon!'

"' D—d good fellow, if he is,' said the other Lieutenant.

"' Maybe,' says the Captain, ' but we can't have him disgracing his uniform in this way.' He then whispered something to the Lieutenants, and while they were talking, Piatte sneaked out and went to dress. I slipped off too, but the Captain followed me and caught me up at the steps of the caravan.

"'It is thus then,' he said, 'that you disgrace your uniform.'

"'Beg your pardon, sir,' I says, 'but I didn't disgrace my uniform, for I had no uniform on.' It was a pity I said that, because it made the Captain real mad.

"'You have the impertinence to reply!' he then cries out; 'I had come here only to lecture you, but as you dare answer me I'll punish you. You will have eight days' *Salle de Police* for having exhibited yourselves in public in a disgraceful way.' Just then he caught sight of Piatte. 'Hallo! here's another one!' he says. 'You shall have eight days, too.'

"'Well, sir,' I says, 'if you will just allow me to say so, it was me who answered you, and I didn't mean any impertinence, but if you remember, you said that you only wanted to give me a lecture, and 'twas only because I answered you that you punished me, so would you mind only punishing me, because Piatte there never answered anything.'

"'You are a plucky one,' said the Captain, 'and a good comrade, but I am sorry that I can't do what you ask me. You both have been guilty of the same offence, and you must both be punished, but I'll reduce your punishment to four days' *Salle de Police*.'

"He then wrote something on a card, and told me to give it to the Sergeant of the Guard. 'Twas an order to put us in the lock-up there and then, and you see we had dressed in such a hurry that we forgot to take off our fleshings, and when the Guv'nor came to ask for them, the Captain, who had waited until we were dressed, told us to go straight to barracks as we were, and I told the Guv'nor that he would get back his fleshings when he had paid us the 50 francs he owed us. But it was rare fun, my boy," concluded Titi.

The following day Titi and Piatte were brought back to the cells at eleven o'clock in the morning, the Colonel having upon the Captain's report altered their punishment into fifteen days' prison.

During the next few days the *Salle de Police* was so crowded at night that, with the exception of the seven prisoners, each of whom had a straw mattress and thus his place marked out, the troopers were so crammed together that they had to lie down on the planks huddled together like herrings in a box.

I had already been twelve days in prison when I began to feel extremely ill. I was suffering from fever and dysentery, probably due to the vitiated air of the place, and it is a wonder to me now how we all escaped typhoid fever. I asked for the doctor, and when he had examined me, he gave orders that I should be immediately removed to hospital, where I was detained for a fortnight before I recovered.

In February came the usual examination, after which the Captain told me that he had hoped to be able to discharge me from the service then, but that my behaviour prevented his doing so. I need not describe for a second time the drudgery of our daily work, which was a mere repetition of what I had gone through the previous year. De Cormet never allowed a week to pass without sending me to the *Salle de Police* on some pretext or other. Lieutenant Amy had also taken a great dislike to me, but I am bound to confess that he never punished me except on one occasion. It was during the month of March; I had been ordered to command the company, and I had to get executed the movement of "Shoulder arms." I was reciting the theory, and explaining the movement as stated in the regulations, when Sergeant de Cormet interrupted me in the middle of my explanation, and told me that I was wrong. He made me begin again, and when I once more reached the passage where he had interrupted me, he asked why I altered the text of the regulations. I replied that I did so because the previous year Sergeant Legros had made us alter the passage, and had made us learn it as I was then reciting it. "So," cried out de Cornet, "now you take it upon yourself to alter the regulations which have been drawn up by the highest authorities in the army!"

"No, Sergeant," I said, "I have not taken it upon myself, but was told to do so."

"Don't tell lies," retorted the Sergeant; "you will have four days' *Salle de Police* for not knowing your theory."

"But, Sergeant," I said, "you can inquire from Sergeant-major Legros whether I am telling you the truth or not."

"You dare answer!" shouted the Sergeant. Just then Lieutenant Amy came along, and, hearing a row, inquired what was the matter. "It's Decle, of course, sir," de Cornet told him.

"What has he done?" queried the Lieutenant.

"The gentleman finds that the regulations are not correct, and he takes it upon himself to correct them, and has the impertinence to answer me that they are written in bad French."

"I am sick of the fellow," replied the Lieutenant; "are you mad, Decle?" he asked.

"No, sir," I answered very calmly, "and I wish to observe that Sergeant de Cornet has not correctly reported what I just now said to him."

"You scoundrel!" exclaimed the Lieutenant. "You have the impudence to tell me that your Sergeant is a liar! You will have four days' prison." I knew by experience that to complain, or appeal to the Colonel, would only mean an increase of my punishment, and I therefore quietly prepared myself to go to prison when I returned to barracks. The overcrowding of the *Salle de Police* had become so great by that time that a special lock-up was used for the prisoners, which was similar to the *Salle*, but much smaller. I had once more Titi for a companion, as he had been up to some more tricks, and he was waiting his trial before *Conseil de discipline*, which had been convened to decide whether he should be sent to a punishment battalion in Africa to finish his time of service there. He didn't feel much depressed at the idea. " It will be a change, old chap," he used to say to me, " and I don't suppose that I shall be bullied there more than I am here; besides, I have only one year and a half more to serve, and that will soon be over." It was this fact which saved him, and he was acquitted by a majority of one, although the General bestowed sixty days' prison on him for his last prank. (He had for the third time absconded for five days.)

I had taken Conway's book to the prison, in order to finish its translation, and only ten pages more were left, when one of the Majors happened to walk in. The door stood open to admit the trooper who was bringing our food, and I had no time to put away my MS. The Major pounced upon it. " That's how you occupy your time," he said; " give me all those papers." I had to hand them over to him, and he tore them up and chucked the pieces into the slop-pail. So ended my first literary attempt.

The four days I spent in prison, coupled with the moral state of despair into which I had fallen, had pretty well broken me down in health. I suffered from incessant headaches and rheumatic pains, and I had to be sent to hospital once more on coming out of prison.

All my thoughts were by that time concentrated upon

devising some means of leaving the hell the regiment had become to me. Desertion was out of the question, not that it would have been difficult for me to pass into Belgium, or cross over to England, but I had too much respect for myself and my family to turn a common deserter.

CHAPTER XVI

I HAVE omitted to mention that in compliance with the regulations I had been obliged before being taken to the prison to hand over to my Sergeant-major whatever money or jewellery I had at the time. Accordingly I handed over to Sergeant-major Vaillant my gold watch and chain, £30 in bank-notes, and two valuable rings, only keeping with me a few pounds in gold and silver, which I carefully hid. The day before I was to leave prison, the Sergeant-major came to see me, and explained that as he was going away on leave he wanted to give me back my belongings. This he did, and he further reminded me that he owed me a long-standing gambling debt of £5, and this he also handed over to me. He added that he might be a long time away, and that I could render him a great service by lending him some civilian clothes. He had allowed me to keep in his room a suit of clothes and an overcoat, and I told him that he was very welcome to them. I also offered to lend him some money, and suggested his paying me the gambling debt on his return; but he absolutely refused to accept either offer. He then bade me good-bye, and I thought no more of the matter until a week later, when de Lanoy having come to see me in hospital, startled me by saying that Sergeant-major Vaillant had deserted, having absconded the day before I left prison, and that he was further accused by the Captain of having stolen 31 francs from the monies belonging to the squadron. I assured de Lanoy that it was quite impossible that Vaillant should have stolen the money, and I told him how he had repaid me the large amount I had entrusted him with, and even £5 that he owed me, and de Lanoy agreed with me that if 32 francs (about 25s.) was missing from the squadron money it was a pure mistake, and not a theft. The following day Captain Hermann, who, as will be remembered, was in command of our squadron, came to the hospital and walked to my bed.

"I am afraid, Decle," he began, "that you are going to find yourself in Queer Street. You probably know that Sergeant-major Vaillant has deserted, but I should like to know if you are aware that he has run off with money belonging to the squadron, and that he has further stolen your civilian clothes?"

"Yes, sir," I said, "I heard that Sergeant-major Vaillant had deserted; but he has not stolen my clothes, for the good reason that I lent them to him; and I don't believe either that he has stolen any money from the squadron."

"Just so," said the Captain; "what you have told me fully confirms my information. You have helped the Sergeant-major to desert, and you have given him £30 to help him to do so."

I grew indignant. "I do not know, sir," I replied, "where you derived your information from. Far from having received money from me, the Sergeant-major came to me while I was in prison and returned the £30 I had entrusted him with, together with my jewellery, when I was sent to prison, so that you see that you have been quite misinformed."

"It's all very well for you to say so," replied the Captain, "but I have only your word for it, while I have distinct information that you lent him £30, and that further he stole your clothes, and that you did not lend them to him. Of course you must remember that if it is proved that you lent the Sergeant-major the money I have mentioned, you will be court-martialled as an accessory to his desertion. If you want, however, to avoid the serious consequences of your act, I am prepared to overlook it provided that you swear that Sergeant-major Vaillant has stolen your clothes."

"I am sorry I cannot do so, sir," I replied, "as that would be committing perjury. I have previously lent the Sergeant-major my clothes on several occasions, and I also lent them to him in the present instance. As to being court-martialled for having lent him £30, I am in no way afraid of the consequences, for I can prove by my solicitor's account that I did not lend him the money, unless I stole it myself. In fact," I added, "I can produce at once the very bank-notes he handed over to me." And so saying, I pulled my pocket-book from under the pillow, and showed the Captain the money.

"Oh," he said, "I know you've got money, but that does not prove that you did not lend the £30. However, you can please yourself; I have warned you, and whatever happens will be your own fault."

"Yes, sir," I answered, "I fully understand."

The Captain retired, but a quarter of an hour later he returned and insisted upon my swearing that the Sergeant-major had stolen my clothes. He even went so far as to promise me, or at least to make me understand, that if I pleased him in the matter, he would see that I was released from the regiment after the following examination. But I was obdurate, and frankly told the Captain that I quite understood his motives, and realised why he was so anxious that I should give testimony as to the theft of my clothes, for otherwise he would not be able to obtain Vaillant's extradition from whatever country he might have taken refuge in, and I once more declared that whatever might be the consequences I would not commit perjury.

The Captain retired in great wrath. The following day the doctor told me that I would have to be at the *gendarmerie* at two o'clock.

When I arrived there I found an old Corporal of the *gendarmes* sitting at a table, with another *gendarme* standing near him. He asked for my name, regimental number, and, as usual in France, I had also to give him full particulars about my father and mother. Having taken all this down, he told me to put up my right hand, and to swear to tell the truth and nothing but the truth. Having thus administered the oath to me he began to question me.

"You had a suit of civilian clothes?" he first asked.

"Well," I replied, "I had, and still have, a good many."

"Why do you have a good many?"

"Because I did not always wear the same suit."

"But you had a suit of clothes which has been stolen from you by the Sergeant-major Vaillant?"

"No," I said, "I have had no suit of clothes stolen from me. I lent Sergeant-major Vaillant a suit of clothes, if that is what you are driving at."

"What!" exclaimed the *gendarme*, evidently much astonished, "how can you say that Sergeant-major Vaillant did not steal a suit of clothes from you when your Captain says he did!"

"I don't know what the Captain says," I replied, "and what he says does not concern me. I am here on my oath, I have sworn to tell the truth, and all you have to do is to take down my words."

"What am I to do?" said the old Corporal, turning

helplessly to his subordinate. "This is a most serious matter. How on earth can I write down that a Dragoon swears that he has had no clothes stolen when his Captain says they have been stolen! That is what discipline has come to nowadays," he went on. "When I was in the Guards, if my Captain had said to me, 'Bouchard, some one has stolen your clothes,' I should have said, 'Yes, sir!' But now, if the Colonel himself were to say to a trooper, 'You're a nigger,' the fellow would reply that he was a white man. And these are the men who are going to lick the Prussians! It breaks my old heart to see such goings on."

"Corporal," I insisted, "whether you like it or not you will have to write down what I say. If you won't I shall decline to sign the declaration, and shall state in writing the reason for my refusal."

"I think you had better take down what he says," suggested the *gendarme,* and the Corporal, with a sigh, proceeded to write out my deposition.

I gave a full account of all I knew about the matter, pointing out that my Sergeant-major had, before leaving, returned a large sum of money I had entrusted to him; finally, having read my deposition through carefully, I signed it.

When the old *gendarme* learned incidentally that I had been in prison, he turned to his subordinate and cried exultingly, "Of course he has! Of course! I knew all along he was a bad un!"

And after I had signed the declaration he could not refrain from a farewell shot. "Now, youngster," he said impressively, "mark my words, for I don't make a mistake often—you'll come to a bad end. It's always the case with fellows who don't respect their betters. You begin with the regimental prison; then, when your time is up, you soon get a month or two, then a year, and it's not long before you are sent to La Nouvelle,* and, if you don't get a 'lifer,' it's ten to one 'The Widow'† ends your days."

With these encouraging words the *gendarme* dismissed me, and the Sergeant took me back to the hospital, chaffing me unmercifully all the way.

I soon discovered that the Captain had only threatened me with a court-martial in order to try and induce me to place documents in his hands which would enable him to obtain an extradition warrant against Vaillant, who was known to have taken refuge in Belgium. My deposition defeated his object, but I afterwards heard that two years later Vaillant surrendered, and was only sentenced to twelve months' imprisonment.

The charge against him of stealing money belonging to the squadron was withdrawn, my testimony showing that he had no inducement to commit a petty theft.

When I left the hospital I entered once more on my duties with the other *Volontaires*, but although I did my best to avoid punishments, I was a "marked man." I had the misfortune too of being senior *Volontaire*, so that whenever we were left without Sergeant or Corporal in the schoolroom I was held responsible in case the others caused a disturbance or indulged in horseplay.

One Saturday—kit inspection day—I discovered, when I returned from the stables in the morning, that my greatcoat had been stolen. It was the only article of outfit of which I had no duplicate, and after searching for it throughout the room I could not find it. I reported the matter to de Lanoy, my Sergeant, and he promised that

* New Caledonia, where convicts sentenced to *travaux forcés* (penal servitude) are sent.
† The guillotine.

when all the great-coats were unrolled before the inspection he would carefully examine the numbers. Although he did this he was, however, unable to trace it. When the officer came to pass the inspection, de Lanoy duly reported the matter to him, but the Lieutenant merely said that I had no business to have my great-coat stolen, and gave me eight days' *Salle de Police*. I was determined to find the thief, and after making careful inquiries, I learnt by accident that a trooper from the fourth squadron had been through our room while we were at morning stables. I heard this while we were coming back from afternoon stables, and I accordingly rushed to the fellow's room, and pulling down the great-coat which was rolled up and placed on the shelf above his bed, I unrolled it, and found that it was my own. Just then the trooper, a Parisian rough, came into the room, and asked me with a volley of oaths what the devil I was doing there. I was in no mood to stand abuse, and I replied in forcible language that he was a thief, and had stolen my great-coat. Thereupon he struck at me, and we had a fierce fight. Twice he knocked me down, and the second time he kicked me viciously before I could rise: we had closed once more, and I had given him a blow which made his teeth rattle, when the Sergeant-major of his squadron, hearing the disturbance, walked into the room. He separated us, and gave each of us four days' *Salle de Police* for fighting in the room. I tried to explain to him what had taken place, but he would not listen to me, and sent me back to my room, where I retired—with my great-coat.

The following day the Colonel ordered " that the troopers Gerbal and Decle, who had fought in the room, would fight a duel on the Monday morning in the riding-school."

I have omitted to mention that all troopers at the end

of six months had to spend one hour every week in the fencing school, where they were taught fencing with the sword and the foils. A good many of the *Volontaires* used also to take extra lessons, and, for my own part, I used to take one daily. The moment I heard that I was to fight a duel on the following day, I went to the fencing-master to ask his advice. He told me that we should have to fight with cavalry swords, not, however, of the kind we were accustomed to use, but with old-fashioned swords of the 1810 pattern. He produced one of these—I had never seen such an unwieldy weapon. The blade was about four feet long, and when you held the sword in your hand, it was so badly balanced that all the weight seemed to be thrown towards the point. The fencing-master explained to me that in regimental duels all strokes were legitimate from the head down to the knee. He then made me practise with the sword in question, but although I was a pretty good fencer, I confess that I was at first absolutely at sea with the weapon I had in my hand. In the evening I took an extra lesson, and got a little more accustomed to the use of the cumbrous sword.

The encounter was to take place at 10 A.M. Each of us had selected a second, and we were told to come to the riding-school in stable costume, being allowed to use whatever shoes we liked. When I arrived with my second I found the two doctors present, with half a dozen officers and the fencing-master, who had brought the swords. We were told to strip to the waist, our weapons were handed over to us, and the fencing-master having put us on guard, stood between us, holding in his hand a scabbard with which he was supposed to stop any deadly stroke. My adversary was a regular bully, and of course a coward, and had imbibed a large quantity of brandy to brace himself up, and when we were placed in position

I noticed that he was flushed, and that he was shaking all over. His second, noticing the state he was in whispered to him, " Buck up, old man ; don't be afraid."

" Afraid," he replied aloud, " I ain't afraid: it's the cold that gives me the shivers."

He was sharply rebuked and warned that he must remain silent. The fencing-master then released our swords, which he held crossed, and gave us the signal " Go." I made a few feints and could have easily touched my opponent, but I meant to inflict a serious injury on the ruffian, and did not take advantage of the chances he gave me. The beginning of the duel was rather a farce, as the fellow kept jumping back whenever I made a feint, and at the end of a minute or two he had already retreated ten paces. The fencing-master ordered us to stop, and warned him that if he went on retreating in that way he would stick him in a corner. We were then placed once more in position, and the second round began. My adversary showed a little more pluck this time, and the moment the signal was given he made a cut at my head, but I easily parried it, and in doing so my sword slightly scratched his arm; we had closed, and I was watching the moment when he would step back, to slip my sword alongside his and with a " *une, deux* " to stick him in the ribs. Just then, however, his second noticed a drop of blood on his arm, and the duel was once more stopped. The doctor came forward to examine the " wound," but he declared that it was just a scratch, and that we must go on. My adversary raised strong objections to this decision, saying that the duel being *au premier sang* (to be stopped the moment blood was drawn), and blood having been drawn, he acknowledged that he was beaten, and that ought to put an end to it, as he was not at all keen to bleed me. The officers, the fencing-master, and even his second could not help laughing, and the fencing-master, without replying, placed us once more in position, and for the third time gave us the signal "Go." I was getting very tired, the weight of the sword telling heavily on my wrist, and I determined to put a speedy end to the encounter. I made a series of quick feints, and as the man uncovered himself well I quickly raised my sword to strike him a *coup de flanc* which would have cut him along the chest from the shoulder to the waist; seeing this the fencing-master put up his scabbard to stop the blow, and instead of striking the man my sword fell on the fencing-master's scabbard, and just as the fencing-master cried "Halt!" my adversary, taking advantage of my defenceless position, stuck the point of his sword in my wrist. The duel was at once stopped, and I dropped my sword, my fingers becoming instantly benumbed.

The doctor bandaged my arm and sent me to the dispensary. It was of course a cowardly act, deliberately done, but the same thing constantly happens in military duels, and even when the two adversaries fight quite fairly. Good fencers have hardly any chance, as the fencing-master, who is responsible for the conduct of the duel, has to stop any strokes which may possibly endanger the life of one of the adversaries, and when he stops the sword of one of them, the other may not stop in time, and he thus wounds the first. In my case things were still worse, as my adversary had deliberately stuck me while I was incapable of defending myself, my sword resting on the fencing-master's scabbard. I must, however, acknowledge that the officers who were present at the duel reported what had taken place, and the ruffian with whom I had been fighting was punished with thirty days' prison. Had I been fairly wounded I should have had eight days' *Salle de Police* myself for having fought a duel under orders, as in my time it was customary to punish the wounded man, absurd as this may appear.

Military duels are certainly a most ridiculous custom, as ridiculous indeed as Parliamentary duels. It is well known beforehand that neither of the adversaries will be seriously hurt, and therefore the point of fighting at all seems obscure. The idea is, I believe, that duelling acts as a deterrent to fights between soldiers—Frenchmen, like most citizens of the other Continental nations, considering the use of fists a low and degrading way of settling a quarrel. Duels between officers are also frequent, but they can only fight if they hold the same rank; for instance, no Captain can fight a duel with a Lieutenant, nor can a Major challenge a Captain. Officers must in any case obtain their Colonel's leave to fight. No officer, challenged by one of his comrades, would dare to refuse to fight; if he did so, he would probably be severely punished by the Colonel and sent to Coventry by his comrades.

When I reached the dispensary my wound was thoroughly washed. It was only then that it began to hurt me; when the sword penetrated my wrist I did not feel it in the least, the only sensation I had being that of sudden numbness in the fingers. On examination the wound proved more serious than it had appeared at first, several of the tendons having been severed. I was therefore detained at the infirmary, and after a couple of days inflammation set in, this being due, I believe, to the fact that during one of the stoppages which had occurred in the course of the duel my adversary had stuck his sword in the ground. It must also be remembered that antiseptics were not known then as they are now, so that my wound had only been washed with a solution of salt and water. This duel (if such a name can be given to such a farce) was, I may add, the first and the last I ever fought or shall fight. It seems incredible that such an absurd custom should subsist among civilised nations. It is due, I suppose, to the lack of means of redress found in the Continental laws in case of slander or libel. In France, for instance, men in a prominent position are daily insulted and dragged through the mire by unscrupulous journalists (some newspapers making it even a specialty to get hold of society scandals and subsisting upon the hush-money they extort from their victims), yet it is very seldom that action is taken in the courts. It is no exaggeration to say that there are hundreds of men in France who would each have recovered damages amounting to at least one million sterling if all the libels which have appeared against them in the French papers within the last ten years had been published in the English press and brought before a British jury. As it is, £20 damages are considered very substantial. This may partly explain why duelling still exists.

CHAPTER XVII

I HAD been a fortnight in the infirmary, when one morning at 10 o'clock one of the Sergeants of my squadron ordered me to dress in tunic and *képi*, saying that he had received orders to take me before the *Conseil*. This word simply means court, and is applied to the *Conseil de discipline* (regimental court-martial) as well as to the *Conseil de réforme* (Invalidation Commission), but I had by that time become so accustomed to threats of being sent before a regimental court-martial, that I could only think of that, and asked the Sergeant on what charge I was going to be tried.

"I can't tell you," he replied, smiling.

He was a friend of mine, and I thought him most heartless to ridicule my trouble. In vain I asked him, while I was dressing, to explain what it meant, but he would not, and tortured me by asking in a jocular way how I would like a change of air and surroundings. At last I lost my temper.

"It's all very fine," I said, "to chaff a fellow when you know that he is going to be sent for three years and a half to hard labour in Algeria. You are simply a brute, that's all I can say."

"But suppose I don't know anything of the kind?" he replied, still smiling. "Why do you think so?"

"Well, I suppose if I am going to be tried before the *Conseil de discipline*——"

TROOPER 3809

"You ass!" he laughingly replied; "who spoke to you of *Conseil de discipline?* Aren't there other *Conseils?*"

I looked astonished.

"Have you never heard of the *Conseil de réforme?*" (Invalidation Commission) he said.

"You don't mean to say——"

"Yes," he replied, "I do mean to say that you are proposed for *invalidation,* and most likely you will cease to be a Dragoon this afternoon."

My heart nearly stopped. The Corporal in charge of the infirmary came in at that moment (I had been put alone in a small ward of only two beds).

"You've heard the news?" he said.

I asked him how it had happened, and how I had not heard of it sooner. He proceeded to explain that, for the last two or three months past, our surgeon had meant to have me invalided, but that the Surgeon-major of the infantry, who was senior surgeon of the district, had always scratched my name off the list, as he had taken a particular dislike to me, and also wished to spite our surgeon, whom he hated. The previous day this infantry surgeon had been suddenly summoned to his mother's bedside in the South of France, so that Surgeon-major Lesage (our own surgeon) was in his absence the head of the medical service, and as such he had included me in the list of men proposed for *invalidation.* My joy knew no bounds, and my only fear was that the Commission would reject the proposal.

I was taken to the hospital with five other Dragoons, and on arriving there we found half a dozen men from the Line regiment, who were also to be examined.

At 11 A.M. the members of the Commission arrived, but we did not see them coming, as they entered the room where we were to be examined by another door.

TROOPER 3809

At the end of a few minutes a Dragoon was called in; he was the Breton of whom I spoke at the beginning of this book, who cried so bitterly at the thought of his cow. Since he had joined the regiment the poor fellow had gradually been sinking, and he was reduced to a mere skeleton. They did not keep him long, and when he came out he was laughing and crying hysterically. " Sergeant," he cried, " oh, Sergeant, let me kiss you! I am going to see her again, my cow, and the hens and the fields, the dear old house!"

He had put his arms round the Sergeant's neck, and was sobbing like a child on his shoulders. He then sat on one of the benches, and kept saying, " I should have died, you know, if they had not sent me home. It's the Blessed Virgin—she has heard my prayers! I prayed so hard to her, and every Sunday I burnt a candle before her altar. I must go and thank her."

He then asked the Sergeant to let him go to the church, but the latter said that he was not allowed to let him leave the hospital until the Commission had retired.

" Then I will thank her here; she will hear all the same." And so saying the poor fellow knelt down and buried his head in his hands, muttering a prayer. It was so genuine, so simple, and yet so beautiful, that not a single one of those coarse soldiers assembled there thought of chaffing him, although he had been unmercifully derided for saying his prayers in the room at the barracks.

In the meantime two other men had been examined, the last one being sent back to his service. Then came the turn of a *Volontaire*, a poor fellow whose knee-cap had been broken. Although the doctors were unanimous in declaring that he would *not be able to walk at all for two years*, and although certificates from two of the greatest French surgeons, who had been sent by his family to operate on him, were produced, stating that he would be lame for life, the Commission refused to invalid him! When my turn came my heart was beating so fast that I could hardly speak.

One of our Majors presided over the Commission, of which the other members were two Captains and four Lieutenants. To my horror, Captain Hermann was one of them. Our Surgeon-major, assisted by the assistant Surgeon-major of the Line regiment, examined each man.

I was presented by Surgeon-major Lesage: "This is Trooper Decle," he said; "he is absolutely unfit for service. He suffers from general weakness of constitution and heart palpitation." The other doctor examined my heart and confirmed my Surgeon-major's diagnosis. The assistant Surgeon-major said that he fully shared Surgeon-major Lesage's views, and was absolutely in favour of my being invalided.

"I should like to listen to the fellow's heart myself," remarked the Major.

"By all means," said the doctor, smiling, for he knew that the Major knew nothing of medicine.

I stood beside the Major and he put his bald head against my chest. Of course my heart was beating furiously, as I was in a blue funk about the decision which would be arrived at.

"I would be sorry to exchange with him," growled the old Major, " he's a regular roarer."

"Well, gentlemen," said the Surgeon-major, "you have heard Major Vian confirm what I told you, and I will ask you to pronounce your decision."

"Allow me to ask you first," said Captain Hermann, "whether the trooper could not do his service in the infantry?"

"I would not have him," replied the infantry doctor.

"But supposing we sent him into the transport service," again suggested Captain Hermann.

"No, sir," replied Surgeon-major Lesage; "you are wasting your time and mine. Invalid him, or don't invalid him—that's for you to decide; but I warn you that if you don't invalid him I shall make him finish his term in hospital."

"Come on, Hermann," said the Major, half asleep, "we have a lot of others to see; let us vote—I want my lunch."

"What do you say?" asked Surgeon-major Lesage from the youngest Lieutenant.

"Oh, invalid him," he quickly replied.

"Yes," said the next Lieutenant.

"Yes," said his neighbour.

"No," replied the fourth Lieutenant, who sat near Captain Hermann.

"Decidedly not," said my Captain.

This looked bad; two nays to three ayes.

"Better invalid him," said the second Captain.

"By all means," murmured the Major with his eyes shut.

I was no longer a trooper! I thought I was going to faint.

"Invalidation No. 1?" queried the doctor.

"Yes, yes," the Major cried, striking his chair with his fist; "but d—— it, let us go on. I want my lunch, and I am off if you don't hurry up."

A form was filled in by the dispensary Corporal acting as clerk: this was signed, and the doctor told me that my papers would be handed over to me in the evening.

When I came out there was no need to ask me what the result was: it was written on my face.

"Must I congratulate you?" asked the Sergeant.

"Yes," I said, shaking him by the hand; "but tell me," I added, "what does 'Invalidation No. 1' mean?"

"You don't mean to say that they have granted you that! Why, man alive! it means a pension of £24 a year for life!"

I was astounded. Half an hour later the Commission had retired, and I suggested stopping at a café on our way back to barracks. The Sergeant assented, and I offered him and my comrades a bottle of champagne to celebrate this glorious day—the happiest day in my existence, I believe. When I returned to the barracks I met Sergeant de Cormet in the yard.

"Where are you coming from?" he cried: "I thought that you were at the infirmary."

"Yes, Sergeant, but I have just come from a turn in the town."

"We shall see about that," he answered.

"I went out on duty, Sergeant."

"I'll make sure of that; but in any case," he sneered, "you won't be always at the infirmary, and when you come out you will soon find yourself in the wrong box."

"I don't think so, Sergeant," I said, laughing; "in fact, I am going to Paris to-night."

"With whose leave, please?"

"Superior authorities," I said.

"If you mean to laugh at me," he replied in angry tones, "I shall have you consigned to prison."

"No, Sergeant, no more *Salle de Police*, prison, or cells for me—in fact, in case I do not see you again, I shall wish you good-bye now, or rather *au revoir*, as I hope I may meet you soon. You see I am no longer a Dragoon: I have just been invalided."

"It can't be," he said, astounded. "*I should have heard of your being proposed for invalidation.*"

"You don't hear everything," I replied; "but if you don't believe me, here comes the dispensary Corporal, and he has my papers."

He did not add a word, and went off shrugging his shoulders eloquently.

The news soon spread through the barracks and many were the congratulations I received.

In the afternoon the Surgeon-major came to the infirmary, where I expressed my deep thanks to him. He told me that I should have to sleep in the barracks again that night, as an error had been made in drawing up my papers, a pension having been granted to me by mistake. As to this I was quite indifferent, for I would willingly have given more than £1000 to have secured my release. The Surgeon-major also advised me to be very careful until I had received my papers, and changed my uniform for civilian clothes, for until this was done I was still under military law. The following morning my papers were handed over to me, and I returned all my outfit to the regimental stores, making a present to Titi and Piatte of all such uniforms and kit as were my personal property.

I gave twenty francs to the troopers of my *peloton* to drink my health, and I did not forget my friends Titi and Piatte. I then took leave of my Sergeants, gave a parting kiss to my charger, and stepped into the street, a free man at last. Half an hour later I had discarded my uniform for ever. Not only had I ceased to be a Dragoon, but I had also altogether ceased to belong to the French army.

A fortnight later I arrived in England, a country I already loved, and, ever since, my life has been spent in travelling through the vast domains of the British Empire; and I feel proud to think that it has fallen to my lot to be numbered among those who have helped to enlighten Englishmen on the glorious work of those great men who have laid the foundation of a gigantic African Empire.

CONCLUSION

It will probably be believed by many readers that in describing my life as a soldier I have at times given the reins to my imagination ; but I can only assure them that this is not the case. I have, fortunately or unfortunately, an excellent memory, and the scenes and conversations I have described are ineffaceably engraved on my mind.

That much of my narrative is occupied with the constantly recurring punishments that befell me, is not my fault—to have slurred over those punishments would have been to paint a misleading picture of my military career, its most salient feature being omitted.

It cannot, at all events, be said with any plausibility that my lot must unfortunately have been cast amongst the scum of the French army. The scum, if any exist, is not to be sought in a cavalry regiment.

Let me, with reference to this point, briefly indicate the relative *status* of the three great branches of the service from an educational point of view. Although it is now possible to secure a commission through the ranks almost as quickly as through the military schools, a preliminary liberal education is absolutely necessary, especially in the cavalry and artillery, as most difficult examinations have to be passed, and the successful candidates must then spend one year in a special military school, as St. Maixant for the infantry, and Saumur for the cavalry. Before leaving the school a final examination has also to be passed in order to obtain a commission. In case of failure in this, candidates are allowed to remain for another year in the school, but, if they are unable to pass at the end of that time, they are sent back to their regiment.

To become an officer without passing through the ranks it is necessary to be admitted to the St. Cyr military school for the infantry and cavalry, and to the *École Polytechnique* for the artillery. At the end of the second year at St. Cyr a competitive examination is undergone, and only those who are at the head of the list have the choice between cavalry and infantry. Those who are thus admitted to serve in the cavalry, spend their third year in a class apart from the Cadets who are to become officers in the Line. At the end of the third year the Cadets pass a final examination, after which they receive their commission. Those who are drafted into the Line at once join a regiment, while those who serve in the cavalry have to spend another year in the cavalry school of Saumur before joining. It will therefore be seen that cavalry officers are, educationally, picked men.

This applies still more strikingly to artillery officers, for these have all passed through the Polytechnic School, the highest engineering school in France. After leaving the Polytechnic they spend a year at the artillery school of Fontainebleau, whence they are drafted into a regiment as full Lieutenants. There are cases of artillery officers having worked their way to a commission through the ranks, but these instances are quite exceptional, and it is very seldom that such officers reach a higher rank than that of Captain. On the contrary, a large percentage of the infantry officers get their commission through the ranks.

That improvements have been effected since my time I gladly admit. The reforms instituted by the much-abused

General Boulanger have been already touched upon, and their value must not be underestimated.

To quote but a few of them—he abolished the *Salle de Police* for non-commissioned officers, replacing it by confinement to the room. He extended from 10 P.M. to 11 P.M. the time at which non-commissioned officers had to be back in barracks, this time being extended to midnight in the case of re-enlisted N.C.O.s. He allowed the latter a higher pay, a separate room, and the right of wearing clothes made of fine cloth of the same quality as that worn by the officers, and gave non-commissioned officers the right to live outside the barracks. He then withdrew from Corporals, Sergeants, and other non-commissioned officers the right of punishing privates with *Salle de Police,* the only punishment they can now inflict being confinement to barracks.

Unfortunately, however, these regulations can be easily evaded, for when a Corporal or a Sergeant wants to send a man to the *Salle de Police* he has only to report him to the Lieutenant of the Week, who hardly ever fails to put down whatever punishment the Corporal or non-commissioned officer asks him to inflict; or, again, if a Corporal or non-commissioned officer wants to have a man punished with *Salle de Police* he has only to give the fellow the maximum number of days of " C.B." (confinement to barracks) he is allowed to give, and justify the punishment by a strong motive, and in that case the Captain will never fail to transform the punishment into lock-up.

General Boulanger also added much to the comfort of privates and Corporals, by ordering that they should have their meals served at table and presided over by a Corporal. The food of the ten to twelve men sitting at each table was to be served in a dish, portions being distributed to each man on an enamelled plate by the Corporal or table president. This regulation, which has remained in force ever since, introduces a great improvement on the way we were fed in my time—as will be obvious from my previous description. Last, but not least, General Boulanger fixed at 9 P.M. instead of 8 P.M., the time at which privates had to return to barracks in the evening. The General's extraordinary popularity is therefore hardly to be wondered at if one remembers that every Frenchman has to be a soldier.

It is, of course, quite clear that one of the greatest blots in the system I have described—that is to say, the system actually adopted, and not the ideal one depicted in the regulations—is that the cavalry officers trust almost entirely to the Sergeants to look after the drill, discipline, and comfort of their men. During my twenty months' service the Colonel did not come fifty times to the barracks, and then rarely stayed there for an hour at a time. Except during the general yearly inspection, the Lieutenant-Colonel or Majors did not pass once a month through our rooms, and then merely marched through them in a perfunctory manner.

The Captain in command of my squadron sometimes, it is true, came to our room, usually on the weekly inspection day, but a fortnight or three weeks often elapsed between his visits. My Lieutenant came to our room on the weekly inspection day, but rarely at other times. None of our officers ever came to look at our food.

As to the drill, until the squadron drilled together the officers hardly ever troubled themselves about it. During the first five months' preliminary training, troopers were left entirely to the care of the Sergeants and Corporals, the Lieutenants looking on for perhaps a few minutes at a time. When, in April, the troopers began to be drilled in squares marked out on the manœuvring ground, the officers used to ride over there, and every quarter of an hour or so glanced at the square where their men were riding under the command of a Sergeant. " Stables " were superintended by the officer of the week, but as in the 1st and 2nd squadrons (as well as in the 4th and 5th) one officer took the week in turn for the two combined squadrons, he could not be expected to see much of what was going on, among the 250 horses or thereabouts he had to superintend. Lieutenants and Sub-lieutenants, except when they were on " week " duty, never came to the stables, so that really everything devolved on the Sergeants, whose power and responsibility were consequently enormous.

Another consequence of the French military system is that officers and rank and file alike are absolutely wanting in that *esprit de corps* which is so remarkable in British regiments. That privates should feel no particular pride in the body to which they are temporarily, and for the most part unwillingly, attached, is not to be wondered at, but in the case of officers a different explanation is forthcoming.

Strange to say, it is a general rule in the French army that officers, on their promotion to a superior rank, are always sent into another regiment (the only exception occurring in the case of Sub-lieutenants, who sometimes —but rarely—remain in the same regiment upon their promotion to the rank of Lieutenant). The consequence of this rule is that an officer who reaches the rank of Colonel has often served in six different regiments. It even often happens, for instance, that a Lieutenant of Dragoons is drafted into the Hussars on his promotion as a Captain, and then passes into the Cuirassiers when he becomes a Major, being transferred to the Chasseurs as

Lieutenant-Colonel, and then being put in command of a regiment of Dragoons as Colonel.

The hard-and-fast lines of social distinction which are drawn between officers of different ranks are also fatal obstacles to the corporate well-being of the regiment. The idea, for instance, that Captains would demean themselves if they sat at the same table with Lieutenants and Sub-lieutenants, and that Majors must also form a separate mess, hinders social intercourse between officers of the different ranks, and seems almost to indicate the possibility of subalterns forgetting themselves in the presence of their superior officers. How different the English system, where all officers mess together, meeting in the simple equality of gentlemen!

There is a general idea in France that German soldiers are subjected to a much stricter discipline than French soldiers, and that German officers may strike their men and treat them like slaves. I believe this was so at the time of the Franco-Prussian War, for I then saw such acts of barbarity committed by officers; but the present system is very different. To begin with, no punishment can be inflicted by a non-commissioned officer or even by a Lieutenant, Captains alone having the right to punish; and I even saw a case, during one of my numerous visits to Germany, when the Captain commanding a company was severely reprimanded by his Colonel, who withdrew from him the right of punishment altogether, because there were too many men punished under his command; the Colonel arguing, with much force, that if an offi ld not maintain discipline without constantly punishing his men it proved that he did not know how to deal with soldiers, and that therefore he was unfit to decide whether a man ought to be punished or not.

So far as my punishments are concerned I have no wish

to pose as a martyr, and I acknowledge that some of them were deserved; but if I had been treated like a free human being and not like a convict—if I had not been bullied, as well as unjustly and unduly punished—I should not have become—as I did—desperate, caring little whether I was punished or not. I fully understand and excuse the motives which prompt so many men to desert —men who have neither position nor reputation to maintain—and I frankly declare that, rather than have served another year, I would have become a deserter myself.

Had war broken out when I was a trooper I am quite sure that the first battle would have resulted in the death of at least three of our officers and four of our Sergeants, and that they would not have fallen under the enemy's bullets. This may be a terrible thing to say, but I knew two troopers who were determined to do the deed. It was not mere brag, for it was by accident that I heard them more than once discussing the matter.

In my own case I am persuaded that my Captain and my Colonel, relying blindly on the N.C.O.s, were honestly convinced that I was a bad character. Five years after I left the regiment I met one of my former officers, who was then military attaché to one of the embassies. He did not recognise me, and did not catch my name. In the course of conversation I inquired whether he had known a man named Decle, who had served in his regiment.

"Don't I remember him!" he said. "He was a most incorrigible rogue! My friend Captain Hermann often spoke to me about him: he was a fellow who would never do any work, and who was most ungrateful. Although fairly intelligent, he worked so little that he was classed last at the final examination, and they had to keep him a second year. I remember that there was some talk of sending him before a court-martial, as he once made serious false allegations against his Sergeant-major. Altogether he was a bad lot. Do you know what has become of him?" I replied in the affirmative, and the military attaché asked me somewhat anxiously if I knew him well.

"He is my best friend," I replied, "and you are now talking to him." The attaché looked much embarrassed, but I soon put him at his ease, and assured him that I was in no way offended. I told him exactly what had happened, and he acknowledged that it was too true that, in many cases, officers formed their opinion entirely from Sergeants' reports, " but," he added helplessly, " what else can we do?" And he really seemed to think the question unanswerable.

I had a good opportunity of personally observing the practical working of French military organisation at the time of the Madagascar war.

Everything was at sixes and sevens.

Plans were made one day and altered the next; the Minister of War wanted one thing, the Commander-in-Chief wanted another; and if these two high authorities had not been seconded by two of the most admirable and practical officers in the French service (General de Torcy and Major, now General, Bailloud), things would have gone even worse than they did. The Intelligence Department, too, was conspicuous by its lack of information. The French military authorities did me the honour to consult me on many points, but unfortunately, as it turned out, the advice I gave was rejected by General Mercier, then Minister of War. I was asked to give my opinion about transport in general, and I first asked how many white men would take part in the Expedition, and inquired how the transport of supplies would be organised. The answer was that 6000 iron carts, drawn by mules, would be used for the service. I pointed out that the use of such carts would be absolute madness, as I knew by my own experience how easily iron carts are broken, and how impossible it is to repair them, and I added that under the circumstances the army would never be able to go forward unless a road was made. I then inquired how the soldiers' knapsacks would be carried, and General Duchesne, the Commander-in-Chief of the Expedition, to whom I put this question, replied that " of course the men would carry them themselves." " In that case," I said, " you may reckon that one half of your force will have died within six months of their landing in Madagascar."

The General said that it was all nonsense—that the men had carried their knapsacks in the Tonkin War, and could do so quite well in Madagascar.

My prediction unfortunately turned out perfectly correct, and nearly six thousand men died within six months of the beginning of the operations. A road had to be made for the iron carts, and if the natives had not proved arrant cowards, the war would have ended in a frightful disaster. It was only due to the untiring energy of Colonel Bailloud, who was in charge of the transport, that the troops were enabled to receive any supplies.

What struck me most, however, in that expedition was the jealousy between the Army and the Navy.

During the Tonkin War, the supreme command of the naval and military forces had been vested in Admiral Corbet, and the military officers strongly objected to being commanded by a sailor. In order, therefore, to avoid a repetition of what had then taken place, the whole of the flotilla which was sent to Madagascar was placed under the command of a mere Captain, who had to take orders from the General commanding the troops. The Navy, of course, resented what they considered a slight, and carefully avoided helping the Army in any way. Of course they did not openly display their rivalry, but they took good care to give no help whatever to the Military Chiefs, allowing them to commit the greatest blunders without warning them beforehand. For instance, the War Office having decided to use the River Betsiboka as far as it was navigable, a large number of steel barges were sent over to Menjunka, which was supposed to be at the mouth of the river. Unfortunately, the real mouth of the river stood nearly thirty miles farther inland, so that unless the weather was perfectly calm the barges were swamped before they had reached the river itself; the water on the other hand being too shallow to enable steamers, except those of the smallest draft, to reach the mouth. When I arrived in Madagascar, in a small 180 ton steamer I had chartered in Zanzibar, I was ordered to follow the course of the river as far as I could go, and to make a survey on my way, as none existed. After considerable trouble I managed to get about seventy miles inland, and on my return to Menjunka, as I was making my report to the General, the naval officer in command walked into the room just as I was asking the General whether he could allow me 24 hours to put my survey on paper. The naval officer inquired what survey I was speaking of, and on being told that it was a survey of the river, he replied that I had been wasting my time, as his officers " had surveyed it long ago, long ago "; and he added that he would send it to the General when he returned to his ship. He knew perfectly well, before I left, that I had been instructed to make a survey, but he had never offered to hand over to the General the map he had in his possession.

Again the Naval Commander was fully aware that a large number of transports were coming, but he carefully abstained from advising the War Office that there was only one steam launch at Menjunka to land the cargo, and the consequence was that at one time there lay as many as 24 steamers in the harbour, with no means of unloading them; an average of £200 per day having to be paid for demurrage on each. I could quote scores of similar instances, but it is not my object to write the history of the Madagascar campaign.

In conclusion, Englishmen regard their own "little army" with a just pride, tempered by a consciousness of its more or less obvious defects; but when any comparison is suggested between the British forces and the "bloated armaments" of the Continent, the pride is apt to become humility, and deprecatory remarks are made to the effect that we do not, of course, profess to be a great military power.

Yet how does the case really stand? Are these armed multitudes as formidable as mere arithmetic would have us think? France, for instance, prides herself upon being able to put in the field millions of trained men. What does this boast amount to? Upon the outbreak of war, in these days of rapid mobilisation, much—perhaps all—would depend upon the troops first in the field. And these troops, upon whose behaviour in the brunt of sudden battle the salvation of their country might depend, would be—not a body of well-trained fighting-men, leavened with veterans, and relying on their leaders with glad confidence—but a crowd of half-taught lads, lacking in thews as well as training, and led—or driven—to battle by officers whom either they have never seen until the day of conflict, or whom they know—and hate.

As for the reserves, suffice it to say that officers of the active army refuse to regard them seriously, and consider them merely in the light of civilians playing at soldiering.

The officers of the reserve (for the most part promoted privates) have received no military education worthy of the name. The non-commissioned officers and men consider the month they have to serve every other year a hateful episode. Awkward in their unaccustomed uniforms, they do not even look like soldiers, and it would take months of training to convert them into such once more. In point of efficiency they are, of course, far inferior to our Volunteers.

But behind these stands yet another " line of defence " —the territorial army and its reserve—an army composed of men who have a faint recollection that they once were drilled. There is something pathetic, as well as absurd, in picturing these middle-aged citizens in time of war, clad in antiquated uniforms, handling unaccustomed weapons, and painfully, if conscientiously, struggling to acquire a knowledge of new regulations and modern drill. To sum all up, it may be true that Providence is still on the side of the big battalions, but chiefly, we think, when those battalions are well officered, well trained, and animated with all the virtues of the soldier.

APPENDIX A

No allusion has been made in the Introduction to the pay of officers, nor to the actual cost of the keep of troopers. Being unable to find any documents on which to base my calculations, I appealed to M. Urbain Gohier, the French writer whose authority on this subject is the greatest, and I append the reply which he very kindly sent me:

[*Translation.*]

Paris, *April* 8, 1899.

Dear Sir,

Subjoined are the chief items of the budget for *pay*—which is the same in all branches of the service so far as officers are concerned.

As to the average cost of the soldier for maintenance, food, &c., it is impossible to arrive at it.

Figures have been given from time to time, but they are purely imaginary.

Expenses of all kinds are scattered under twenty different headings in our budget, and the Reporter-General for that of 1899 has announced that nobody, either at the War Office or in Parliament, can accurately dissect the expenditure.

The actual pay—of which I give you the amounts—is in practice augmented by a mass of "indemnities," so-called, for residence, travelling, mustering, lodging, high price of food, office expenses, maintenance of dignity, first equipment, &c., varying with the nature of the employment and the individuals employed.

APPENDIX A

Some officers draw their bare pay, whilst others make a large income, of which no official trace can anywhere be found.

Similarly, in the case of the men: the cost of provisions, firing, lighting, sleeping accommodation, medical treatment in or out of hospital, is reckoned in a lump sum, without distinction between different branches of the service.

This extraordinary confusion is cunningly contrived to prevent any control.

These are the items of pay:

	FRANCS.
Colonel	8564.21
Lieutenant-colonel	6934.74
Major and Chef d'Escadron	5797.90
Captain	3221.05
1st Lieutenant	2842.11
2nd Lieutenant	2652.63
Sub-lieutenant	2463.16
Adjudant	1022.00
Sergeant-major	511.00
Sergeant	401.50
Farrier	346.75
Corporal	200.75
Trumpeter	127.75
Trooper	109.50

(The N.C.O.s have 91.25 francs extra in the field.)

Note the exactitude of the above figures to a single centime, and yet there may be in addition hundreds or even thousands of francs handled in reality, either in money or in kind.

Always, &c.,
(*Signed*)   URBAIN GOHIER.

APPENDIX A

I leave to M. Gohier the whole responsibility for these statements, as I am not in a position to test their correctness. I may add, however, that French officers, whatever their faults, have always seemed to me remarkably straightforward in money matters, and even M. Gohier—whom I cannot follow in his virulent attacks upon all officers indiscriminately—has never even hinted that any of them enrich themselves by dishonourable means.

APPENDIX B

ACCUSED persons are examined by a *Juge d'instruction* (examining magistrate) *in camera*. Prisoners are considered guilty until they can prove their innocence. The examining magistrate can use any means he likes to obtain a confession; he can send a prisoner to solitary confinement (*au secret*) for weeks, if he chooses. He collects all information respecting the prisoner, bewilders him, lies to him if he thinks fit, and can keep him for months in confinement, before committing him for trial or releasing him.

In most of the cases which would be disposed of in England by a Police Magistrate, within twenty-four hours of arrest, the accused is kept, in France, for a period of from one to three months under lock and key, before being tried by the *Police Correctionnelle* (Police Court), and in case of crimes which have to be tried by a jury the preliminary inquiry or *instruction* lasts from three to *eighteen* months. Three or four years ago in one of the celebrated cases which ended in an acquittal, the *instruction* of the case lasted eighteen months, during the whole of which time the accused was kept in prison, being for a considerable period, in the strictest solitary confinement.

It is only during the last two years that a new law has been passed, enabling accused persons to be assisted by counsel during the *instruction*—counsel being present during the examination of the accused. Formerly, the

APPENDIX B

accused was not allowed to be assisted by counsel until the examination was closed.

As I said before, bail does not exist in France, except in rare instances with the approval of the Minister for Justice. In such cases bail takes the form of a deposit in cash, usually amounting to many hundreds or even thousands of pounds.

The *Juge d'instruction* can, however, release a prisoner off hand, or grant him provisional liberty, but this is also very rarely done.

Limitation in the case of criminal offences, however, exists in France. For offences which entail a maximum punishment of five years' imprisonment, no prosecution can take place after a lapse of three years from the date of the commission of the crime.

In the case of felonies (even in the case of murder), no prosecution can take place after thirty years have elapsed since the crime was committed.

On the other hand, if a citizen is accused of any crime or felony, and he absconds, he can be tried and sentenced *par contumace* in his absence.

APPENDIX C

CONSTITUTION OF A SQUADRON.

Captain in Command.

Second Captain.

1st *Peloton*	2nd *Peloton*	3rd *Peloton*	4th *Peloton*
(30 men)	(30 men)	(30 men)	(30 men)
1st Lieutenant	Sub-lieutenant	Sub-lieutenant	2nd Lieutenant
(In command)	(In command)	(In command)	(In command)
Sergeant-Major	Sergeant	Sergeant	*Sergent-fourrier*
2 Sergeants	*Caporal-fourrier*		2 Sergeants
Trumpeter	Trumpeter	Trumpeter	Trumpeter

Each *peloton* (company) consists of three *esconades* (squads) of ten men, each under a corporal.

Total.

2 Captains.
2 Lieutenants.
2 Sub-lieutenants.
1 Sergeant-major.
1 *Sergent-fourrier.*
1 *Caporal-fourrier.*
6 Sergeants.
12 Corporals.
4 Trumpeters.
120 Troopers.

www.ingramcontent.com/pod-product-compliance
Lightning Source LLC
Chambersburg PA
CBHW022027240426
43667CB00042B/1210